S0-BBR-183

CHICAGO PUBLIC LIBRARY
BEVERLY BRANCH
1962 W. 95th STREET
CHICAGO, ILLINOIS 60643

ALSO BY JAMES MERRILL

POETRY
The Black Swan
First Poems
The Country of a Thousand Years of Peace
Water Street
Nights and Days
The Fire Screen
Braving the Elements
The Yellow Pages
Divine Comedies
Mirabell: Books of Number
Scripts for the Pageant
The Changing Light at Sandover
From the First Nine: Poems 1946–1976
Late Settings
The Inner Room
Selected Poems 1946–1985
A Scattering of Salts

FICTION
The (Diblos) Notebook
The Seraglio

PLAYS
The Immortal Husband
The Bait

ESSAYS
Recitative

MEMOIR
A Different Person

JAMES MERRILL OMNIBUS TITLES
Collected Poems
Collected Prose
Collected Novels and Plays
The Changing Light at Sandover

Selected Poems

CHICAGO PUBLIC LIBRARY
BEVERLY BRANCH
1962 W. 95th STREET
CHICAGO, ILLINOIS 60643

James Merrill

Selected Poems

Edited by J. D. McClatchy and Stephen Yenser

ALFRED A. KNOPF   *New York*   2008

THIS IS A BORZOI BOOK
PUBLISHED BY ALFRED A. KNOPF

Copyright © 2008 by The Literary Estate of James Merrill at Washington University

All rights reserved.
Published in the United States by Alfred A. Knopf,
a division of Random House, Inc., New York, and in Canada
by Random House of Canada, Limited, Toronto.

www.aaknopf.com

Knopf, Borzoi Books, and the colophon are registered
trademarks of Random House, Inc.

The poems in this collection were originally published in the following: *Braving the Elements* (Atheneum, 1972);
The Changing Light at Sandover (Atheneum, 1982); *Collected Poems* (Alfred A. Knopf, 2001); *The Country of a Thousand
Years of Peace* (Alfred A. Knopf, 1959); *Divine Comedies* (Atheneum, 1976); *The Fire Screen* (Atheneum, 1969);
First Poems (Alfred A. Knopf, 1951); *The Inner Room* (Alfred A. Knopf, 1988); *Late Settings* (Atheneum, 1985);
Nights and Days (Atheneum, 1966), *A Scattering of Salts* (Alfred A. Knopf, 1995),
and *Water Street* (Atheneum, 1962).

Library of Congress Cataloging-in-Publication Data
Merrill, James Ingram.
[Poems. Selections]
Selected poems / by James Merrill ; a new selection edited by J. D. McClatchy and Stephen Yenser.—1st ed.
p. cm.
ISBN 978-0-375-71166-4
I. McClatchy, J. D., 1945–   II. Yenser, Stephen.   III. Title.
PS3525 E6645A6 2008
811'.54—dc22   2008020194

Manufactured in the United States of America
First Edition

R042984940q

Contents

Introduction

As the second half of the twentieth century got under way, American poetry was often at odds with itself. The flood tide of modernism was receding, and the poets of the next generation were restless, uncertain, and ambitious as they experimented with different styles and hesitated over their predecessors' inventions. New figures emerged along with competing claims of authenticity. Movements as different as those associated with Black Mountain College and the New York School flourished, and confessional verse, Language poetry, and the new formalism began to take shape. When James Merrill's first book of poems appeared in 1951, it seemed unlikely that he would eventually emerge as one of the era's crucial poets. He was not political, enterprising, dogmatic, addicted, or suicidal. At first his poems seemed cautious except in their implications. Later—the Sphinx always smiled—they seemed enigmatic but dazzling. His originality was a part of his respect for tradition. His wisdom came from his shrugging off any pretense to it. He was, he said, just "a man choosing the words he lives by." From those words he made some of the most ravishing, surprising, intimate, and memorable poems written in English. Merrill himself once called his body of work "chronicles of love and loss," and in twenty books written over four decades he used the details of his own life—comic and haunting, exotic and domestic—to fashion a portrait that in turn mirrored back to us the image of our world and our moment.

The thing about James Merrill's writing is that there were two things: he never stopped growing and he never left anything behind. While this minor paradox might seem to state the obvious about a poet's career, it is dramatically demonstrable in his case.

He began, like other enduring poets of his generation, as a writer of formalist lyrics who had been reared on the principles of New Criticism (the poem should be an object of art, formally sophisticated, richly but definably ambiguous, self-contained, and thus detached from authorial intention and critical impressionism), but early in his career he turned his hand to other genres as well. He wrote a Jamesian roman à clef *(The Seraglio)* and before long a couple of plays (themselves quite different: *The Immortal Husband* is a Chekhovian drama and *The Bait* is a surrealistic comedy of manners) and then began to incorporate techniques sharpened in those undertakings into his poems, which began to lengthen—and often to grow denser. He wrote an experimental novel *(The [Diblos] Notebook)*, and his poems increasingly revealed his lifelong interest in the symbolists and their dedication to the autonomy of language. Yet at the same time, the two long poems written during the middle of his career, "Days of 1935" and "The Summer People," were ballads with plots based on transparently autobiographical material. The hardly predictable but natural evolution of these dissimilar elements led to the lyrical, meditative narratives in *Divine Comedies* ("Lost in Translation," "Chimes for Yahya," "Yánnina") and then to "The Book of Ephraim," his longest poetic work at that juncture (1976), which he thought was complete—before he realized that it was the first part of an epic trilogy-with-coda that he would call *The Changing Light at Sandover,* finally completed in 1982.

The driving forces here—to build on what had been done and to break new ground—embody his thoroughgoing commitment to nourishing contrary impulses. In an interview, he speculated that from an early age he had been predisposed to "understand the relativity, even the reversibility of truths" and to consider that "there was truth on both sides" of most crucial issues. Such a dual perspective comported, he thought, with "the nature of poetry—and of science too, for that matter," so that "the ability to see both ways at once isn't merely an idiosyncrasy but corresponds to how the world needs to be seen: cheerful *and* awful, opaque *and* transparent." His characteristic pairing of science and poetry, fields all too often seen as opposed, informs much of *The Changing Light at Sandover,* the third part of which, *Scripts for the Pageant,* contains three main parts tellingly entitled "YES," "&," and "NO." At the heart of all his work is this effort to remain of two minds, to recognize (and sometimes reconcile) apparently conflicting sides of life.

Merrill sets his epic in two realms, the worldly and the spiritual, traffic between which takes place by way of a Ouija board operated by the poet and his longtime companion David Jackson—a means unlikely and even at first blush preposterous (though rooted in a tradition of otherworldly inspiration stretching from Hesiod's Muses' "voice divine" through Milton's female Holy Spirit's "nightly visitation" to the revelations of Yeats's "instructors"), but understood in the course of things to be an epitome of language itself, the medium between the real and the imagined. The need to think of both realms simultaneously perhaps derives from the poet's most traumatic youthful experience, the divorce of his parents, themselves strangely matched—a dynamic, hard-living, free-spirited financier whose name was to become legendary and a conventional, decorous journalist. It is as if their divorce displayed the elements in Merrill's own complex personality. As much his father's son as his mother's boy, he had a temperament that by turns revealed both paternal and maternal sides. He was drawn equally to the ardent and the ironic, idea and fact, the rational and the fanciful, tradition and innovation, America and Europe. And from the very beginning, his aspiration as a poet had been—like the child attempting to bring his warring parents back together—to harmonize his life's discordant factors.

Here is the whole of his small poem "Log" on confronting life's resistless divisions:

> Then when the flame forked like a sudden path
> I gasped and stumbled, and was less.
> Density pulsing upward, gauze of ash,
> Dear light along the way to nothingness,
> What could be made of you but light, and this?

"Burn always with [a] hard, gemlike flame" was Pater's advice to those of us proceeding "along the way to nothingness." In Merrill's poem, the inevitable splitting of the self, the forking of the vital flame, diminishes the speaker thus reminded of his mortality, but the very bifurcation produces sudden illumination and even gaiety. (The poet can *make light* of the dilemma after all, and as soon as "upward" suggests "up word," the word "Log" itself in retrospect breaks into two meanings, a journal entry and a piece of fuel. So it is that dark is made light—and "light" becomes heavy, dense with implication.)

"The Broken Home," the pivotal sequence in the volume carefully entitled *Nights and Days* that recalls the domestic rupture, which is Merrill's version of the Fall, concludes with an evocation of the fate of the family's mansion (designed by the noted architect Stanford White) on Long Island:

> The real house became a boarding school.
> Under the ballroom ceiling's allegory
> Someone at last may actually be allowed
> To learn something; or, from my window, cool
> With the unstiflement of the entire story,
> Watch a red setter stretch and sink in cloud.

If the broken home became "a boarding school," Merrill lets us infer that he learned lessons there ever after. Now we can see that the phrase was indeed prescient, since a photo of a room in that "real house" graced the cover of *The Changing Light at Sandover*, in which "Sandover" is the name of the "academy" where the poet takes (by way of the "board") those further seminars on cosmogony and the structure of reality.

On his way to *Sandover*, Merrill habitually declined to leave a road not taken. As his writing kept branching out, so did his life. The title of his second full volume, *The*

Country of a Thousand Years of Peace (1959), which refers to Switzerland, portends the degree to which his poems would be cosmopolitan. They would also be deeply American—and how could they not be, in view of the influence on his character of the zealous and extravagant co-founder of Merrill Lynch? His next book, *Water Street* (1962), took its name from his address in Stonington, Connecticut, a town, with a well-preserved history, on a "tongue of land" that projects into Fishers Island Sound, where he and David Jackson moved in 1955. Later years would find him establishing a second home in Athens, Greece, and in another interview he mused in characteristic terms on his motivations: "Now it may sound—it may *be*—childish, but haven't we all dreamed [of leading two lives]? To disappear and reemerge as a new person without any ties, the slate wiped clean. Sometimes one even puts the dream into action. . . . I began going to Greece . . . in the spirit of one who embarks on a double life. The life I lived there seemed I can't tell you how different from the life in America."

"Days of 1964," the concluding poem in *Nights and Days* (1966), testifies to the poet's passion for that life in Greece. As pure a love poem as Merrill ever wrote, it begins sedately but richly:

> Houses, an embassy, the hospital,
> Our neighborhood sun-cured if trembling still
> In pools of the night's rain . . .
> Across the street that led to the center of town
> A steep hill kept one company part way
> Or could be climbed in twenty minutes
> For some literally breathtaking views,
> Framed by umbrella pines, of city and sea.
> Underfoot, cyclamen, autumn crocus grew
> Spangled as with fine sweat among the relics
> Of good times had by all. If not Olympus,
> An out-of-earshot, year-round hillside revel.

Not a word "underfoot" but that contributes to his ends. The "embassy" foreshadows international relations on a personal level. The nature of that relationship? We look again from our post-Freudian vantage at the details of the "twenty minutes" of "literally breathtaking" climbing. And the effect of the relationship? We note the influential presence of "the hospital" and the "sun-cured if trembling" neighborhood. "The Thousand and Second Night," one of the two long poems in *Nights and Days*, which also begins with a malady involving division and leads to recuperation, is therefore set partly in Athens and partly in Istanbul, as well as in the United States, while the other long poem, "From the Cupola," overlays Merrill's routine in Stonington Village with the Hellenistic myth of Psyche and Eros.

Matters Greek gave him the occasion for a number of vivacious poems in *The Fire Screen* (1969), *Braving the Elements* (1972), and *Divine Comedies* (1976), and by that time his personal experience was so integral to his work that it seemed his life was falling into verse and stanza for him. People he had met—his rough-and-ready lover Strato, a sibylline Greek woman named Maria, his godchild Urania, his Greek housekeeper, his former nanny—became both characters in his poems (and sometimes speakers of them) and instances of archetypes. As late as *Late Settings* (1985), poems like "Santorini: Stopping the Leak" and the magisterial "Bronze" would owe a good deal to the Hellenophile in Merrill, but by then his "other life" had shifted materially to Key West, Florida, a location that had been important to Wallace Stevens and Elizabeth Bishop, the one a literary model (quoted in "The Book of Ephraim" and elsewhere) and the other a model *and* a friend (addressed in "The Victor Dog" and commemorated in "Overdue Pilgrimage to Nova Scotia").

If there is such a thing as a *typical* Merrill poem, how does it work? At its core is the mercurial and transforming power of metaphor. This is one aspect of his "double-seeing"—the impulse to understand something by seeing it first or momentarily as something else. Whether observed or imagined, sensuous details are what give the poem its momentum. Merrill was shy of brandishing ideas. (He once compared coming across Great Ideas in a poem to seeing one's grandparents nude.) His poems are intelligent but not cerebral, allusive but rarely obscure. Their tone is darting and silvery, with long periodic sentences brought up sharply by fragments, and their diction a vivid blend of the elegant and the colloquial. "In poetry," he once reflected, "I look for English in its billiard-table sense—words that have been set spinning against their own gravity." That is to say, the grave may be disguised by the glamorous, and the depths of his poems may often be found in their surfaces, where wit and wordplay carom. By temperament, he was a man, as he said, with a "fondness for given arrangements," and his poems tend to be *arranged*. He was a master of poetic forms, and his books abound with traditional schemes like the sonnet and the villanelle as well as with intricate patterns of his own devising. He never wanted merely to submit to experience; he wanted to weigh and balance it, and his use of meter and rhyme facilitated a moral perspective on otherwise volatile emotional material. "Form's what affirms," one poem says, and it is important to remember that for him form is not an order imposed, but an order revealed.

As his affinity for the past might suggest, more than any other American poet of the late twentieth century, perhaps more than any other American poet, period, Merrill was a citizen of the world. Some work we have omitted here in the name of economy and with great regret will bear colorful witness to that claim. Two substantial such pieces, both originally in *The Inner Room*, are the closet drama "The Image Maker," which derives from his interest in Santeria, and "Prose of Departure," which reflects his fascination with and visits to Japan in part because it adapts Basho's genre. Shorter poems that indicate his inveterate cultural sophistication and that we have found space for include "After Cavafy," a recasting of the Alexandrian poet's "Waiting for the Barbarians," and "Rhapsody on Czech Themes," both completed after Merrill had seen through the press his final volume, *A Scattering of Salts* (1995).

As a whole, these *Selected Poems* make a verbal version of the jacket in "Self-Portrait in Tyvek(™) Windbreaker," which appears in that last book. The article of clothing pictures a "world map" whose details allow the poet to bring together the Italian street-singer Roberto Murolo, an Albanian doorman, "Americans, blithe as the last straw," a "carrot-haired" French "Girl in the bakery" in Manhattan, and much more, including, from this country alone, "Dead white males in malls. / Prayer breakfasts. Pay-phone sex. 'Ring up as meat.' / Oprah. The GNP. The contour sheet. / The painless death of History. The stick / Figures on Capitol Hill." There is even room, magically, for a negative version of his jacket, an image of "my windbreaker / In black, with starry longitudes, Archer, Goat, / Clothing an earphoned archangel of Space." The world's sweet and scandalous plenty—itself a reflection of heavenly orders above us—is conjured up, its relations revealed.

One of the great love poets of the century, able to dramatize what love can grant and withhold, Merrill believed, with Marcel Proust, that the only true paradise is a lost paradise. Love is not fully itself until it is lost, until it becomes memory, then becomes art. That same impulse—to look over his shoulder at what might have been—goes to the heart of many poems in this book, whether they have love or merely (merely!) life as their subject, and accounts for the poignance of their playfulness. Beneath the elegiac tone is a palpable gratitude, and the very process of turning loss into art celebrates the regenerating power of the human imagination. "As for me," he once said, "I can't imagine my life without poetry. It created me." He was right, of course. The poems James Merrill wrote created the person whose life he had borrowed to make his art. He was indeed a man choosing the words he lives by.

JDMcC and SY

Selected Poems

THE BLACK SWAN

Black on flat water past the jonquil lawns
    Riding, the black swan draws
A private chaos warbling in its wake,
Assuming, like a fourth dimension, splendor
That calls the child with white ideas of swans
    Nearer to that green lake
  Where every paradox means wonder.

Though the black swan's arched neck is like
    A question-mark on the lake,
The swan outlaws all possible questioning:
A thing in itself, like love, like submarine
Disaster, or the first sound when we wake;
    And the swan-song it sings
  Is the huge silence of the swan.

Illusion: the black swan knows how to break
    Through expectation, beak
Aimed now at its own breast, now at its image,
And move across our lives, if the lake is life,
And by the gentlest turning of its neck
    Transform, in time, time's damage;
  To less than a black plume, time's grief.

Enchanter: the black swan has learned to enter
    Sorrow's lost secret center
Where like a maypole separate tragedies
Are wound about a tower of ribbons, and where
The central hollowness is that pure winter
    That does not change but is
  Always brilliant ice and air.

Always the black swan moves on the lake; always
    The blond child stands to gaze
As the tall emblem pivots and rides out
To the opposite side, always. The child upon
The bank, hands full of difficult marvels, stays
    Forever to cry aloud
  In anguish: I love the black swan.

THE HOUSE

Whose west walls take the sunset like a blow
Will have turned the other cheek by morning, though
The long night falls between, as wise men know:

Wherein the wind, that daily we forgot,
Comes mixed with rain and, while we seek it not,
Appears against our faces to have sought

The contours of a listener in night air,
His profile bent as from pale windows where
Soberly once he learned what houses were.

Those darkening reaches, crimsoned with a dust
No longer earth's, but of the vanishing West,
Can stir a planet nearly dispossessed,

And quicken interest in the avid vein
That dyes a man's heart ruddier far than stain
Of day does finial, cornice and windowpane:

So that whoever strolls on his launched lawn
At dusk, the hour of recompense, alone,
May stumbling on a sunken boundary stone

The loss of deed and structure apprehend.
And we who homeless toward such houses wend
May find we have dwelt elsewhere. Scholar and friend,

After the twelve bright houses that each day
Presume to flatter what we most display,
Night is a cold house, a narrow doorway.

This door to no key opens, those to brass.
Behind it, warning of a deep excess,
The winds are. I have entered, nevertheless,

And seen the wet-faced sleepers the winds take
To heart; have felt their dreadful profits break
Beyond my seeing: at a glance they wake.

THE COUNTRY OF A THOUSAND YEARS OF PEACE

to Hans Lodeizen (1924–1950)

Here they all come to die,
Fluent therein as in a fourth tongue.
But for a young man not yet of their race
It was a madness you should lie

Blind in one eye, and fed
By the blood of a scrubbed face;
It was a madness to look down
On the toy city where

The glittering neutrality
Of clock and chocolate and lake and cloud
Made every morning somewhat
Less than you could bear;

And makes me cry aloud
At the old masters of disease
Who dangling high above you on a hair
The sword that, never falling, kills

Would coax you still back from that starry land
Under the world, which no one sees
Without a death, its finish and sharp weight
Flashing in his own hand.

THE LOVERS

They met in loving like the hands of one
Who having worked six days with creature and plant
Washes his hands before the evening meal.
Reflected in a basin out-of-doors
The golden sky receives his hands beneath
Its coldly wishing surface, washing them

Of all perhaps but what of one another
Each with its five felt perceptions holds:
A limber warmth, fitness of palm and nail
So long articulate in his mind before
Plunged into happening, that all the while
Water laps and loves the stirring hands

His eye has leisure for the young fruit-trees
And lowing beasts secure, since night is near,
Pasture, lights of a distant town, and sky
Molten, atilt, strewn on new water, sky
In which for a last fact he dips his face
And lifts it glistening: what dark distinct

Reflections of his features upon gold!
—Except for when each slow slight water-drop
He sensed on chin and nose accumulate,
Each tiny world of sky reversed and branches,
Fell with its pure wealth to mar the image:
World after world fallen into the sky

And still so much world left when, by the fire
With fingers clasped, he set in revolution
Certitude and chance like strong slow thumbs;
Or read from an illuminated page
Of harvest, flood, motherhood, mystery:
These waited, and would issue from his hands.

A RENEWAL

Having used every subterfuge
To shake you, lies, fatigue, or even that of passion,
Now I see no way but a clean break.
I add that I am willing to bear the guilt.

You nod assent. Autumn turns windy, huge,
A clear vase of dry leaves vibrating on and on.
We sit, watching. When I next speak
Love buries itself in me, up to the hilt.

UPON A SECOND MARRIAGE

for H. I. P.

Orchards, we linger here because
Women we love stand propped in your green prisons,
Obedient to such justly bending laws
        Each one longs to take root,
        Lives to confess whatever season's
Pride of blossom or endeavor's fruit
        May to her rustling boughs have risen.

        Then autumn reddens the whole mind.
No more, she vows, the dazzle of a year
Shall woo her from your bare cage of loud wind,
        Promise the ring and run
        To burn the altar, reappear
With apple blossoms for the credulous one.
        Orchards, we wonder that we linger here!

        Orchards we planted, trees we shook
To learn what you were bearing, say we stayed
Because one winter dusk we half-mistook
        Frost on a bleakened bough
        For blossoms, and were half-afraid
To miss the old persuasion, should we go.
        And spring did come, and discourse made

        Enough of weddings to us all
That, loving her for whom the whole world grows
Fragrant and white, we linger to recall
        As down aisles of cut trees
        How a tall trunk's cross-section shows
Concentric rings, those many marriages
        That life on each live thing bestows.

THE CHARIOTEER OF DELPHI

Where are the horses of the sun?

Their master's green bronze hand, empty of all
But a tangle of reins, seems less to call
His horses back than to wait out their run.

To cool that havoc and restore
The temperance we had loved them for
I have implored him, child, at your behest.

Watch now, the flutings of his dress hang down
From the brave patina of breast.
His gentle eyes glass brown

Neither attend us nor the latest one
Blistered and stammering who comes to cry
Village in flames and river dry,

None to control the chariot
And to call back the killing horses none
Now that their master, eyes ashine, will not.

For watch, his eyes in the still air alone
Look shining and nowhere
Unless indeed into our own

Who are reflected there
Littler than dolls wound up by a child's fear
How tight, their postures only know.

And loosely, watch now, the reins overflow
His fist, as if once more the unsubdued
Beasts shivering and docile stood

Like us before him. Do you remember how
A small brown pony would
Nuzzle the cube of sugar from your hand?

Broken from his mild reprimand
In fire and fury hard upon the taste
Of a sweet license, even these have raced

Uncurbed in us, where fires are fanned.

MIRROR

I grow old under an intensity
Of questioning looks. *Nonsense,*
I try to say, *I cannot teach you children
How to live.—If not you, who will?*
Cries one of them aloud, grasping my gilded
Frame till the world sways. *If not you, who will?*
Between their visits the table, its arrangement
Of Bible, fern and Paisley, all past change,
Does very nicely. If ever I feel curious
As to what others endure,
Across the parlor *you* provide examples,
Wide open, sunny, of everything I am
Not. You embrace a whole world without once caring
To set it in order. That takes thought. Out there
Something is being picked. The red-and-white bandannas
Go to my heart. A fine young man
Rides by on horseback. Now the door shuts. Hester
Confides in me her first unhappiness.
This much, you see, would never have been fitted
Together, but for me. Why then is it
They more and more neglect me? Late one sleepless
Midsummer night I strained to keep
Five tapers from your breathing. *No,* the widowed
Cousin said, *let them go out.* I did.
The room brimmed with gray sound, all the instreaming
Muslin of your dream . . .
Years later now, two of the grown grandchildren
Sit with novels face-down on the sill,
Content to muse upon your tall transparence,
Your clouds, brown fields, persimmon far
And cypress near. One speaks. *How superficial
Appearances are!* Since then, as if a fish
Had broken the perfect silver of my reflectiveness,
I have lapses. I suspect
Looks from behind, where nothing is, cool gazes
Through the blind flaws of my mind. As days,
As decades lengthen, this vision
Spreads and blackens. I do not know whose it is,
But I think it watches for my last silver

To blister, flake, float leaf by life, each milling-
Downward dumb conceit, to a standstill
From which not even you strike any brilliant
Chord in me, and to a faceless will,
Echo of mine, I am amenable.

MARSYAS

I used to write in the café sometimes:
Poems on menus, read all over town
Or talked out before ever written down.
One day a girl brought in his latest book.
I opened it—stiff rhythms, gorgeous rhymes—
And made a face. Then crash! my cup upset.
Of twenty upward looks mine only met
His, that gold archaic lion's look

Wherein I saw my wiry person skinned
Of every skill it labored to acquire
And heard the plucked nerve's elemental twang.
They found me dangling where his golden wind
Inflicted so much music on the lyre
That no one could have told you what he sang.

THE DOODLER

Most recent in the long race that descends
From me, welcome! and least askew of ikons
That grow on a new page like rapid lichens
Among the telephone numbers of new friends.

These I commune with every day. Hellos,
Goodbyes. Often by dusk a pair of eyes
Is all I draw; the pencil stupefies
Their lids with kohl until they almost close

But then do not, as if, more animate
Than any new friend's voice flattened by news,
Guessing some brilliant function I refuse,
And why, and wanting to accept their fate.

Noses as yet, alas, revert to profile.
Lips, too, are pursed in this or that direction,
Or raised to other lips from sheer distraction;
To mine, not once. While still, just as at Deauville

Off-season, tiny hands are better hidden
By great muffs of albino porcupine.
Indeed, nothing I do is at all fine
Save certain abstract forms. These come unbidden:

Stars, oblongs linked, or a baroque motif
Expressed so forcibly that it indents
A blank horizon generations hence
With signs and pressures, massing to relief

Like thunderheads one day in sultry foretaste
Of flashes first envisioned as your own
When, squat and breathless, you inscribe on stone
Your names for me, my inkling of an artist—

He-Who-endures-the-disembodied-Voice
Or *Who-in-wrath-puts-down-the-Black-Receiver*—
And, more than image then, a rain, a river
Of prescience, you reflect and I rejoice!

Far, far behind already is that aeon
Of pinheads, bodies each a ragged weevil,
Slit-mouthed and spider-leggèd, with eyes like gravel,
Wavering under trees of purple crayon.

Shapes never realized, were you dogs or chairs?
That page is brittle now, if not long burned.
This morning's little boy stands (I have learned
To do feet) gazing down a flight of stairs.

And when A. calls to tell me he enjoyed
The evening, I begin again. Again
Emerge, O sunbursts, garlands, creatures, men,
Ever more lifelike out of the white void!

VOICES FROM THE OTHER WORLD

Presently at our touch the teacup stirred,
Then circled lazily about
From A to Z. The first voice heard
(If they are voices, these mute spellers-out)
Was that of an engineer

Originally from Cologne.
Dead in his 22nd year
Of cholera in Cairo, he had KNOWN
NO HAPPINESS. He once met Goethe, though.
Goethe had told him: PERSEVERE.

Our blind hound whined. With that, a horde
Of voices gathered above the Ouija board,
Some childish and, you might say, blurred
By sleep; one little boy
Named Will, reluctant possibly in a ruff

Like a large-lidded page out of El Greco, pulled
Back the arras for that next voice,
Cold and portentous: ALL IS LOST.
FLEE THIS HOUSE. OTTO VON THURN UND TAXIS.
OBEY. YOU HAVE NO CHOICE.

Frightened, we stopped; but tossed
Till sunrise striped the rumpled sheets with gold.
Each night since then, the moon waxes,
Small insects flit round a cold torch
We light, that sends them pattering to the porch . . .

But no real Sign. New voices come,
Dictate addresses, begging us to write;
Some warn of lives misspent, and all of doom
In ways that so exhilarate
We are sleeping sound of late.

Last night the teacup shattered in a rage.
Indeed, we have grown nonchalant
Towards the other world. In the gloom here,

Our elbows on the cleared
Table, we talk and smoke, pleased to be stirred

Rather by buzzings in the jasmine, by the drone
Of our own voices and poor blind Rover's wheeze,
Than by those clamoring overhead,
Obsessed or piteous, for a commitment
We still have wit to postpone

Because, once looked at lit
By the cold reflections of the dead
Risen extinct but irresistible,
Our lives have never seemed more full, more real,
Nor the full moon more quick to chill.

IN THE HALL OF MIRRORS

The parquet barely gleams, a lake.
The windows weaken the dark trees.
The mirrors to their bosoms take
Far glints of water, which they freeze
And wear like necklaces.

Some pause in front of others with
Glimmers of mutual admiration.
Even to draw breath is uncouth.
Steps make the silver marrow spin
Up and down every spine.

You feel that something must begin.
To clickings from the chandeliers
A woman and a man come in
And creak about. She sighs, he peers.
A guide hisses in their ears,

"Your seeresses of sheer Space
In argent colloquy despise
Anything personal or commonplace."
Looked at, the mirrors close their eyes.
Through the guide's good offices

In one glass brow a tree is lit
That multiplies itself in tiers,
Tempting the pair to populate
Those vistas from which visitors
Ricochet in fours,

Eights, sixteens, till the first two gaze
At one another through a glazed crush
Of their own kind, and the man says,
"Complex but unmysterious,
This is no life for us."

He shuts the camera whose cold eye
Far outshone his own or hers.
The woman, making no reply,

Scans the remotest mirrors within mirrors
For grander figures,

Not just those of herself and him
Repeated soothingly, as though
Somebody's wits were growing dim—
Those! those beyond! The guide says, "Time to go."
They turn to do so,

And of a million likenesses
The two had thought to leave behind
Not one but nimble as you please
Turns with them, masterfully aligned.
Then all slip out of mind

And in the solitary hall
The lobes of crystal gather dust.
From glass to glass an interval
Widens like moonrise over frost
No tracks have ever crossed.

A DEDICATION

Hans, there are moments when the whole mind
Resolves into a pair of brimming eyes, or lips
Parting to drink from the deep spring of a death
That freshness they do not yet need to understand.
These are the moments, if ever, an angel steps
Into the mind, as kings into the dress
Of a poor goatherd, for their acts of charity.
There are moments when speech is but a mouth pressed
Lightly and humbly against the angel's hand.

AN URBAN CONVALESCENCE

Out for a walk, after a week in bed,
I find them tearing up part of my block
And, chilled through, dazed and lonely, join the dozen
In meek attitudes, watching a huge crane
Fumble luxuriously in the filth of years.
Her jaws dribble rubble. An old man
Laughs and curses in her brain,
Bringing to mind the close of *The White Goddess.*

As usual in New York, everything is torn down
Before you have had time to care for it.
Head bowed, at the shrine of noise, let me try to recall
What building stood here. Was there a building at all?
I have lived on this same street for a decade.

Wait. Yes. Vaguely a presence rises
Some five floors high, of shabby stone
—Or am I confusing it with another one
In another part of town, or of the world?—
And over its lintel into focus vaguely
Misted with blood (my eyes are shut)
A single garland sways, stone fruit, stone leaves,
Which years of grit had etched until it thrust
Roots down, even into the poor soil of my seeing.
When did the garland become part of me?
I ask myself, amused almost,
Then shiver once from head to toe,

Transfixed by a particular cheap engraving of garlands
Bought for a few francs long ago,
All calligraphic tendril and cross-hatched rondure,
Ten years ago, and crumpled up to stanch
Boughs dripping, whose white gestures filled a cab,
And thought of neither then nor since.
Also, to clasp them, the small, red-nailed hand
Of no one I can place. Wait. No. Her name, her features
Lie toppled underneath that year's fashions.
The words she must have spoken, setting her face
To fluttering like a veil, I cannot hear now,
Let alone understand.

So that I am already on the stair,
As it were, of where I lived,
When the whole structure shudders at my tread
And soundlessly collapses, filling
The air with motes of stone.
Onto the still erect building next door
Are pressed levels and hues—
Pocked rose, streaked greens, brown whites.
Who drained the pousse-café?
Wires and pipes, snapped off at the roots, quiver.

Well, that is what life does. I stare
A moment longer, so. And presently
The massive volume of the world
Closes again.

Upon that book I swear
To abide by what it teaches:
Gospels of ugliness and waste,
Of towering voids, of soiled gusts,
Of a shrieking to be faced
Full into, eyes astream with cold—

With cold?
All right then. With self-knowledge.

Indoors at last, the pages of *Time* are apt
To open, and the illustrated mayor of New York,
Given a glimpse of how and where I work,
To note yet one more house that can be scrapped.

Unwillingly I picture
My walls weathering in the general view.
It is not even as though the new
Buildings did very much for architecture.

Suppose they did. The sickness of our time requires
That these as well be blasted in their prime.
You would think the simple fact of having lasted
Threatened our cities like mysterious fires.

There are certain phrases which to use in a poem
Is like rubbing silver with quicksilver. Bright
But facile, the glamour deadens overnight.
For instance, how "the sickness of our time"

Enhances, then debases, what I feel.
At my desk I swallow in a glass of water
No longer cordial, scarcely wet, a pill
They had told me not to take until much later.

With the result that back into my imagination
The city glides, like cities seen from the air,
Mere smoke and sparkle to the passenger
Having in mind another destination

Which now is not that honey-slow descent
Of the Champs-Elysées, her hand in his,
But the dull need to make some kind of house
Out of the life lived, out of the love spent.

AFTER GREECE

Light into the olive entered
And was oil. Rain made the huge pale stones
Shine from within. The moon turned his hair white
Who next stepped from between the columns,
Shielding his eyes. All through
The countryside were old ideas
Found lying open to the elements.
Of the gods' houses only
A minor premise here and there
Would be balancing the heaven of fixed stars
Upon a Doric capital. The rest
Lay spilled, their fluted drums half sunk in cyclamen
Or deep in water's biting clarity
Which just barely upheld me
The next week, when I sailed for home.
But where is home—these walls?
These limbs? The very spaniel underfoot
Races in sleep, toward what?
It is autumn. I did not invite
Those guests, windy and brittle, who drink my liquor.
Returning from a walk I find
The bottles filled with spleen, my room itself
Smeared by reflection onto the far hemlocks.
I some days flee in dream
Back to the exposed porch of the maidens
Only to find my great-great-grandmothers
Erect there, peering
Into a globe of red Bohemian glass.
As it swells and sinks, I call up
Graces, Furies, Fates, removed
To my country's warm, lit halls, with rivets forced
Through drapery, and nothing left to bear.
They seem anxious to know
What holds up heaven nowadays.
I start explaining how in that vast fire
Were other irons—well, Art, Public Spirit,
Ignorance, Economics, Love of Self,
Hatred of Self, a hundred more,
Each burning to be felt, each dedicated

To sparing us the worst; how I distrust them
As I should have done those ladies; how I want
Essentials: salt, wine, olive, the light, the scream—
No! I have scarcely named you,
And look, in a flash you stand full-grown before me,
Row upon row, Essentials,
Dressed like your sister caryatids
Or tombstone angels jealous of their dead,
With undulant coiffures, lips weathered, cracked by grime,
And faultless eyes gone blank beneath the immense
Zinc and gunmetal northern sky . . .
Stay then. Perhaps the system
Calls for spirits. This first glass I down
To the last time
I ate and drank in that old world. May I
Also survive its meanings, and my own.

FOR PROUST

Over and over something would remain
Unbalanced in the painful sum of things.
Past midnight you arose, rang for your things.
You had to go into the world again.

You stop for breath outside the lit hotel,
A thin spoon bitter stimulants will stir.
Jean takes your elbow, Jacques your coat. The stir
Spreads—you are known to all the personnel—

As through packed public rooms you press (impending
Palms, chandeliers, orchestras, more palms,
The fracas and the fragrance) until your palms
Are moist with fear that you will miss the friend

Conjured—but she is waiting: a child still
At first glance, hung with fringes, on the low
Ottoman. In a voice reproachful and low
She says she understands you have been ill.

And you, because your time is running out,
Laugh in denial and begin to phrase
Your questions. There had been a little phrase
She hummed, you could not sleep tonight without

Hearing again. Then, of that day she had sworn
To come, and did not, was evasive later,
Would she not speak the truth two decades later,
From loving-kindness learned if not inborn?

She treats you to a look you cherished, light,
Bold: "Mon ami, how did we get along
At all, those years?" But in her hair a long
White lock has made its truce with appetite.

And presently she rises. Though in pain
You let her leave—the loved one always leaves.
What of the little phrase? Its notes, like leaves
In the strong tea you have contrived to drain,

Strangely intensify what you must do.
Back where you came from, up the strait stair, past
All understanding, bearing the whole past,
Your eyes grown wide and dark, eyes of a Jew,

You make for one dim room without contour
And station yourself there, beyond the pale
Of cough or of gardenia, erect, pale.
What happened is becoming literature.

Feverish in time, if you suspend the task,
An old, old woman shuffling in to draw
Curtains, will read a line or two, withdraw.
The world will have put on a thin gold mask.

SCENES OF CHILDHOOD

for Claude Fredericks

My mother's lamp once out,
I press a different switch:
A field within the dim
White screen ignites,
Vibrating to the rapt
Mechanical racket
Of a real noon field's
Crickets and gnats.

And to its candid heart
I move with heart ajar,
With eyes that smart less
From pollen or heat
Than from the buried day
Now rising like a moon,
Shining, unwinding
Its taut white sheet.

Two or three bugs that lit
Earlier upon the blank
Sheen, all peaceable
Insensibility, drowse
As she and I cannot
Under the risen flood
Of thirty years ago—
A tree, a house

We had then, a late sun,
A door from which the primal
Figures jerky and blurred
As lightning bugs
From lanterns issue, next
To be taken for stars,
For fates. With knowing smiles
And beaded shrugs

My mother and two aunts
Loom on the screen. Their plucked
Brows pucker, their arms encircle
One another.
Their ashen lips move.
From the love seat's gloom
A quiet chuckle escapes
My white-haired mother

To see in that final light
A man's shadow mount
Her dress. And now she is
Advancing, sister-
less, but followed by
A fair child, or fury—
Myself at four, in tears.
I raise my fist,

Strike, she kneels down. The man's
Shadow afflicts us both.
Her voice behind me says
It might go slower.
I work dials, the film jams.
Our headstrong old projector
Glares at the scene which promptly
Catches fire.

Puzzled, we watch ourselves
Turn red and black, gone up
In a puff of smoke now coiling
Down fierce beams.
I switch them off. A silence.
Your father, she remarks,
Took those pictures; later
Says pleasant dreams,

Rises and goes. Alone
I gradually fade and cool.
Night scatters me with green
Rustlings, thin cries.
Out there between the pines
Have begun shining deeds,

Some low, inconstant (these
Would be fireflies),

Others as in high wind
Aflicker, staying lit.
There are nights we seem to ride
With cross and crown
Forth under them, through fumes,
Coils, the whole rattling epic—
Only to leap clear-eyed
From eiderdown,

Asleep to what we'd seen.
Father already fading—
Who focused your life long
Through little frames,
Whose microscope, now deep
In purple velvet, first
Showed me the skulls of flies,
The fur, the flames

Etching the jaws—father:
Shrunken to our true size.
Each morning, back of us,
Fields wail and shimmer.
To go out is to fall
Under fresh spells, cool web
And stinging song new-hatched
Each day, all summer.

A minute galaxy
About my head will easily
Needle me back. The day's
Inaugural *Damn*
Spoken, I start to run,
Inane, like them, but breathing
In and out the sun
And air I am.

The son and heir! In the dark
It makes me catch my breath
And hear, from upstairs, hers—

That faintest hiss
And slither, as of life
Escaping into space,
Having led its characters
To the abyss

Of night. Immensely still
The heavens glisten. One broad
Path of vague stars is floating
Off, a shed skin
Of all whose fine cold eyes
First told us, locked in ours:
You are the heroes without name
Or origin.

ANGEL

Above my desk, whirring and self-important
(Though not much larger than a hummingbird)
In finely woven robes, school of Van Eyck,
Hovers an evidently angelic visitor.
He points one index finger out the window
At winter snatching to its heart,
To crystal vacancy, the misty
Exhalations of houses and of people running home
From the cold sun pounding on the sea;
While with the other hand
He indicates the piano
Where the Sarabande No. 1 lies open
At a passage I shall never master
But which has already, and effortlessly, mastered me.
He drops his jaw as if to say, or sing,
"Between the world God made
And this music of Satie,
Each glimpsed through veils, but whole,
Radiant and willed,
Demanding praise, demanding surrender,
How can you sit there with your notebook?
What do you think you are doing?"
However he says nothing—wisely: I could mention
Flaws in God's world, or Satie's; and for that matter
How did he come by *his* taste for Satie?
Half to tease him, I turn back to my page,
Its phrases thus far clotted, unconnected.
The tiny angel shakes his head.
There is no smile on his round, hairless face.
He does not want even these few lines written.

SWIMMING BY NIGHT

A light going out in the forehead
Of the house by the ocean,
Into warm black its feints of diamond fade.
Without clothes, without caution

Plunging past gravity—
Wait! Where before
Had been floating nothing, is a gradual body
Half remembered, astral with phosphor,

Yours, risen from its tomb
In your own mind,
Haunting nimbleness, glimmerings a random
Spell had kindled. So that, new-limned

By this weak lamp
The evening's alcohol will feed
Until the genie chilling bids you limp
Heavily over stones to bed,

You wear your master's robe
One last time, the far break
Of waves, their length and sparkle, the spinning globe
You wear, and the star running down his cheek.

A TENANCY

for David Jackson

Something in the light of this March afternoon
Recalls that first and dazzling one
Of 1946. I sat elated
In my old clothes, in the first of several
Furnished rooms, head cocked for the kind of sound
That is recognized only when heard.
A fresh snowfall muffled the road, unplowed
To leave blanker and brighter
The bright, blank page turned overnight.

A yellow pencil in midair
Kept sketching unfamiliar numerals,
The 9 and 6 forming a stereoscope
Through which to seize the Real
Old-Fashioned Winter of my landlord's phrase,
Through which the ponderous *idées reçues*
Of oak, velour, crochet, also the mantel's
Baby figures, value told me
In some detail at the outset, might be plumbed
For signs I should not know until I saw them.

But the objects, innocent
(As we all once were) of annual depreciation,
The more I looked grew shallower,
Pined under a luminous plaid robe
Thrown over us by the twin mullions, sashes,
And unequal oblong panes
Of windows and storm windows. These,
Washed in a rage, then left to dry unpolished,
Projected onto the inmost wall
Ghosts of the storm, like pebbles under water.

And indeed, from within, ripples
Of heat had begun visibly bearing up and away
The bouquets and wreaths of a quarter century.
Let them go, what did I want with them?

It was time to change that wallpaper!
Brittle, sallow in the new radiance,
Time to set the last wreath floating out
Above the dead, to sweep up flowers. The dance
Had ended, it was light; the men looked tired
And awkward in their uniforms.
I sat, head thrown back, and with the dried stains
Of light on my own cheeks, proposed
This bargain with—say with the source of light:
That given a few years more
(Seven or ten or, what seemed vast, fifteen)
To spend in love, in a country not at war,
I would give in return
All I had. All? A little sun
Rose in my throat. The lease was drawn.

I did not even feel the time expire.

I feel it though, today, in this new room,
Mine, with my things and thoughts, a view
Of housetops, treetops, the walls bare.
A changing light is deepening, is changing
To a gilt ballroom chair a chair
Bound to break under someone before long.
I let the light change also me.
The body that lived through that day
And the sufficient love and relative peace
Of those short years, is now not mine.
Would it be called a soul?
It knows, at any rate,
That when the light dies and the bell rings
Its leaner veteran will rise to face
Partners not recognized
Until drunk young again and gowned in changing
Flushes; and strains will rise,
The bone-tipped baton beating, rapid, faint,
From the street below, from my depressions—

From the doorbell which rings.
One foot asleep, I hop
To let my three friends in. They stamp
Themselves free of the spring's

Last snow—or so we hope.

One has brought violets in a pot;
The second, wine; the best,
His open, empty hand. Now in the room
The sun is shining like a lamp.
I put the flowers where I need them most

And then, not asking why they come,
Invite the visitors to sit.
If I am host at last
It is of little more than my own past.
May others be at home in it.

NIGHTGOWN

A cold so keen,
My speech unfurls tonight
As from the chattering teeth
Of a sewing machine.

Whom words appear to warm,
Dear heart, wear mine. Come forth
Wound in their flimsy white
And give it form.

THE THOUSAND AND SECOND NIGHT

for Irma Brandeis

I / RIGOR VITAE

Istanbul. 21 March. I woke today
With an absurd complaint. The whole right half
Of my face refuses to move. I have to laugh
Watching the rest of it reel about in dismay

Under the double burden, while its twin
Sags on, though sentient, stupefied.
I'm here alone. Not quite—through fog outside
Loom wingèd letters: PAN AMERICAN.

Twenty-five hundred years this city has stood between
The passive Orient and our frantic West.
I see no reason to be depressed;
There are too many other things I haven't seen,

Like Hagia Sophia. Tea drunk, shaved and dressed . . .
Dahin! Dahin!

The house of Heavenly Wisdom first became
A mosque, is now a flame-
less void. The apse,
Militantly dislocated,
Still wears those dark-green epaulettes
On which (to the pilgrim who forgets
His Arabic) a wild script of gold whips
Has scribbled glowering, dated
Slogans: "God is my grief!" perhaps,
Or "Byzantine,
Go home!"
Above you, the great dome,
Bald of mosaic, senile, floated
In a gilt wash. Its old profusion's
Hypnotic shimmer, back and forth between
That of the abacus, that of the nebula,

38 *Nights and Days*

Had been picked up from the floor,
The last of numberless handfuls,
By the last 18th-century visitor.
You did not want to think of yourself for once,
But you had held your head erect
Too many years within such transcendental skulls
As this one not to feel the usual, if no
Longer flattering kinship. You'd let go
Learning and faith as well, you too had wrecked
Your precious sensibility. What else did you expect?

Outdoors. Uprooted, turban-crested stones
Lie side by side. It's as I might have feared.
The building, desperate for youth, has smeared
All over its original fine bones

Acres of ocher plaster. A diagram
Indicates how deep in the mudpack
The real façade is. I want *my* face back.
A pharmacist advises

The Hamam

After the hour of damp heat
One is addressed in gibberish, shown
Into a marble cell and thrown
On marble, there to be scrubbed clean,

Is wrapped in towels and a sheet
And led upstairs to this lean tomb
Made all of panes (red, amber, green)
With a glass star hung in the gloom,

Here sits effaced by gemlike moods,
Tastes neither coffee nor loukoum,
And to the attendant who intrudes

(Or archeologist or thief)
Gravely uptilts one's mask of platinum
Still dripping, in a sign of life.

And now what? Back, I guess, to the modern town.
Midway across the bridge, an infantile
Memory promises to uncramp my style.
I stop in deepening light to jot it down:

On the crest of her wrist, by the black watered silk of the watchband, his grandmother had a
wen, a hard mauve bubble up from which bristled three or four white hairs. How often he
had lain in her lap and been lulled to a rhythm easily the whole world's then—the yellowish
sparkle of a ring marking its outer limit, while in the foreground, silhouetted like the mosque
of Suleiman the Magnificent, mass and minarets felt by someone fallen asleep on the deck of
his moored caïque, that principal landmark's rise and fall distinguished, from any other, her
beloved hand.

Cold. A wind rising. An entire city
Dissolved by rhetoric. And out there, past
The mirror of the Bosporos, what black coast
Reflecting us into immobility?

On this side, crowds, a magic-lantern beam—
Belgians on bicycles, housewives with red hair,
Masts, cries of crows blown high in the rose-blue air,
Ataturk's tailcoat . . . It is like a dream,

The "death-in-life and life-in-death" of Yeats'
Byzantium; and, if so, by the same token,
Alone in the sleepwalking scene, my flesh has woken
And sailed for the fixed shore beyond the straits.

2 / THE CURE

The doctor recommended cortisone,
Diathermy, vitamins, and rest.
It worked. These months in Athens, no one's guessed
My little drama; I appear my own

Master again. However, once you've cracked
That so-called mirror of the soul,
It is not readily, if at all, made whole.
("Between the motion and the act

Falls the Shadow"—T. S. Eliot.)
Part of me has remained cold and withdrawn.
The day I went up to the Parthenon
Its humane splendor made me think *So what?*

One May noon in the Royal Park, among
The flora of l'Agneau Mystique—
Cypress, mimosa, laurel, palm—a Greek
Came up to name them for me in his tongue.

I thanked him; he thanked me, sat down. Peacocks
Trailed by, hard gray feet mashing overripe
But bitter oranges. I knew the type:
Superb, male, raucous, unclean, Orthodox

Ikon of appetite feathered to the eyes
With the electric blue of days that will
Not come again. My friend with time to kill
Asked me the price of cars in Paradise.

By which he meant my country, for in his
The stranger is a god in masquerade.
Failing to act that part, I am afraid
I was not human either—ah, who is?

He is, or was; had brothers and a wife;
Chauffeured a truck; last Friday broke his neck
Against a tree. We have no way to check
These headlong emigrations out of life.

Try, I suppose, we must, as even Valéry said,
And said more grandly than I ever shall—
Turning shut lids to the August sun, and all
Such neon figments (amber, green, and red)

Of incommunicable energy
As in my blindness wake, and at a blink
Vanish, and were the clearest hint, I think,
Of what I have been, am, and care to be.

Three good friends in as many months have complained,
"You were nice, James, before your trip. Or so
I thought. But you have changed. I know, I know,
People do change. Well, I'm surprised, I'm pained."

Before they disappeared into the night
Of what they said, I'd make a stab at mouthing
Promises that meant precisely nothing
And never saved my face. For they were right.

These weren't young friends, what's more. Youth would explain
Part of it. I have kept somewhere a page
Written at sixteen to myself at twice that age,
Whom I accuse of having become the vain

Flippant unfeeling monster I now am—
To hear them talk—and exhorting me to recall
Starlight on an evening in late fall
1943, and the walk with M,

To die in whose presence seemed the highest good.
I met M and his new wife last New Year's.
We rued the cold war's tainted atmospheres
From a corner table. It was understood

Our war was over. We had made our peace
With—everything. The heads of animals
Gazed in forbearance from the velvet walls.
Great drifts of damask cleaned our lips of grease.

Then L—her "Let's be friends" and her clear look
Returned in disbelief. I had a herd
Of *friends*. I wanted love, if love's the word
On the foxed spine of the long-mislaid book.

A thousand and one nights! They were grotesque.
Stripping the blubber from my catch, I lit
The oil-soaked wick, then could not see by it.
Mornings, a black film lay upon the desk

. . . Where just a week ago I thought to delve
For images of those years in a Plain Cover.
Some light verse happened as I looked them over:

Postcards from Hamburg, Circa 1912

The ocelot's yawn, a sepia-dim
Shamelessness from nun's coif to spike heels,
She strokes his handlebar who kneels
To do for her what a dwarf does for him.
The properties are grim,

Are, you might want to say, unsexed
By use. A divan covered with a rug,
A flat Methusalem of Krug
Appear from tableau to tableau. The next
Shows him with muscle flexed

In resurrection from his underwear,
Gaining an underworld to harrow.
He steers her ankles like—like a wheelbarrow.
The dwarf has slipped out for a breath of air,
Leaving the monstrous pair.

Who are they? What does their charade convey?
Maker and Muse? Demon and Doll?
"All manners are symbolic"—Hofmannsthal.
Here's the dwarf back with cronies . . . oh I *say*!
Forget about it. They,

In time, in pain, unlearned their tricks.
Only the shrouded focusser of the lens
May still be chasing specimens
From his lone bathysphere deep in the Styx.
St. Pauli's clock struck six;

Sighing, "The death of sin is wages,"
He paid his models, bade them dress and go,
Earthlings once more, incognito
Down swarming boulevards, the contagious-
ly easy, final stages,

Dodged even by the faithful, one of whom
(Morose Great-Uncle Alastair)
Brought back these effigies and would shortly bear
Their doctrine unconfessed, we may assume,
Into his brazen tomb.

We found the postcards after her divorce,
I and Aunt Alix. She turned red with shame,
Then white, then thoughtful. "Ah, they're all the same—
Men, I mean." A pause. "Not you, of course."

And then: "We'll burn them. Light the fire." I must
Meanwhile have tucked a few into my shirt.
I spent the night rekindling with expert
Fingers—but that phase needn't be discussed . . .

"The soul, which in infancy could not be told from the body, came with age to resemble *a body one no longer had*, whose transports went far beyond what passes, now, for sensation. All irony aside, the libertine *was* 'in search of his soul'; nightly he labored to regain those firelit lodgings . . . Likewise, upon the Earth's mature body we inflict a wealth of gross experience—drugs, drills, bombardments—with what effect? A stale *frisson*, a waste of resources all too analogous to our own. Natural calamities (tumor and apoplexy no less than flood and volcano) may at last be hailed as positive reassurances, perverse if you like, of life in the old girl yet."

—GERMAINE NAHMAN

". . . faced with such constant bickering, Cynthia would have to pinch herself to recall how warmly and deeply those two did, in fact, love one another."

—A. H. CLARENDON, *Psyche's Sisters*

Love. Warmth. Fist of sunlight at last
Pounding emphatic on the gulf. High wails
From your white ship: The heart prevails!
Affirm it! Simple decency rides the blast!—
Phrases that, quick to smell blood, lurk like sharks
Within a style's transparent lights and darks.

The lips part. The plume trembles. You're afloat
Upon the breathing, all-reflecting deep.
The past recedes and twinkles, falls asleep.
Fear is unworthy, say the stars by rote;
What destinations have been yours till now
Unworthy, says the leaping prow.

O skimmer of deep blue
Volumes fraught with rhyme and reason,
Once the phosphorescent meshes loosen
And the objects of your quest slip through,
Almost you can overlook a risen
Brow, a thin, black dawn on the horizon.

Except that in this virgin hemisphere
One city calls you—towers, drums, conches, bells
Tolling each year's more sumptuous farewells
To flesh. Among the dancers on the pier
Glides one figure in a suit of bones,
Whose savage grace alerts the chaperones.

He picks you out from thousands. He intends
Perhaps no mischief. Yet the dog-brown eyes
In the chalk face that stiffens as it dries
Pierce you with the eyes of those three friends.
The mask begins to melt upon your face.
A hush has fallen in the marketplace,

And now the long adventure

Let that wait.
I'm tired, it's late at night.

Tomorrow, if it is given me to conquer
An old distrust of imaginary scenes,
Scenes not lived through yet, the few final lines
Will lie on the page and the whole ride at anchor.

I'm home, of course. It's winter. Real
Snow fills the road. On the unmade
Brass bed lies my adored Scheherazade,
Eight-ninths asleep, tail twitching to the steel

Band of the steam heat's dissonant calypso.
The wind has died. Where would I be
If not here? There's so little left to see!
Lost friends, my long ago

Voyages, I bless you for sore
Limbs and mouth kissed, face bronzed and lined,
An earth held up, a text not wholly undermined
By fluent passages of metaphor.

4

Now if the class will turn back to this, er,
Poem's first section—Istanbul—I shall take
What little time is left today to make
Some brief points. So. The rough pentameter

Quatrains give way, you will observe, to three
Interpolations, prose as well as verse.
Does it come through how each in turn refers
To mind, body, and soul (or memory)?

It does? Good. No, I cannot say offhand
Why this should be. I find it vaguely satis—
Yes please? The poet quotes too much? Hm. That is
One way to put it. Mightn't he have planned

For his own modest effort to be seen
Against the yardstick of the "truly great"
(In Spender's phrase)? Fearing to overstate,
He lets *them* do it—lets their words, I mean,

Enhance his—Yes, what now? Ah. How and when
Did he "affirm"? Why, constantly. And how else
But in the form. Form's what affirms. That's well
Said, if I do—*[Bells ring.]* Go, gentlemen.

5

And when the long adventure reached its end,
I saw the Sultan in a glass, grown old,
While she, his fair wife still, her tales all told,
Smiled at him fondly. "O my dearest friend,"

Said she, "and lord and master from the first,
Release me now. Your servant would refresh
Her soul in that cold fountain which the flesh
Knows not. Grant this, for I am faint with thirst."

And he: "But it is I who am your slave.
Free me, I pray, to go in search of joys
Unembroidered by your high, soft voice,
Along that stony path the senses pave."

They wept, then tenderly embraced and went
Their ways. She and her fictions soon were one.
He slept through moonset, woke in blinding sun,
Too late to question what the tale had meant.

TIME

for B. V. Winebaum

Ever that Everest
Among concepts, as prize for fruitful
Grapplings with which
The solved crossword puzzle has now and then
Eclipsed Blake's "Sun-Flower"
(Not that one wanted a letter changed in either)
And jazz believed at seventeen
So parodied the slopes
That one mistook the mountain for a cloud . . .

Or there was blessed Patience:
Fifty-two chromosomes permitting
Trillions of "lives"—some few
Triumphant, the majority
Blocked, doomed, yet satisfying, too,
In that with each, before starting over,
You could inquire beneath
The snowfield, the vine-monogram, the pattern
Of winged cyclists, to where the flaw lay
Crocus-clean, a trail inching between
Sheer heights and drops, and reach what might have been.

All day you had meant
To write letters, turn the key
In certain friendships, be ticked through at dusk
By hard, white, absent faces.

Let's say you went
So far as to begin: "It's me! Forgive . . ."
Too late. From the alcove came his cough,
His whimper—the old man whom sunset wakes.
Truly, could you bear another night
Keeping him company while he raved, agreeing
To Persia on horseback, just you two! when even
The garden path had been forbidden,
He was so feeble. Feeble!

He grasped your pulse in his big gray-haired hand,
Crevasses opening, numb azure. *Wait*
He breathed and glittered: *You'll regret*
You want to   Read my will first   Don't
Your old father   All he has   Be yours

Hours you raised the dark rum to his lips.
Your eyes burned. Your voice said:
"All right, we'll read Cervantes, we'll take trips.
She you loved lives. You'll see her in the morning.
You'll get well, you'll be proud of me. Don't smile!
I love you. I'll find work. You'll—I'll—"

It was light and late.
You could not remember
Sleeping. It hurt to rise.
There stood
Those features' ice-crowned, tanned—by what?—
Landmark, like yours, unwrinkled in repose.
Pouring tea strong and hot,
You swiftly wrote:

". . . this long silence. I don't know what's the matter with me. All winter I have been trying
to discipline myself—'Empty the mind,' as they say in the handbooks, 'concentrate upon one
thing, any thing, the snowflake, the granite it falls upon, the planet risen opposite, etc., etc.'—
and failing, failing. Quicksands of leisure! Now summer's here, I *think*. Each morning a fog
rolls in from the sea. It would lift, perhaps, if you were to come and speak to it. Will you? Do!
One catches the ferry at . . ."

The pen reels from your hand. Were you asleep?
Who were you writing to? Annette? Me? Jake?
Later, smoothing the foothills of the sheet,
You take up your worn pack.

Above their gay crusaders' dress
The monarchs' mouths are pinched and bleak.
Staggering forth in ranks of less and less
Related cards, condemned to the mystique

Of a redeeming One,
An Ace to lead them home, sword, stave, and ax,
Power, Riches, Love, a place to lay them down
In dreamless heaps, the reds, the blacks,

Old Adams and gray Eves
Escort you still. Perhaps this time . . . ?
A Queen in the discarded suit of Leaves,
Earth dims and flattens as you climb

And heaven, darkened, steams
Upon the trembling disk of tea.
Sixty or seventy more games
And you can go the rest alone maybe—

Arriving then at something not unlike
Meaning relieved of sense,
To plant a flag there on that needle peak
Whose diamond grates in the revolving silence.

CHARLES ON FIRE

Another evening we sprawled about discussing
Appearances. And it was the consensus
That while uncommon physical good looks
Continued to launch one, as before, in life
(Among its vaporous eddies and false calms),
Still, as one of us said into his beard,
"Without your intellectual and spiritual
Values, man, you are sunk." No one but squared
The shoulders of his own unloveliness.
Long-suffering Charles, having cooked and served the meal,
Now brought out little tumblers finely etched
He filled with amber liquor and then passed.
"Say," said the same young man, "in Paris, France,
They do it this way"—bounding to his feet
And touching a lit match to our host's full glass.
A blue flame, gentle, beautiful, came, went
Above the surface. In a hush that fell
We heard the vessel crack. The contents drained
As who should step down from a crystal coach.
Steward of spirits, Charles's glistening hand
All at once gloved itself in eeriness.
The moment passed. He made two quick sweeps and
Was flesh again. "It couldn't matter less,"
He said, but with a shocked, unconscious glance
Into the mirror. Finding nothing changed,
He filled a fresh glass and sank down among us.

THE BROKEN HOME

Crossing the street,
I saw the parents and the child
At their window, gleaming like fruit
With evening's mild gold leaf.

In a room on the floor below,
Sunless, cooler—a brimming
Saucer of wax, marbly and dim—
I have lit what's left of my life.

I have thrown out yesterday's milk
And opened a book of maxims.
The flame quickens. The word stirs.

Tell me, tongue of fire,
That you and I are as real
At least as the people upstairs.

My father, who had flown in World War I,
Might have continued to invest his life
In cloud banks well above Wall Street and wife.
But the race was run below, and the point was to win.

Too late now, I make out in his blue gaze
(Through the smoked glass of being thirty-six)
The soul eclipsed by twin black pupils, sex
And business; time was money in those days.

Each thirteenth year he married. When he died
There were already several chilled wives
In sable orbit—rings, cars, permanent waves.
We'd felt him warming up for a green bride.

He could afford it. He was "in his prime"
At three score ten. But money was not time.

When my parents were younger this was a popular act:
A veiled woman would leap from an electric, wine-dark car
To the steps of no matter what—the Senate or the Ritz Bar—
And bodily, at newsreel speed, attack

No matter whom—Al Smith or José María Sert
Or Clemenceau—veins standing out on her throat
As she yelled *War mongerer! Pig! Give us the vote!*,
And would have to be hauled away in her hobble skirt.

What had the man done? Oh, made history.
Her business (he had implied) was giving birth,
Tending the house, mending the socks.

Always that same old story—
Father Time and Mother Earth,
A marriage on the rocks.

One afternoon, red, satyr-thighed
Michael, the Irish setter, head
Passionately lowered, led
The child I was to a shut door. Inside,

Blinds beat sun from the bed.
The green-gold room throbbed like a bruise.
Under a sheet, clad in taboos
Lay whom we sought, her hair undone, outspread,

And of a blackness found, if ever now, in old
Engravings where the acid bit.
I must have needed to touch it
Or the whiteness—was she dead?
Her eyes flew open, startled strange and cold.
The dog slumped to the floor. She reached for me. I fled.

Tonight they have stepped out onto the gravel.
The party is over. It's the fall
Of 1931. They love each other still.

She: Charlie, I can't stand the pace.
He: Come on, honey—why, you'll bury us all!

A lead soldier guards my windowsill:
Khaki rifle, uniform, and face.
Something in me grows heavy, silvery, pliable.

How intensely people used to feel!
Like metal poured at the close of a proletarian novel,
Refined and glowing from the crucible,
I see those two hearts, I'm afraid,
Still. Cool here in the graveyard of good and evil,
They are even so to be honored and obeyed.

. . . Obeyed, at least, inversely. Thus
I rarely buy a newspaper, or vote.
To do so, I have learned, is to invite
The tread of a stone guest within my house.

Shooting this rusted bolt, though, against him,
I trust I am no less time's child than some
Who on the heath impersonate Poor Tom
Or on the barricades risk life and limb.

Nor do I try to keep a garden, only
An avocado in a glass of water—
Roots pallid, gemmed with air. And later,

When the small gilt leaves have grown
Fleshy and green, I let them die, yes, yes,
And start another. I am earth's no less.

A child, a red dog roam the corridors,
Still, of the broken home. No sound. The brilliant
Rag runners halt before wide-open doors.
My old room! Its wallpaper—cream, medallioned
With pink and brown—brings back the first nightmares,
Long summer colds, and Emma, sepia-faced,
Perspiring over broth carried upstairs
Aswim with golden fats I could not taste.

The real house became a boarding school.
Under the ballroom ceiling's allegory
Someone at last may actually be allowed
To learn something; or, from my window, cool
With the unstiflement of the entire story,
Watch a red setter stretch and sink in cloud.

THE CURRENT

Down the dawn-brown
River the charcoal woman
Swept in a boat thin
As the old moon.
White tremblings darted and broke
Under her hat's crown.
A paddle-stroke
And she was gone, in her wake
Only miniature
Whirlpools, her faint
Ritualistic cries.

Now up the stream,
Urging an unwilling
Arc of melon-rind
Painted red to match
His wares, appeared
The meat-vendor.
The young, scarred face
Under the white brim
Glowed with strain
And flamelike ripplings.
He sat in a cloud of flies.

If, further on,
Someone was waiting to thread
Morsels of beef
Onto a green
Bamboo sliver
And pose the lean brochette
Above already glowing
Embers, the river,
Flowing in one direction
By moon, by sun,
Would not be going
To let it happen yet.

THE MAD SCENE

Again last night I dreamed the dream called Laundry.
In it, the sheets and towels of a life we were going to share,
The milk-stiff bibs, the shroud, each rag to be ever
Trampled or soiled, bled on or groped for blindly,
Came swooning out of an enormous willow hamper
Onto moon-marbly boards. We had just met. I watched
From outer darkness. I had dressed myself in clothes
Of a new fiber that never stains or wrinkles, never
Wears thin. The opera house sparkled with tiers
And tiers of eyes, like mine enlarged by belladonna,
Trained inward. There I saw the cloud-clot, gust by gust,
Form, and the lightning bite, and the roan mane unloosen.
Fingers were running in panic over the flute's nine gates.
Why did I flinch? I loved you. And in the downpour laughed
To have us wrung white, gnarled together, one
Topmost mordent of wisteria,
As the lean tree burst into grief.

FROM THE CUPOLA

for H. M.

The sister who told fortunes prophesied
A love-letter. In the next mail it came.
You didn't recognize the writer's name
And wondered he knew yours. Ah well. That seed

Has since become a world of blossom and bark.
The letters fill a drawer, the gifts a room.
No hollow of your day is hidden from
His warm concern. Still you are in the dark.

Too much understanding petrifies.
The early letters struck you as blackmail.
You have them now by heart, a rosy veil
Colors the phrase repaired to with shut eyes.

Was the time always wrong for you to meet?—
Not that he ever once proposed as much.
Your sisters joke about it. "It's too rich!
Somebody Up There loves you, Psyche sweet."

Tell me about him, then. Not a believer,
I'll hold my tongue while you, my dear, dictate.
Him I have known too little (or, of late,
Too well) to trust my own view of your lover.

Oh but one has many, many tongues!
And you will need a certain smouldering five
Deep in the ash of something I survive,
Poke and rummage with as reluctant tongs

As possible. The point won't be to stage
One of our torchlit hunts for truth. Truth asks
Just this once to sleep with fiction, masks
Of tears and laughter on the moonstruck page;

To cauterize what babbles to be healed—
Just this once not by candor. Here and now,
Psyche, I quench that iron lest it outglow
A hovering radiance your fingers shield.

Renaissance features grafted onto Greek
Revival, glassed, hexagonal lookouts crown
Some of the finest houses in this town.
By day or night, cloud, sunbeam, lunatic streak,

They alternately ravish and disown
Earth, sky, and water—Are you with me? Speak.

SUNLIGHT   Crossfire
of rays and shadows each
glancing off a windowpane a stone
You alone my correspondent

have remained sheer
projection   Hurt   Not gravely   Not at all
Your bloodlessness a glaze
of thin thin varnish where I kneel

Were the warm drop
upon your letter oil and were that page
your sleeping person then
all would indeed be lost

Our town is small
its houses built like temples
The rare stranger I let pass with lowered
eyes   He also could be you

Nights the last red
wiped from my lips the harbor
blinking out gem by gem how utterly
we've been undressed

You will not come
to the porch at noon will you rustling your wings
or masked as crone or youth
The mouths behind our faces kiss

Kindlings of truth
Risen from the dawn mist
some wriggling silver in a tern's beak scrawls
joyous memoranda onto things

TODAY I have your letter from the South
where as a child I   but of course you know
Three times I've read it at my attic window
A city named for palms half mummy and half myth
pools flashing talking birds the world of my
first vision of you Psyche   Though it's May

that could be frost upon the apple trees
silvery plump as sponges above the pale
arm of the Sound and the pane is chill to feel
I live now by the seasons burn and freeze
far from that world where nothing changed or died
unless to be reborn on the next tide

You daylong in the saddles of foaming opal
ride   I am glad   Come dusk lime juice and gin
deepen the sunset under your salt skin
I've tasted that side of the apple
A city named for palms half desert and half dream
its dry gold settles on my mouth   I bloom

Where nothing died   Breaking on us like waves
the bougainvillea bloomed fell bloomed again
The new sea wall rose from the hurricane
and no less staunchly from the old freed slave's
ashes each night her grandchild climbed the stairs
to twitch white gauze across the stinging stars

City half dream half desert where at dawn
the sprinkler dervish whirled and all was crystalline
within each house half brothel and half shrine
up from the mirror tabletop had flown
by noon the shadow of each plate each spoon to float
in light that warbled on the ceiling   Wait

ALICE has entered talking

Any mirage if seen from a remote stand
point is refreshing   Yes but dust and heat
lie at its heart   Poor Psyche you forget
That was a cruel impossible wonderland

The very sidewalks suffered   Ours that used
to lead can you remember to the beach
I felt it knew and waited for us each
morning to trot its length in teardrop punctured shoes

when in fact the poor dumb thing lay I now know
under a dark spell cast from quite another
quarter the shadow of a towering mother
smooth as stone and thousandbreasted though

her milk was watery scant so much for love
false like everything in that whole world
However   This shadow that a royal palm hurled
onto the sidewalk from ten yards above

day night rustling and wrestling never shattered
except to mend back forth or lost its grip
the batwing offspring of her ladyship
Our orchid stucco house looked on greenshuttered

stoic   But the sidewalk suffered most
Like somebody I shall not name it lacked
perspective   It failed absolutely to detect
the root of all that evil   The clues it missed

Nights after a windstorm great yellow paper
dry branches lying on the curb in heaps
like fancy dress don't ask me whose someone who steps
forth and is changed by the harsh moonlight to vapor

the sidewalk could only grit itself and shift
Some mornings respite   A grisaille opaque
as poured concrete   And yet by ten o'clock
the phantom struck again in a first sunshaft

Off to the beach   Us nurse in single file
Those days we'd meet our neighbor veiled and hatted
tanagra leading home out of the sun she hated
a little boy with water wings   We'd smile

then hold our breaths to pass a barricade
of black smells rippling up from the soft hot
brink of the mirage past which sidewalks could not
follow   Ours stood there crumbling then obeyed

a whisper back of it and turned   The sea the loose
unshadowed sand too free white heterodox
ever to be congealed into sidewalks
ours never saw   GIVE ME THE SNAPPED SHOELACE

LIZARDS ANTS SCRAPS OF SILVER FOIL
hoarse green tongues begged from each new crack   No use
The shadow trod it as our nightmares us
Then we moved here where gray skies are the rule

What   Why not simply have cut down the tree
Psyche I can't believe my   Hush   You child
Cut down the   I've got gooseflesh   Feel   I'm chilled
My sister's hyperthyroid eyes fix me

The whites lackluster shot with miniature
red brambles abruptly glitter overspill
down powdered cheeks   Alice can weep at will
How to convey the things I feel for her

She is more strange than Iceland bathed all night
an invalid in sunshine   Lava cliffs
The geyser that erupts the loon that laughs
I move to kiss her but she hums a note

and licks her lips   *Well darling I must fly*
before you read what it does not intend
about yourself and your mysterious friend
say or some weird rivalry that I

may once have harbored though I harbor none
now nor does Gertrude not the tiniest pang
into this long but kindly meant harangue
She nods and leaves the room   And I am here alone

I place the ladder hoist from rung to rung
my pail and cloths into a cupola glassed
entirely with panes some tinted amethyst
it is my task to clean   Up here among

spatterings and reflections wipe as I will
these six horizons still the rain's dry ghost
and my own features haunt the roofs the coast
How does one get to know a landscape well

When did we leave the South   Why do we live indoors
I wonder sweating to the cadence   Even
on sunless days the cupola is an oven
Views blur   This thing we see them through endures

MIDNIGHT   I dream I dream   The slow moon eludes
one stilled cloud   Din of shimmerings   From across the Sound
what may have begun as no more
than a willow's sleepwalking outline quickens detaches
comes to itself in the cupola
panics from pane to pane and then impulsively
surrendering fluttering by now the sixteenfold
wings of the cherubim unclipped by faith or reason
stands there my dream made whole

over whose walls again
a red vine black in moonlight crawls
made habitable   Each cell of the concrete
fills with sweet light   The wave breaks
into tears   Come if it's you   Step down
to where I   Stop   For at your touch the dream
cracks the angel tenses flees

NOON finds me faced by a small troop of furies
They are my senses shrill and ominous
We who were trained they cry *to do your pleasure*
are kept like children   Is this fair to us

Dear ones I say bending to kiss their faces
trust me   One day you'll understand   Meanwhile
suppose we think of things to raise our spirits
and leading the two easiest to beguile

into the kitchen feed them shots of bourbon
Their brother who loves Brahms conceives a wish
for gems from L'Africana played at volumes
that make the dwarf palm shudder in its dish

The pale one with your eyes restively flashing
takes in the dock the ashen Sound the sky
The fingers of the eldest brush my features
But you are smiling she says coldly   *Why*

STAR or candle being lit
    but to shed itself
    into blackness partly night's
sure that no less golden warm than it
            is our love
    will have missed the truth by half
    We see according to our lights

Eros   husband   names distort
          you who have no name
Peace upon your neophytes
Help me when the christenings shall start
                    o my love
          to defend your sleep from them
          and see according to our lights

Ah and should discernment's twin
          tyrants adamant
          for their meal of pinks and whites
be who call those various torches in
                    help me love
          This is nothing I shall want
          We see according to our lights

When as written you have lapsed
          back into the god
          darts and wings and appetites
what of him the lover all eclipsed
                    by sheer love
          Shut my eyes it does no good
          Who will ever put to rights

Psyche, hush. This is me, James.
          Writing lest he think
Of the reasons why he writes—
Boredom, fear, mixed vanities and shames;
                    Also love.
          From my phosphorescent ink
          Trickle faint unworldly lights

Down your face. Come, we'll both rest.
          Weeping? You must not.
All our pyrotechnic flights
Miss the sleeper in the pitch-dark breast.
                    He is love:
          He is everyone's blind spot.
          We see according to our lights.

"What's that sound? Is it you, dear?"

"Yes. I was just eating something."

"What?"

"I don't know—I mean, an apricot . . ."

"Hadn't you best switch on the light and make sure?"

"No, thank you, Gertrude."

A hurt silence ensued.

"Oh, Psyche!" her sister burst out at length. "Here you you are, surrounded by loving kin, in a house crammed with lovely old things, and what do you crave but the unfamiliar, the 'transcendental'? I declare, you're turning into the classic New England old maid!"

· ·

Psyche's hands dropped from her wet, white face. The time had come—except that Time, like Love, wears a mask in this story, whose action requires perhaps thirty-six hours of Spring, perhaps thirty-six Springs of a life—a moment nevertheless had come to take the electric torch and leave her sisters without a word. Later she was to recall a tear-streaked muzzle, the marvelous lashed golds of an iris reflecting her own person backed by ever tinier worlds of moonlight and tossing palms, then, at the center, blackness, a fixed point, a spindle on which everything had begun to turn. Piercing her to the brain.

Spelt out in brutal prose, all had been plain.

RAIN   Evening   The drive in   My sisters' gold sedan's
   eyes have gone dim and dark   windows are sealed
      For vision's sake two wipers wield
   the automatic coquetry of fans

In the next car young Eros and his sweetheart sit
   fire and saltwater still from their embrace
      Grief plays upon his sated face
   Her mask of tears does not exactly fit

The love goddess his mother overflows a screen
   sixty feet wide or seems to   Who can plumb
      those motes of rose and platinum
   At once they melt back into the machine

throbbing dry and dispassionate beyond our ken
   to spool her home whose beauty flabbergasts
      The nervous systems of her guests
   drink and drink the sparkling staleness in

Now in her element steam she looms up from a bath
   The hero's breastplate mirrors her red lips
      It burns and clouds   As waterdrops
   course down the monumental cheeks of both

they kiss   My sisters turn on me from either side
   shrieking with glee under the rainlight mask
      fondle and pinch in mean burlesque
   of things my angel you and I once tried

In no time he alone is left of a proud corps
   That dustcloud hides triumphant fleeing Huns
      Lips parched by a montage of suns
   he cannot taste our latter night's downpour

while she by now my sisters fatten upon fact
   is on location in Djakarta where
      tomorrow's sun illumines her
   emoting in strange arms   It's all an act

Eros are you like her so false a naked glance
   turns you into that slackjawed fleshproud youth
      driving away   Was he your truth
   Is it too late to study ignorance

These fictive lives these loves of the comedian
   so like so unlike ours which hurt and heal
      are what the gods know   You can feel
   lust and fulfillment Eros no more than

ocean its salt depths or uranium its hot
   disintegrative force or I our fable
      My interest like the rain grown feeble
   a film of sorrow on my eyes they shut

I may already be part god   Asleep awake
   some afterglow as of a buried heaven
      keeps flickering through me   I may even
   learn to love it Eros for your sake

MORNING   The task is done   When my sisters wake
they will look once more upon pale water and clear sky
a fair far brow of land
with its fillet of Greek trees oak apple willow
and here below in the foreground
across a street finished down to the last detail
a red clapboard temple   The neat outlines
it's a warehouse really have been filled with colors
dull red flaking walls   white trim
and pediment   tar roof patched black on black
Greek colors   An effect I hope
not too much spoiled by a big yellow legend
BOAT WORKS on the roof which seagulls helicopters
the highup living and the happy dead
are in a position to read
Outside indeed a boat lies covered with tarpaulin
Old headlines mend a missing pane   The warehouse
seems but in the time it takes to say *abandoned*
a face male old molepale in sun
though blinded by the mullion's shadow
has floated to an eerie scale the rising
wind flutes out of the oaken depths
I look away   When I look back
the panic's over   It is afternoon
Now the window reflects my sisters' white
mock Ionic portico and me emerging
blinking   Too bright to bear or turn from
spring's first real sun burns on the numb blue Sound
Beyond the warehouse past the round GULF sign
whose warning it ignores a baby dock has waded
The small waves stretch their necks gulls veer and scold
I walk the length of our Greek Revival village
from library to old blind lighthouse
Like one entranced who talks as awake she cannot
a potpourri of dead chalkpetal dialects
dead anyhow all winter
lips caulked with faded pollen and dust of cloves
I find that I can break the cipher
come to light along certain humming branches
make out not only *apple blossom* and *sun*
but perfectly the dance of darker undertones
on pavement or white wall   It is this dance I know

that cracks the pavement   I do know
Finally I reach a garden where I am to uproot
the last parsnips for my sisters' dinner
Not parsnips mastodons   But this year's greens
already frill them and they pull easily
from the soft ground   Two of the finest
are tightly interlocked have grown that way   They lie
united in the grave of sunny air
as in their breathing living dark
I look at them a long while
mealy and soiled in one another's arms
and blind full to the ivory marrow
with tender blindness   Then I bury them
once more in memory of us
Back home   Gold skies   My basket full
Lifting it indoors I turn   The little dock
It is out there still on stilts in freezing water
It must know by now
that no one is coming after it that it must wait
for morning for next week for summer
by which time it will have silvered and splintered
and the whitewinged boats and the bridegroom's burning sandals
will come too late   It's dark   It's dinner time
Light the lamp my sisters call from where they eat
There follows a hushed preening and straining
wallpaper horsehair glass wood pewter glue
Now is their moment when all else goes black
and what is there but substance to turn to
Sister the lamp   The round
moon mallet has risen and struck   Of the warehouse pulverized
one faintest blueprint glimmers by which to build it
on the same spot tomorrow somehow right
Light your lamp Psyche dear
My hand is on the switch   I have done this
faithfully each night since the first
Tonight I think will not be different
Then soft light lights the room the furniture
a blush invades even the dropped lid
yes and I am here alone
I and my flesh and blood

Thank you, Psyche. I should think those panes
Were just about as clear as they can be.
It's time I turned my light on. Child, leave me.
Here on the earth we loved alone remains

One shrunken amphitheater, look, to moon
Hugely above. Ranked glintings from within
Hint that a small articulate crowd has been
Gathered for days now, waiting. None too soon,

Whether in lower or in upper case,
Will come the Moment for the metal of each
To sally forth—once more into the breach!
Beyond it, glory lies, a virgin space

Acrackle in white hunger for the word.
We've seen what comes next. There is no pure deed.
A black-and-red enchanter, a deep-dyed
Coil of—No matter. One falls back, soiled, blurred.

And on the page, of course, black only. Damned
If I don't tire of the dark view of things.
I think of your "Greek colors" and it rings
A sweet bell. Time to live! Haven't I dimmed

That portion of the ribbon—whose red glows
Bright with disuse—sufficiently for a bit?
Tomorrow mayn't I start to pay my debt,
In wine, in heart's blood, to la vie en rose?

This evening it will do to be alone,
Here, with your girlish figures: parsnip, Eros,
Shadow, blossom, windowpane. The warehouse.
The lamp I smell in every other line.

Do you smell mine? From its rubbed brass a moth
Hurtles in motes and tatters of itself
—Be careful, tiny sister, drabbest sylph!—
Against the hot glare, the consuming myth,

Drops, and is still. My hands move. An intense,
Slow-paced, erratic dance goes on below.
I have received from whom I do not know
These letters. Show me, light, if they make sense.

DAYS OF 1964

Houses, an embassy, the hospital,
Our neighborhood sun-cured if trembling still
In pools of the night's rain . . .
Across the street that led to the center of town
A steep hill kept one company part way
Or could be climbed in twenty minutes
For some literally breathtaking views,
Framed by umbrella pines, of city and sea.
Underfoot, cyclamen, autumn crocus grew
Spangled as with fine sweat among the relics
Of good times had by all. If not Olympus,
An out-of-earshot, year-round hillside revel.

I brought home flowers from my climbs.
Kyria Kleo who cleans for us
Put them in water, sighing *Virgin, Virgin.*
Her legs hurt. She wore brown, was fat, past fifty,
And looked like a Palmyra matron
Copied in lard and horsehair. How she loved
You, me, loved us all, the bird, the cat!
I think now she *was* love. She sighed and glistened
All day with it, or pain, or both.
(We did not notably communicate.)
She lived nearby with her pious mother
And wastrel son. She called me her real son.

I paid her generously, I dare say.
Love makes one generous. Look at us. We'd known
Each other so briefly that instead of sleeping
We lay whole nights, open, in the lamplight,
And gazed, or traded stories.

One hour comes back—you gasping in my arms
With love, or laughter, or both,
I having just remembered and told you
What I'd looked up to see on my way downtown at noon:
Poor old Kleo, her aching legs,
Trudging into the pines. I called,
Called three times before she turned.

Above a tight, skyblue sweater, her face
Was painted. Yes. Her face was painted
Clown-white, white of the moon by daylight,
Lidded with pearl, mouth a poinsettia leaf,
Eat me, pay me—the erotic mask
Worn the world over by illusion
To weddings of itself and simple need.

Startled mute, we had stared—was love illusion?—
And gone our ways. Next, I was crossing a square
In which a moveable outdoor market's
Vegetables, chickens, pottery kept materializing
Through a dream-press of hagglers each at heart
Leery lest he be taken, plucked,
The bird, the flower of that November mildness,
Self lost up soft clay paths, or found, foothold,
Where the bud throbs awake
The better to be nipped, self on its knees in mud—
Here I stopped cold, for both our sakes;

And calmer on my way home bought us fruit.

Forgive me if you read this. (And may Kyria Kleo,
Should someone ever put it into Greek
And read it aloud to her, forgive me, too.)
I had gone so long without loving,
I hardly knew what I was thinking.

Where I hid my face, your touch, quick, merciful,
Blindfolded me. A god breathed from my lips.
If that was illusion, I wanted it to last long;
To dwell, for its daily pittance, with us there,
Cleaning and watering, sighing with love or pain.
I hoped it would climb when it needed to the heights
Even of degradation, as I for one
Seemed, those days, to be always climbing
Into a world of wild
Flowers, feasting, tears—or was I falling, legs
Buckling, heights, depths,
Into a pool of each night's rain?
But you were everywhere beside me, masked,
As who was not, in laughter, pain, and love.

LORELEI

The stones of kin and friend
Stretch off into a trembling, sweatlike haze.

They may not after all be stepping-stones
But you have followed them. Each strands you, then

Does not. Not yet. Not here.
Is it a crossing? Is there no way back?

Soft gleams lap the base of the one behind you
On which a black girl sings and combs her hair.

It's she who some day (when your stone is in place)
Will see that much further into the golden vagueness

Forever about to clear. Love with his chisel
Deepens the lines begun upon your face.

THE FRIEND OF THE FOURTH DECADE

When I returned with drinks and nuts my friend
Had moved to the window seat, back to the view.

The clear central pane around which ran
Smaller ones stained yellow, crimson, blue,

Framed our country's madly whipping flag,
Its white pole above roofs, the sea beyond.

That it was time for the flag to be lowered shed
Light on my friend's tactful disinvolvement—

Or did he feel as chastening somehow
Those angry little stripes upon his shoulders?

A huge red sun flowed positively through
Him in spots, glazing, obscuring his person

To that of Anyman with ears aglow,
On a black cushion, gazing inward, mute.

After dinner he said, "I'm tired of understanding
The light in people's eyes, the smells, the food.

(By the way, those veal birds were delicious.
They're out of Fannie Farmer? I thought so.)

Tired of understanding what I hear,
The tones, the overtones; of knowing

Just what clammy twitchings thrive
Under such cold flat stones

As We-are-profoundly-honored-to-have-with-us
Or This-street-has-been-torn-up-for-your-convenience.

As for what I catch myself saying,
Don't believe me! I *despise* Thoreau.

I mean to learn, in the language of where I am going,
Barely enough to ask for food and love.

Listen," he went on. "I have this friend—
What's that face for? Did you think I had only one?

You are my oldest friend, remember. Well:
Karlheinrich collects stamps. I now spend mornings

With a bowl of water and my postcard box.
Cards from all over. God! Those were the years

I never used to throw out anything.
Each card then soaks five minutes while its ink

Turns to exactly the slow formal swirls
Through which a phoenix flies on Chinese silk.

These leave the water darker but still clear,
The text unreadable. It's true!

Cards from my mother, my great-uncle, you!
And the used waters deepen the sea's blue.

I cannot tell you what this does to me.
Scene upon scene's immersion and emergence

Rinsed of the word. The Golden Gate, Moroccan
Dancing boys, the Alps from Interlaken,

Fuji, the Andes, Titian's Venus, two
Mandrills from the Cincinnati zoo—

All *that* survives the flood, as does a lighter
Heart than I have had in many a day.

Salt lick big as a fist, heart, hoard
Of self one grew up prizing above rubies—

To feel it even by a grain dissolved,
Absolved I mean, recipient with writer,

By water holy from the tap, by air that dries,
Of having cared and having ceased to care . . ."

I nodded and listened, envious. When my friend
Had gone where he was going, I tried it, too.

The stamp slid off, of course, and the ink woke.
I watched my mother's *Dearest Son* unfurl

In blue ornate brief plungings-up:
Almost a wild iris taking shape.

I heard oblivion's thin siren singing,
And bore it bravely. At the hour's end

I had my answer. Chances are it was
Some simple matter of what ink she used,

And yet her message remained legible,
The memories it stirred did not elude me.

I put my postcards back upon the shelf.
Certain things die only with oneself.

"You should see Muhammed's taxi," wrote my friend.
"Pure junkyard Bauhaus, angular, dented white,

It trails a wedding veil of squawking dust.
Each ride is worth your life—except I'm just

Not afraid. I'm not.
Those chiefly who discern us have the juju

To take our lives. Bouncing beside Muhammed,
I smile and smoke, am indestructible.

Or else I just can't picture dying
On foreign soil. These years are years of grace.

The way I feel towards home is . . . dim.
Don't worry, I'll go back. Honeymoons end.

Nor does the just man cheat his native earth
Of its inalienable right to cover him."

Finally a dung-and-emerald oasis,
No place I knew of. "Here," he wrote on the back,

"Individual and type are one.
Do as I please, I *am* the simpleton

Whose last exploit is to have been exploited
Neck and crop. In the usual bazaar,

Darker, more crisscrossed than a beggar's palm,
Smell of money draws them after me,

I answer to whatever name they call,
Drink the sweet black condescending dregs,

Try on their hungers like a shirt of flame
(Well, a sports shirt of flame) whereby I've been

Picked clean, reborn each day increasingly
Conspicuous, increasingly unseen."

Behind a door marked DANGER
(This is a dream I have about my friend)

Swaddlings of his whole civilization,
Prayers, accounts, long priceless scroll,

Whip, hawk, prow, queen, down to some last
Lost comedy, all that fine writing

Rigid with rains and suns,
Are being gingerly unwound.

There. Now the mirror. Feel the patient's heart
Pounding—oh please, this once—

Till nothing moves but to a drum.
See his eyes darken in bewilderment—

No, in joy—and his lips part
To greet the perfect stranger.

Unjeweled in black as ever comedienne
Of mourning if not silent star of chic,
You drift, September nightwind at your back,
The half block from your flat to the Bon Goût,
Collapse, order a black
Espresso and my ouzo in that Greek
Reserved for waiters, crane to see who's who
Without removing your dark glasses, then,
Too audibly: "Eh, Jimmy, qui sont ces deux strange men?"

Curiosity long since killed the cat
Inside you. Sweet good nature, lack of guile,
These are your self-admitted foibles, no?
My countrymen, the pair in question, get
Up, glance our way, and go,
And we agree it will not be worthwhile
To think of funny nicknames for them yet,
Such as Le Turc, The Missing Diplomat,
Justine, The Nun, The Nut—ah now, speaking of that,

I'm calling *you* henceforth The Lunatic.
Today at 4 a.m. in a snack bar
You were discovered eating, if you please,
Fried squid; alone. Aleko stood aghast.
"Sit down, try some of these,"
You said and gave your shrug, as when, the car
Door shutting on your thumb, a faint sigh passed
Uninterpreted till Frederick
At table glimpsed your bloodstained Kleenex and was sick.

Sapphó has been to your new flat, she *says*.
Tony, who staggered there with the Empire
Mirror you wanted from his shop, tells how
You had him prop it in a chair and leave
That instant. Really now!
Let's plan a tiny housewarming. "My dear,
Impossible with L'Eternel Convive."
Tall, gleaming, it could sit for years, I guess,
Drinking the cool black teas of your appearances.

Not that you're much at home this season. By
Ten you are being driven to the shore—
A madness known as Maria's Gardening Phase.
I went along once, watched you prune, transplant,
Nails ragged, in a daze
Of bliss. A whitewashed cube with tout confort
You'd built but would not furnish. "Bah, one can't
Spend day and night in Eden. Chairs, beds—why?
Dormir, d'ailleurs, this far from the Bon Goût? I'd die!"

In smarter weeds than Eve's (Chanel, last year's)
You kneel to beds of color and young vines.
The chauffeur lounges smoking in the shade . . .
Before you know it, sunset. Brass-white, pink-
Blue wallowings. Dismayed
You recollect a world in which one dines,
Plays cards, endures old ladies, has to think.
The motor roars. You've locked up trowel and shears.
The whole revived small headland lurches, disappears

To float pale black all night against the sea,
A past your jasmines for the present grow
Dizzyingly from. About what went before
Or lies beneath, how little one can glean.
Girlhood, marriage, the war . . .
I'd like once (not now, here comes Giulio)
Really to hear—I mean—I didn't mean—
You paint a smiling mouth to answer me:
"Since when does L'Enfant care for archaeology?"

"Some people are not charmed. I'm among those,"
Sapphó said, livid. "Fond of one? Pure myth.
Fond of her chauffeur—period. I refuse
Flatly to see her." As for me, I've come
To take you for the muse
Of my off-days, and tell you so herewith
If only to make you smile, shrug, run a comb
Through foam-grayed hair the wind from Egypt blows
Across a brow of faint lines powdered tuberose.

TO MY GREEK

Dear nut
Uncrackable by nuance or debate,
Eat with your fingers, wear your bloomers to bed,

Under my skin stay nude. Let past and future

Perish upon our lips, ocean inherit
Those paper millions. Let there be no word
For justice, grief, convention; *you* be convention—
Goods, bads, kaló-kakó, cockatoo-raucous

Coastline of white printless coves

Already strewn with offbeat echolalia.
Forbidden   Salt   Kiss   Wardrobe   Foot   Cloud   Peach
—Name it, my chin drips sugar. Radiant dumbbell, each

Noon's menus and small talk leave you

Likelier, each sunset yawned away,
Hair in eyes, head bent above the strummed
Lexicon, gets by heart about to fail
This or that novel mode of being together

Without conjunctions. Still

I fear for us. Nights fall
We toss through blindly, drenched in her appraising
Glare, the sibyl I turn to

When all else fails me, when you do—

The mother tongue!
Her least slip a mirror triptych glosses,
Her automation and my mind are one.
Ancient in fishscale silver-blue,

What can she make of you? Her cocktail sweats

With reason: speech will rise from it,
Quite beyond your comprehension rise
Like blood to a slapped face, stingingly apt

If unrepeatable, tones one forgets

Even as one is changed for life by them,
Veins branching a cold coral,
Common sense veering into common scenes,
Tears, incoherent artifice,

Altar upset, cut glass and opaline

Schools ricocheting through the loud cave
Where lie my Latin's rusted treasure,
The bones, picked clean, of my Italian,

Where some blue morning also she may damn

Well find her windpipe slit with that same rainbow
Edge a mere weekend with you gives
To books, to living (anything to forego
That final drunken prophecy whereby,

Lacking her blessing, you my siren grow

Stout, serviceable, gray.
A fishwife shawled in fourth-hand idiom
Spouting my views to earth and heaven)—Oh,

Having chosen the way of little knowledge,

Trusted each to use the other
Kindly except in moments of gross need,
Come put the verb-wheel down
And kiss my mouth despite the foot in it.

Let schoolboys brave her shallows. Sheer

Lilting azure float them well above
Those depths the surfacer
Lives, when he does, alone to sound and sound.
The barest word be what I say in you.

LAST WORDS

My life, your light green eyes
Have lit on me with joy.
There's nothing I don't know
Or shall not know again,
Over and over again.
It's noon, it's dawn, it's night,
I am the dog that dies
In the deep street of Troy
Tomorrow, long ago—
Part of me dims with pain,
Becomes the stinging flies,
The bent head of the boy.
Part looks into your light
And lives to tell you so.

ANOTHER AUGUST

Pines. The white, ocher-pocked houses. Sky unflawed. Upon so much former strangeness a calm settles, glaze of custom to be neither shattered nor shattered by. Home. Home at last.

Years past—blind, tattering
wind, hail, tears—my head was in those clouds
that now are dark pearl in my head.

Open the shutters. Let variation
abandon the swallows one by one.
How many summer dusks were needed
to make that single skimming form!
The very firefly kindles to its type.
Here is each evening's lesson. First
the hour, the setting. Only then
the human being, his white shirtsleeve
chalked among treetrunks, round a waist,
or lifted in an entrance. Look for him.
Be him.

Envoi for S.

Whom you saw mannerless and dull of heart,
Easy to fool, impossible to hurt,
I wore that fiction like a fine white shirt
And asked no favor but to act the part.

MORNINGS IN A NEW HOUSE

And still at dawn the fire is lit
By whom a cold man hardly cares,
Reflection gliding up the legs of chairs,
Flue choking with the shock of it.

Next a frozen window thaws
In gradual slow stains of field,
Snow fence and birches more or less revealed.
This done, the brightness sheathes its claws.

The worst is over. Now between
His person and that tamed uprush
(Which to recall alone can make him flush)
Habit arranges the fire screen.*

Crewelwork. His mother as a child
Stitched giant birds and flowery trees
To dwarf a house, *her* mother's—see the chimney's
Puff of dull yarn! Still vaguely chilled,

Guessing how even then her eight
Years had foreknown him, nursed him, all,
Sewn his first dress, sung to him, let him fall.
Howled when his face chipped like a plate,

He stands there wondering until red
Infraradiance, wave on wave,
So enters each plume-petal's crazy weave,
Each worsted brick of the homestead,

That once more, deep indoors, blood's drawn,
The tiny needlewoman cries,
And to some faintest creaking shut of eyes
His pleasure and the doll's are one.

*Days later. All framework & embroidery rather than any slower looking into things. Fire screen—screen *of* fire. The Valkyrie's baffle, pulsing at trance pitch, godgiven, elemental. Flames masking that cast-iron plaque—"contrecoeur" in French—which backs the hearth with charred Loves & Graces. Some such meaning might have caught, only I didn't wait, I settled for the obvious—by lamplight as it were. Oh well. Our white heats lead us on no less than words do. Both have been devices in their day.

MATINÉES

for David Kalstone

A gray maidservant lets me in
To Mrs. Livingston's box. It's already begun!
The box is full of grown-ups. She sits me down
Beside her. Meanwhile a ravishing din

Swells from below—Scene One
Of *Das Rheingold*. The entire proscenium
Is covered with a rippling azure scrim.
The three sopranos dart hither and yon

On invisible strings. Cold lights
Cling to bare arms, fair tresses. Flat
And natural aglitter like paillettes
Upon the great green sonorous depths float

Until with pulsing wealth the house is filled,
No one believing, everybody thrilled.

Lives of the Great Composers make it sound
Too much like cooking: "Sore beset,
He put his heart's blood into that quintet . . ."
So let us try the figure turned around

As in some Lives of Obscure Listeners:
"The strains of Cimarosa and Mozart
Flowed through his veins, and fed his solitary heart.
Long beyond adolescence [One infers

Your elimination, sweet Champagne
Drunk between acts!] the aria's remote
Control surviving his worst interval,

Tissue of sound and tissue of the brain
Would coalesce, and what the Masters wrote
Itself compose his features sharp and small."

Hilariously Dr. Scherer took the guise
Of a bland smoothshaven Alberich whose age-old
Plan had been to fill my tooth with gold.
Another whiff of laughing gas,

And the understanding was implicit
That we must guard each other, this gold and I,
Against amalgamation by
The elemental pit.

Vague as to what dentist and tooth "stood for,"
One patient dreamer gathered something more.
A voice said in the speech of birds,

"My father having tampered with your mouth,
From now on, metal, music, myth
Will seem to taint its words."

We love the good, said Plato? He was wrong.
We love as well the wicked and the weak.
Flesh hugs its shaved plush. Twenty-four-hour-long
Galas fill the hulk of the Comique.

Flesh knows by now what dishes to avoid,
Tries not to brood on bomb or heart attack.
Anatomy is destiny, said Freud.
Soul is the brilliant hypochondriac.

Soul will cough blood and sing, and softer sing,
Drink poison, breathe her joyous last, a waltz
Rubato from his arms who sobs and stays

Behind, death after death, who fairly melts
Watching her turn from him, restored, to fling
Kisses into the furnace roaring praise.

The fallen cake, the risen price of meat,
Staircase run ten times up and down like scales
(Greek proverb: He who has no brain has feet)—
One's household opera never palls or fails.

The pipes' aubade. Recitatives.—Come back!
—I'm out of pills!—We'd love to!—What?—*Nothing,*
Let me be!—No, no, I'll drink it black . . .
The neighbors' chorus. The quick darkening

In which a prostrate figure must inquire
With every earmark of its being meant
Why God in Heaven harries him/her so.

The love scene (often cut). The potion. The tableau:
Sleepers folded in a magic fire,
Tongues flickering up from humdrum incident.

When Jan Kiepura sang His Handsomeness
Of Mantua those high airs light as lust
Attuned one's bare throat to the dagger-thrust.
Living for them would have been death no less.

Or Lehmann's Marschallin!—heartbreak so shrewd,
So ostrich-plumed, one ached to disengage
Oneself from a last love, at center stage,
To the beloved's dazzled gratitude.

What havoc certain Saturday afternoons
Wrought upon a bright young person's morals
I now leave to the public to condemn.

The point thereafter was to arrange for one's
Own chills and fever, passions and betrayals,
Chiefly in order to make song of them.

You and I, caro, seldom
Risk the real thing any more.
It's all too silly or too solemn.
Enough to know the score

From records or transcription
For our four hands. Old beauties, some
In advanced stages of decomposition,

Float up through the sustaining
Pedal's black and fluid medium.
Days like today

Even recur (wind whistling themes
From *Lulu,* and sun shining
On the rough Sound) when it seems
Kinder to remember than to play.

Dear Mrs. Livingston,
I want to say that I am still in a daze
From yesterday afternoon.
I will treasure the experience always—

My very first Grand Opera! It was very
Thoughtful of you to invite
Me and am so sorry
That I was late, and for my coughing fit.

I play my record of the Overture
Over and over. I pretend
I am still sitting in the theater.

I also wrote a poem which my Mother
Says I should copy out and send.
Ever gratefully, Your little friend . . .

THE SUMMER PEOPLE

. . . et l'hiver resterait la saison intellectuelle créatrice.
—MALLARMÉ

On our New England coast was once
A village white and neat
With Greek Revival houses,
Sailboats, a fishing fleet,

Two churches and two liquor stores,
An Inn, a Gourmet Shoppe,
A library, a pharmacy.
Trains passed but did not stop.

Gold Street was rich in neon,
Main Street in rustling trees
Untouched as yet by hurricanes
And the Dutch elm disease.

On Main the summer people
Took deep-rooted ease—
A leaf turned red, to town they'd head.
On Gold lived the Portuguese

Whose forebears had manned whalers.
Two years from the Azores
Saw you with ten gold dollars
Upon these fabled shores.

Feet still pace the whaler's deck
At the Caustic (Me.) Museum.
A small stuffed whale hangs overhead
As in the head a dream.

Slowly the fleet was shrinking.
The good-sized fish were few.
Town meetings closed and opened
With the question what to do.

Each year when manufacturers
Of chemicals and glues
Bid to pollute the harbor
It took longer to refuse.

Said Manuel the grocer,
"Vote for that factory,
And the summer people's houses
Will be up for sale, you'll see.

Our wives take in their laundry.
Our kids, they cut the grass
And baby-sit. The benefit
Comes home to all of us."

Someone else said, "Next winter
You'll miss that Chemical Plant."
Andrew breathed in Nora's ear:
"Go, grasshopper! Go, ant!"

These two were summer neighbors.
They loved without desire.
Both, now pushing fifty,
Had elsewhere played with fire.

Of all the summer people
Who dwelt in pigeonholes,
Old Navy or Young Married,
The Bad Sports, the Good Souls,

These were the Amusing,
The Unconventional ones—
Plus Andrew's Jane (she used a cane
And shook it at his puns)

And Nora's mother Margaret
With her dawn-colored hair,
Her novels laid in Europe
That she wrote in a garden chair.

"Where's Andrew?" Margaret queried
As Nora entered the room.

"Didn't he want to come over?
It seems to be my doom

To spend long lonely evenings.
Don't we *know* anyone?"
"Dozens of people, Mother."
"But none of them are fun!

The summer already seems endless
And it's only the first of July.
My eyes are too weak for reading
And I am too strong to cry.

I wish I weren't a widow,
I wish you weren't divorced—
Oh, by the way, I heard today
About a man named Frost

Who's bought the Baptist church
And means to do it over."
"Mother, he sounds like just the type
I don't need for a lover."

Andrew at the piano
Let the ice in his nightcap melt.
Mendelssohn's augmentations
Were very deeply felt.

Jane cleaned her paintbrushes
With fingers rheumatic and slow.
Their son came back from the movies,
She called a vague hello

But he'd bounded upstairs already,
Jarring three petals loose
From today's bunch of roses
Not dry yet—pink, cream, puce.

A young man spoke to Margaret
At a party: "Don't be bored.
I've read your books, I like your looks"—
Then vanished in the horde.

Her hostess said when questioned,
"Why, that's Interesting Jack Frost.
He's fixing up that eyesore
With no regard for cost.

Don't ask me where he comes from
Or why he settled here.
He's certainly attractive,
To judge by the veneer."

One thing led to another,
And long before summer's end,
Margaret, Nora, Andrew, Jane
Had found them a new friend.

Jack Frost was years older
Than his twenty-year-old face.
He loved four-hand piano
And gladly took the bass,

Loved also bridge but did not play
So well as to offend,
Loved to gossip, loved croquet,
His money loved to spend

On food and drink and flowers,
Loved entertaining most.
The happy few who'd been there knew
Him as a famous host.

The church was now a folly
Cloud-white and palest blue—
Lanterns, stained glass, mirrors,
Polar bear rugs, bamboo,

Armchairs of gleaming buffalo-horn,
The titter of wind chimes,
A white cat, a blue cushion
Stitched with the cat's name, Grimes.

"Proud Grimes, proud loyal kitty,"
Jack said, "I love you best."

Two golden eyes were trimmed to slits,
Gorgeously unimpressed.

Ken the Japanese "houseboy"
(Though silver-haired and frail)
Served many a curious hot hors d'oeuvre
And icy cold cocktail.

The new friends, that first evening,
Sat on till half past two.
"This man," said Andrew on the street,
"Is too good to be true.

One views with faint misgivings
The bounty of the young."
"Speak for yourself," said Nora
Or the Cointreau on her tongue.

"Well, *I* think he's enchanting,"
Said Margaret, "and what's more
In the long run he'll find, for fun,
No one to match us four."

October came too quickly,
The leaves turned red and sere,
Time for the summer people
To pack up and call it a year.

In the mind's mouth summers later
Ken's farewell banquet melts.
Where would Jack spend the winter?
Why, here of course—where else?

"Stay here all winter? Really,
The things some people do!"
"Whither thou goest, Margaret,
To thee I will be true."

"Come see us in the city."
"My lovely Nora, no.
Too full of dull, dull people
And dirty, dirty snow."

"Come see *us* in Barbados."
"Forgive me, dearest Jane.
I've planned a Northern winter."
So they cajoled in vain.

The next days Jack lay drowsing,
Grimes in the bend of his knees.
He woke one dusk to eat a rusk
And smile at the bare trees.

The first huge flakes descended
Hexagonal, unique.
The panes put forth white leafage.
The harbor froze in a week.

The shrieking children skated
Upon its harsh white jewel,
Whose parents stayed indoors and paid
Outrageous bills for fuel.

Great lengths of gnarled crystal
Glittered from porch and eave.
It was, in short, a winter
You had to see to believe.

Whole nights, a tower window
Threw light upon the storm.
"Jack's sure artistic," Manuel said,
"But how does he keep warm?"

Ken climbed the stair one March dusk.
"Dear Jack-san, now am ord,
Dream of my Kyushu virrage
Where nobody catch cord."

"Together, Ken, we'll go there,
But for the moment stay.
What would I do without you?"
Ken bowed and turned away.

Jack stood up. The cat scuttled
Discreetly out of sight.
Jack's eyes were wet. Pride and regret
Burned in his heart all night.

A mild sun rose next morning.
The roofs began to steam
Where snow had melted. Winter
Was ending like a dream.

Alerted and elated
The summer friends came back.
Their exile had been tiresome,
Each now confessed to Jack.

His garden made them welcome;
Ken had spent May on his knees
Among the plots. From Chinese pots
On the church porch small trees

Rose thick with purple blossoms
Pendulous as Turks.
Said Andrew gravely, "I have seen
The fuchsia, and it works."

That summer was the model
For several in a row—
High watermarks of humor
And humankindness, no

Discord at cards, at picnics,
Charades or musicales.
Their faces bright with pleasure might
Not have displeased Frans Hals.

Jane, speaking of pictures,
Had started one of Grimes
Drugged on Jack's lap. Those sessions
Made for the merriest times.

Margaret brought out her gripping
Stories of love and war,
Peking and Nice. They held their peace
Who'd heard them told before.

Nora, one August afternoon,
Burst in with currant fool
Enough for the whole village.
Its last sweet molecule

Eaten, they blushed like truants.
"Shame on us every one,"
Jane sighed, "we've got no fiber."
And Margaret: "Oh, the fun!

Let's stay for Christmas. Andrew,
You can play Santa Claus!"
Jack gave a cry. Into his thigh
The cat had dug its claws.

Jane's canvas, scarred and peeling
Turned up at the village fair
The other day. I'm sad to say
It found a customer.

The Chemical Plant director
Bought it for his wife
To overpaint with symbols
Flat as her palette knife.

They're a perfectly nice couple
So long as you steer clear
Of art and politics and such—
But to resume. That year

Jack's friends did stay for Christmas,
The next year into Lent,
A third year stayed all winter
To their own astonishment.

Logs burned, the sparks flew upward.
The whiteness when they woke
Struck them as of a genius
Positively baroque,

Invention's breast and plumage,
Flights of the midnight Swan . . .
The facts are in Margaret's journal
To be published when she's gone.

I should perhaps have trusted
To dry-eyed prose like hers.
The meter grows misleading,
Given my characters.

For figures in a ballad
Lend themselves to acts
Passionate and simple.
A bride weeps. A tree cracks.

A young king, an old outlaw
Whose temperament inclines
To strife where breakers thunder
Bleeds between the lines.

But I have no such hero,
No fearful deeds—unless
We count their quiet performance
By Time or Tenderness.

These two are the past masters
Of rime, tone, overtone.
They write upon our faces
Until the pen strikes bone.

Time passes softly, scarcely
Felt by me or you.
And then, at an odd moment,
Tenderness passes, too.

That January midday
Jack's head fell to his knee.
Margaret stopped in mid-sentence—
Whatever could it be?

"He's sound asleep," said Nora.
"So clever of him. If
Only I were! Your stories
Bore everybody stiff."

"What can she mean," said Margaret,
"Speaking to me like that?"
"I mean you're gaga, Mother."
"And you, my child, are fat."

Jack murmured in his slumber,
"I didn't sleep a wink
All during last night's blizzard.
Where am I? Where's my drink?"

His eyes flew wide. "I'm sorry,
I'm sick, I have to go."
He took his coat and tottered
Out into windless snow.

The dogwood at the corner,
Unbending in a burst
Of diamond levity, let drop:
Old friend, think! First things first,

Not June in January—
"Be still!" cried Jack, and bit
His stupid tongue. A snowflake stung
Silence back into it.

Ken helped him up the tower stair,
"Rie down, Jack-san, now rest."
He fell among white blankets,
Grimes heavy on his chest.

Margaret went round next morning
And rang. No one replied.
She found Ken sleeping on the stair,
A wineglass at his side.

A white blur sped to meet her—
Was it that ghastly cat?
Grimes spat, crouched, sprang and sank a fang
Into her, just like that!

She screamed. A stern young doctor,
Summoned out of the void,
Dressed her wound, then telephoned
To have the cat destroyed.

Jack flew to the Police Chief,
Called the SPCA,
Despairing thought that Margaret
Herself might save the day.

She kept him standing, coldly
Displayed her bandaged calf.
He spoiled it all by failing
To check a thoughtless laugh.

Two men with gloves were waiting.
They caught Grimes in a sack.
Two good whiffs of ether
And his gold eyes shut on Jack.

That same night, Grimes in ermine
And coronet of ice
Called him by name, cried vengeance,
Twitching his long tail twice.

Jack woke in pitch dark, burning,
Freezing, leapt dry-lipped
From bed, threw clothes on, neither
Packed nor reflected, slipped

Money between pages
Of Ken's dog-eared almanac,
Then on the sleeping village
Forever turned his back.

He must have let a month go by
Before he sent them all
Postcards of some Higher Thing—
The Jungfrau, white and tall.

"Well, that answers our question,"
Said Margaret looking grim.
They dealt with Jack from then on
By never mentioning him.

Languid as convalescents,
Dreading the color green,
They braced themselves for summer's
Inexorable routine.

Andrew at the piano,
Six highballs gone or more,
Played Brahms, his "venerable beads"
Fixed on the flickering score.

Kneeling in her muggy
Boxwood garden Jane
Stopped weeding, tried to rise
But could not move for pain.

She saw her son's tanned fingers
Lowering the blind
Of an attic window.
She did not know his mind.

Croquet and hectic banter
From Margaret's backyard
Broke up her twinges.
"En," shrieked Nora, *"garde!"*

"Oh God, this life's so pointless,
So wearing," Margaret said.
"You're telling me," Andrew agreed.
"High time we both were dead."

"It *is*. I have pills—let's take them!"
He looked at her with wit.
"Just try. You know we'd never
Hear the end of it."

Their laughter floated on the dusk.
Ken thought of dropping in,
But his nails were cracked and dirty
And his breath smelled of gin.

"Missed you at Town Meeting
Last night," said Manuel
As Nora fingered honeydews.
"Things didn't go too well.

Fact is, the Plant got voted in.
I call it a downright
Pity you summer people
Didn't care enough to fight."

"Manuel, there have been winters
We stayed here," Nora said.
"That makes us year-round people."
The grocer scratched his head.

"I guess I don't mean season
So much as a point of view."
It made her mad. She'd meant to add,
"And we do care, we *do*,"

But it was too late, she didn't,
Didn't care one bit.
Manuel counted out her change:
". . . *and* ten. Will that be it?"

"Insufferable rudeness!
Of course by now it's clear,"
Said Margaret, laying down her trumps,
"We must all get out of here."

"We go next week," admitted
Jane with a guilty air.
"Old friends in Locust Valley
Keep asking us down there."

"Besides," said Andrew quickly,
"This climate's bothersome.
I may take Jane to Port-of-Spain—
All *my* roads lead to rum."

"So they do. Well, that's lovely,
Leaving us in the lurch,"
Said Nora, "just like what's-his-name
Who had the Baptist church."

"The summer's over," said Margaret.
"But you misunderstood:
I meant this town was ruined.
We must all get out for good."

Ken wrapped some Canton saucers
Like a conspirator,
To be exchanged for credit
At the corner liquor store.

September. Dismal rainstorms
Made everything a blur,
Lashed Margaret into action—
City life for her!

"I'll stay up here," said Nora,
"A month or two. I need
Time to think things over,
Listen to records, read."

She drove home from Caustic
Where Margaret caught her plane.
The windshield streamed in silence,
The wipers thrashed in vain.

October. Early twilights.
To the wharf came a blue
And silver haul of fish too small
For anything but glue.

The boatyard was a boneyard,
Bleached hull, moon-eaten chain.
The empty depot trembled
At the scream of a passing train.

Nora long past midnight
Lay rereading *Emma*,
Unmoved for once by a daughter's
Soon-to-be-solved dilemma.

And late dawns. The first victim
Of Main Street's seventeen
Doomed elms awoke and feebly shook
Its sparrow-tambourine.

In the November mildness
Rose delicate green spears—
Spring flowers Ken had planted.
His small eyes filled with tears:

They were coming up too early!
He sniffed and went indoors.
He dusted all the objects,
Polished the bare floors,

Bathed and oiled his person;
Now put on his best clothes,
Thought up a huge sweet cocktail,
And sipping at it chose

The first words of a letter
He had long meant to write.
But wait, his glass was empty—
A foolish oversight.

Nora heard him coughing.
She stopped her evening stroll
And went to see. With courtesy
Both sinister and droll

Ken bowed low, made her welcome,
Concocted a new drink.
Darkly hilarious he said,
"Rong rife!" and gave a wink.

One didn't need to be Nora
To see that things weren't right.
In his brown silk kimono
Ken sat there high as a kite.

His talk was incoherent:
Jack—his mother's loom—
The weather—his green island—
Flowers he'd not see bloom—

The dead cat—a masked actor—
Ghosts up in the hills . . .
And then those frightful spasms
Followed by small white pills.

Nora thought food might help him
And ran back for a cup
Of homemade soup. He took a sip,
Set down the cup, got up:

"Dear Missy-san, too sorty.
Night-night now. Kissing hand."
This done, Ken headed for the stair,
Though hardly able to stand.

Next day she found him lying
Cold on his bed. "I knew,
I *knew*!" sobbed Nora over the phone.
"But what was there to do?

He wasn't kin or even friend,
Just old and sick, poor dear.
It was his right to take his life,
Not mine to interfere."

"Exactly," said her mother.
"I'll come tomorrow. Jack?
Try the address on Ken's letter.
A wire may bring him back."

It did not. The two ladies
Arranged the funeral,
Then sat at home in silence
Deeper than I can tell.

Jack sent a check weeks later
And wrote them from Tibet
A long sad charming letter,
But friendship's sun had set.

December. "I think sometimes,"
Said Margaret dreamily,
"That Jack was a delusion
Of the whole community.

No reasonable adult
Starts acting like a child.
How else can you explain it?
He had us all beguiled."

Nora looked up. The mirror
Struck her a glancing blow.
Her hair once blonde as summer
Was dull and streaked with snow.

"Oh tell me, Mother, tell me
Where do the years go?
I'm old, my life is ending!"
"Baby, I know, I know."

As soon as they were calmer,
"I also," Margaret said,
"Know what to do about it.
So get up from that bed.

I know a clever fairy
Who puts gold back in hair.
I know of jets to Rio.
It will be summer there."

Come May, Ken's garden blossomed
In memory of him—
Hyacinth, narcissus
White as seraphim.

Jane and Andrew saw it.
They'd driven up to sell
Their house at a tidy profit
To the Head of Personnel.

It had grown so big, so empty.
Their lawn was choked with weeds,
Their son in California
Barefoot, all beard and beads.

They stood among Ken's flowers
Gazing without a word.
Jane put her hand in Andrew's.
The cat in heaven purred.

And then a faint piano
Sounded—from where? They tried
The door, it floated open,
Inviting them inside.

Sitting at the keyboard
In a cloud of brilliant motes
A boy they'd both seen somewhere
Was playing random notes.

He rose as if uncertain
Whether to speak or run.
Jane said, "I know who you are,
You're Joey, Manuel's son,

Who used to cut the grass for us.
Look at you, grown so tall!"
He grinned. "I won a scholarship
At M.I.T. this fall

To study cybernetics
And flute—it's worth a try.
I used to come and talk to Ken.
I miss that little guy."

"One by one, like swallows . . ."
Said Andrew in the gloom
That fell when Joe departed.
"Dear God, look at this room."

Full ashtrays, soft-drink bottles
Told an artless tale
Of adolescent revels.
Tan stacks of ninth-class mail

Lay tumbled helter-skelter.
A chill in the stirred air
Sent Jane outdoors and Andrew
To brave the tower stair.

Moon after moon had faded
The papers on Jack's desk:
Unfinished calculation,
Doodle and arabesque.

One window framed the sunset
Transfiguring Main Street,
Its houses faintly crimson
But upright in defeat.

The other faced the harbor.
Lights of the Chemical Plant
Gloated over water.
"The grasshopper, the ant,"

Breathed Andrew, recollecting
His long ago remark,
Then shut both views behind him
And felt his way down in dark.

LOG

Then when the flame forked like a sudden path
I gasped and stumbled, and was less.
Density pulsing upward, gauze of ash,
Dear light along the way to nothingness,
What could be made of you but light, and this?

AFTER THE FIRE

Everything changes; nothing does. I am back,
The doorbell rings, my heart leaps out of habit,
But it is only Kleo—how thin, how old!—
Trying to smile, lips chill as the fallen dusk.

She has brought a cake "for tomorrow"
As if tomorrows were still memorable.
We sit down in the freshly-painted hall
Once used for little dinners. (The smoke cleared
On no real damage, yet I'd wanted changes,
Balcony glassed in, electric range,
And wrote to have them made after the fire.)
Now Kleo's eyes begin to stream in earnest—
Tears of joy? Ah, troubles too, I fear.
Her old mother has gone off the deep end.

From their basement window the yiayia, nearly ninety,
Hurls invective at the passing scene,
Tea bags as well, the water bill, an egg
For emphasis. A strange car stops outside?
She cackles *Here's the client! Paint your face,*
Putana! to her daughter moistening
With tears the shirt she irons. Or locks her out
On her return from watering, with tears,
My terrace garden. (I will see tomorrow
The white oleander burst from its pot in the rains.)
Nor is darling Panayióti, Kleo's son,
Immune. Our entire neighborhood now knows
As if they hadn't years before
That he is a *Degenerate!* a *Thieving*
Faggot! just as Kleo is a *Whore!*

I press Kleo's cold hand and wonder
What could the poor yiayia have done
To deserve this terrible gift of hindsight,
These visions that possess her of a past
When Kleo really was a buxom armful
And "Noti" cruised the Naval Hospital,
Slim then, with teased hair. Now he must be forty,

Age at which degeneration takes
Too much of one's time and strength and money.
My eyes brim with past evenings in this hall,
Gravy-spattered cloth, candles minutely
Guttering in the love-blinded gaze.
The walls' original old-fashioned colors,
Cendre de rose, warm flaking ivory—
Colors last seen as by that lover's ghost
Stumbling downstairs wound in a sheet of flame—
Are hidden now forever but not lost
Beneath this quiet sensible light gray.

Kleo goes on. The yiayia's *warm*,
What can it mean? She who sat blanketed
In mid-July now burns all day,
Eats only sugar, having ascertained
Poison in whatever Kleo cooks.
Kill me, there'll be an autopsy,
Putana, matricide, I've seen to that!
I mention my own mother's mother's illness,
Querulous temper, lucid shame.
Kleo says weeping that it's not the same,
There's nothing wrong, according to the doctor,
Just that she's old and merciless. And warm.

Next day I visit them. Red-eyed Kleo
Lets me in. Beyond her, bedclothes disarrayed,
The little leaden oven-rosy witch
Fastens her unrecognizing glare
Onto the lightest line that I can spin.
"It's me, yiayia! Together let us plumb
Depths long dry"—getting no further, though,
Than Panayioti's anaconda arms:

"Ah Monsieur Tzim, bon zour et bon retour!
Excuse mon déshabillé. Toute la nuit
Z'ai décoré l'église pour la fête
Et fait l'amour, le prêtre et moi,
Dans une alcove derrière la Sainte Imaze.
Tiens, z'ai un cadeau pour toi,
Zoli foulard qui me va pas du tout.
Mais prends-le donc, c'est pas volé—
Ze ne suis plus voleur, seulement volaze!"

Huge, powerful, bland, he rolls his eyes and r's.
Glints of copper wreathe his porcelain brow
Like the old-time fuses here, that blow so readily.
I seem to know that crimson robe,
And on his big fat feet—my slippers, ruined.
Still, not to complicate affairs,
Remembering also the gift of thumb-sized garnet
Bruises he clasped round Aleko's throat,
I beam with gratitude. Meanwhile
Other translated objects one by one
Peep from hiding: teapot, towel, transistor.
Upon the sideboard an old me
Scissored from its glossy tavern scene—
I know that bare arm too, flung round my shoulder—
Buckles against a ruby glass ashtray.
(It strikes me now, as happily it did not
The insurance company, that P caused the fire.
Kleo's key borrowed for a rendezvous,
A cigarette left burning . . . Never mind.)
Life like the bandit Somethingopoulos
Gives to others what it takes from us.

Some of those embers can't be handled yet.

I mean to ask whose feast it is today
But the room brightens, the yiayia shrieks my name—
It's Tzimi! He's returned!
—And with that she returns to human form,
The snuffed-out candle-ends grow tall and shine,
Dead flames encircle us, which cannot harm,
The table's spread, she croons, and I
Am kneeling pressed to her old burning frame.

DAYS OF 1935

Ladder horned against moonlight,
Window hoisted stealthily—
That's what I'd steel myself at night
To see, or sleep to see.

My parents were out partying,
My nurse was old and deaf and slow.
Way off in the servants' wing
Cackled a radio.

On the Lindbergh baby's small
Cold features lay a spell, a swoon.
It seemed entirely plausible
For my turn to come soon,

For a masked and crouching form
Lithe as tiger, light as moth,
To glide towards me, clap a firm
Hand across my mouth,

Then sheer imagination ride
Off with us in its old jalopy,
Trailing bedclothes like a bride
Timorous but happy.

A hundred tenuous dirt roads
Dew spangles, lead to the web's heart.
That whole pale night my captor reads
His brow's unwrinkling chart.

Dawn. A hovel in the treeless
Trembling middle of nowhere,
Hidden from the world by palace
Walls of dust and glare.

A lady out of *Silver Screen*,
Her careful rosebud chewing gum,
Seems to expect us, lets us in,
Nods her platinum

Spit curls deadpan (I will wait
Days to learn what makes her smile)
At a blue enamel plate
Of cold greens I can smell—

But swallow? Never. The man's face
Rivets me, a lightning bolt.
Lean, sallow, lantern-jawed, he lays
Pistol and cartridge belt

Between us on the oilskin (I
Will relive some things he did
Until I die, until I die)
And clears his throat: "Well, Kid,

You've figured out what's happening.
We don't mean to hurt you none
Unless we have to. Everything
Depends on, number one,

How much you're worth to your old man,
And, number two, no more of this—"
Meaning my toothprints on his hand,
Indenture of a kiss.

With which he fell upon the bed
And splendidly began to snore.
"Please, I'm sleepy too," I said.
She pointed to the floor.

The rag rug, a rainbow threadbare,
Was soft as down. For good or bad
I felt her watching from her chair
As no one ever had.

Their names were Floyd and Jean. I guess
They lived in what my parents meant
By sin: unceremoniousness
Or common discontent.

"Gimme—Wait—Hey, watch that gun—
Why don't these dumb matches work—
See you later—Yeah, have fun—
Wise guy—Floozie—Jerk—"

Or else he bragged of bygone glories,
Stores robbed, cars stolen, dolls betrayed,
Escape from two reformatories.
Said Jean, "Wish you'd of stayed."

To me they hardly spoke, just watched
Or gave directions in dumb show.
I nodded back like one bewitched
By a violent glow.

Each morning Floyd went for a ride
To post another penciled note.
Indignation nationwide
Greeted what he wrote.

Each afternoon, brought papers back.
One tabloid's whole front page was spanned
By the headline bold and black:
FIEND ASKS 200 GRAND.

Photographs too. My mother gloved,
Hatted, bepearled, chin deep in fur.
Dad glowering—was it true he loved
Others beside her?

Eerie, speaking likenesses.
One positively heard her mild
Voice temper some slow burn of his,
"Not before the child."

The child. That population map's
Blanknesses and dots were me!
Mine, those swarming eyes and lips,
Centers of industry

Italics under which would say
(And still do now and then, I fear)
Is This Child Alive Today?
Last Hopes Disappear.

Toy ukelele, terrorstruck
Chord, the strings so taut, so few—
Tingling I hugged my pillow. *Pluck,*
Some deep nerve went. I knew

That life was fiction in disguise.
My teeth said, chattering in Morse,
"Are you a healthy wealthy wise
Red-blooded boy? Of course?

Then face the music. Stay. Outwit
Everyone. Captivity
Is beckoning—make a dash for it!
It will set you free."

Sometimes as if I were not there
He put his lips against her neck.
Her head lolled sideways, just like Claire
Coe in *Tehuantepec.*

Then both would send me looks so heaped
With a lazy, scornful mirth,
This was growing up, I hoped,
The first flushed fruits of earth.

One night I woke to hear the room
Filled with crickets—no, bedsprings.
My eyes dilated in the gloom,
My ears made out things.

Jean: The kid, he's still awake . . .
Floyd: Time he learned . . . Oh baby . . . God . . .
Their prone tango, for my sake,
Grew intense and proud.

And one night—pure *Belshazzar's Feast*
When the slave-girl is found out—
She cowered, face a white blaze ("Beast!")
From his royal clout.

Mornings, though, she came and went,
Buffed her nails and plucked her brows.
What had those dark doings meant?
Less than the fresh bruise

Powdered over on her cheek.
I couldn't take my eyes away.
Let hers meet them! Let her speak!
She put down *Photoplay*:

"Do you know any stories, Kid?
Real stories—but not real, I mean.
Not just dumb things people did.
Wouldja tell one to Jean?"

I stared at her—*she* was the child!—
And a tale came back to me.
Bluebeard. At its end she smiled
Half incredulously.

I spun them out all afternoon.
Wunspontime, I said and said . . .
The smile became a dainty yawn
Rose-white and rose-red.

The little mermaid danced on knives,
The beauty slept in her thorn bower.
Who knows but that our very lives
Depend on such an hour?

The fisherman's hut became Versailles
Because he let the dolphin go . . .
Jean's lids have shut. I'm lonely. I
Am pausing on tiptoe

To marvel at the shimmer breath
Inspires along your radii,
Spider lightly running forth
To kiss the simple fly

Asleep. A chance to slip the net,
Wriggle down the dry stream bed,
Now or never! This child cannot.
An iridescent thread

Binds him to her slumber deep
Within a golden haze made plain
Precisely where his fingertip
Writes on the dusty pane

In spit his name, address, age nine
—Which the newspapers and such
Will shortly point to as a fine
Realistic touch.

Grown up, he thinks how S, T, you—
Second childhood's alphabet
Still unmastered, it is true,
Though letters come—have yet

Touched his heart, occasioned words
Not quickened by design alone,
Responses weekly winging towards
Your distance from his own,

Distance that much more complex
For its haunting ritornel:
Things happen to a child who speaks
To strangers, mark it well!

Thinks how you or V—where does
It end, will *any*one have done?—
Taking the wheel (cf. those "Days
Of 1971")

Have driven, till his mother's Grade
A controls took charge, or handsome
Provisions which his father made
Served once again as ransom,

Driven your captive far enough
For the swift needle on the gauge
To stitch with delicate kid stuff
His shoddy middle age.

Here was Floyd. The evening sun
Filled his eyes with funny light.
"Junior, you'll be home real soon."
To Jean, "Tomorrow night."

What was happening? Had my parents
Paid? pulled strings? Or maybe I
Had failed in manners, or appearance?
Must this be goodbye?

I'd hoped I was worth more than crime
Itself, which never paid, could pay.
Worth more than my own father's time
Or mother's negligée

Undone where dim ends barely met,
This being a Depression year . . .
I'd hoped, I guess, that they would let
Floyd and Jean keep me here.

We ate in silence. He would stop
Munching and gaze into the lamp.
She wandered out on the dark stoop.
The night turned chill and damp.

When she came in, she'd caught a bug.
She tossed alone in the iron bed.
Floyd dropped beside me on the rug;
Growled, "Sleep." I disobeyed.

Commenced a wary, mortal heat
Run neck by nose. Small fingers felt,
Sore point of all that wiry meat,
A nipple's tender fault.

Time stopped. His arm somnambulist
Had circled me, warm, salt as blood.
Mine was the future in his fist
To get at if I could,

While his heart beat like a drum
And *Oh baby* faint and hoarse
Echoed from within his dream . . .
The next day Jean was worse

—Or I was. Dawn discovered me
Sweating on my bedroom floor.
Was there no curbing fantasy
When one had a flair?

Came those nights to end the tale.
I shrank to see the money tumble,
All in 20s, from a teal
Blue Studebaker's rumble

Down a slope of starlit brush.
Sensed with anguish the foreseen
Net of G-men, heard the hush
Deepen, then Floyd's voice ("Jean,

Baby, we've been doublecrossed!")
Drowned out by punctual crossfire
That left the pillow hot and creased.
By three o'clock, by four,

They stood in handcuffs where the hunt
Was over among blood-smeared rocks
—Whom I should not again confront
Till from the witness-box

I met their stupid, speechless gaze.
How empty they appeared, how weak
By contrast with my opening phrase
As I began to speak:

"You I adored I now accuse . . ."
Would imagination dare
Follow that sentence like a fuse
Sizzling towards the Chair?

See their bodies raw and swollen
Sagging in a skein of smoke?
The floor was reeling where I'd fallen.
Even my old nurse woke

And took me in her arms. I pressed
My guilty face against the void
Warmed and scented by her breast.
Jean, I whispered, Floyd.

A rainy day. The child is bored.
While Emma bakes he sits, half-grown.
The kitchen dado is of board
Painted like board. Its grain

Shiny buff on cinnamon
Mimics the real, the finer grain.
He watches icing sugar spin
Its thread. He licks in vain

Heavenly flavors from a spoon.
Left in the metallic bowl
Is a twenty-five-watt moon.
Somewhere rings a bell.

Wet walks from the east porch lead
Down levels manicured and rolled
To a small grove where pets are laid
In shallow emerald.

The den lights up. A Sazerac
Helps his father face the *Wall
Street Journal.* Jules the colored (black)
Butler guards the hall.

Tel & Tel executives,
Heads of Cellophane or Tin,
With their animated wives
Are due on the 6:10.

Upstairs in miles of spangled blue
His mother puts her make-up on.
She kisses him sweet dreams, but who—
Floyd and Jean are gone—

Who will he dream of? True to life
He's played them false. A golden haze
Past belief, past disbelief . . .
Well. Those were the days.

18 WEST 11TH STREET

In what at least
Seemed anger the Aquarians in the basement
Had been perfecting a device

For making sense to us
If only briefly and on pain
Of incommunication ever after.

Now look who's here. Our prodigal
Sunset. Just passing through from Isfahan.
Filled by him the glass

Disorients. The swallow-flights
Go word by numbskull word
—Rebellion . . . Pentagon . . . Black Studies—

Crashing into irreality,
Plumage and parasites
Plus who knows what of the reptilian,

Till wit turns on the artificial lights
Or heaven changes. The maid,
Silent, pale as any victim,

Comes in, identifies;
Yet brings new silver, gives rise to the joint,
The presidency's ritual eclipse.

Take. Eat. His body to our lips. The point
Was anger, brother? Love? Dear premises
Vainly exploded, vainly dwelt upon.

Item: the carpet.
Identical bouquets on black, rose-dusted
Face in fifty funeral parlors,

Scentless and shaven, wall-to-wall
Extravagance without variety . . .
That morning's buzzing vacuum be fed

By ash of metropolitan evening's
Smoker inveterate between hot bouts
Of gloating over scrollwork,

The piano (three-legged by then like a thing in a riddle)
Fingered itself provocatively. Tones
Jangling whose tuner slept, moon's camphor mist

On the parterre compounding
Chromatic muddles which the limpid trot
Flew to construe. Up from camellias

Sent them by your great-great-grandfather,
Ghosts in dwarf sateen and miniver
Flitted once more askew

Through *Les Sylphides*. The fire was dead. Each summer,
While onto white keys miles from here
Warm salt chords kept breaking, snapping the strings,

The carpet—its days numbered—
Hatched another generation
Of strong-jawed, light-besotted saboteurs.

A mastermind
Kept track above the mantel. The cold caught,
One birthday in its shallows, racked

The weak frame, glazed with sleet
Overstuffed aunt and walnut uncle. Book
You could not read. Some utterly

Longed-for present meeting other eyes'
Blue arsenal of homemade elegies,
Duds every one. The deed

Diffused. Your breakfast *Mirror* put
Late to bed, a fever
Flashing through the veins of linotype:

NIX ON PEACE BID   PROPHET STONED
FIVE FEARED DEAD IN BOMBED DWELLING
—Bulletin-pocked columns, molten font

Features would rise from, nose for news
Atwitch, atchoo, God bless you!
Brought to your senses (five feared? not one bit)

Who walking home took in
The ruin. The young linden opposite
Shocked leafless. Item: the March dawn.

Shards of a blackened witness still in place.
The charred ice-sculpture garden
Beams fell upon. The cold blue searching beams.

Then all you sought
No longer, B came bearing. An arrangement
In time known simply as That June—

Fat snifter filled with morbidest
Possibly meat-eating flowers,
So hairy-stemmed, red-muscled, not to be pressed.

Pinhead notions underwater, yours,
Quicksilvered them afresh.
You let pass certain telltale prints

Left upon her in the interim
By that winter's person, where he touched her.
Still in her life now, was he, feeling the dim

Projection of your movie on his sheet?
Feeling how you reached past B towards him,
Brothers in grievance? But who grieves!

The night she left ("One day you'll understand")
You stood under the fruitless tree. The streetlight
Cast false green fires about, a tragic

Carpet of shadows of blossoms, shadows of leaves.
You understood. You would not seek rebirth
As a Dalmatian stud or Tiny Tim.

Discolorations from within, dry film
Run backwards, parching, scorching, to consume
Whatever filled you to the brim,

Fierce tongue, black
Fumes massing forth once more on
Waterstilts that fail them. The

Commissioner unswears his oath. Sea serpent
Hoses recoil, the siren drowns in choking
Wind. The crowd has thinned to a coven

Rigorously chosen from so many called. Our
Instant trance. The girl's
Appearance now among us, as foreseen

Naked, frail but fox-eyed, head to toe
(Having passed through the mirror)
Adorned with heavy shreds of ribbon

Sluggish to bleed. She stirs, she moans the name
Adam. And is *gone*. By her own
Broom swept clean, god, stop, behind this

Drunken backdrop of debris, airquake,
Flame in bloom—a pigeon's throat
Lifting, the puddle

Healed. To let:
Cream paint, brown ivy, brickflush. Eye
Of the old journalist unwavering

Through gauze. Forty-odd years gone by.
Toy blocks. Church bells. Original vacancy.
O deepening spring.

WILLOWWARE CUP

Mass hysteria, wave after breaking wave
Blueblooded Cantonese upon these shores

Left the gene pool Lux-opaque and smoking
With dimestore mutants. One turned up today.

Plum in bloom, pagoda, blue birds, plume of willow—
Almost the replica of a prewar pattern—

The same boat bearing the gnat-sized lovers away,
The old bridge now bent double where her father signals

Feebly, as from flypaper, minding less and less.
Two smaller retainers with lanterns light him home.

Is that a scroll he carries? He must by now be immensely
Wise, and have given up earthly attachments, and all that.

Soon, of these May mornings, rising in mist, he will ask
Only to blend—like ink in flesh, blue anchor

Needled upon drunkenness while its destroyer
Full steam departs, the stigma throbbing, intricate—

Only to blend into a crazing texture.
You are far away. The leaves tell what they tell.

But this lone, chipped vessel, if it fills,
Fills for you with something warm and clear.

Around its inner horizon the old odd designs
Crowd as before, and seem to concentrate on you.

They represent, I fancy, a version of heaven
In its day more trouble to mend than to replace:

Steep roofs aslant, minutely tiled;
Tilted honeycombs, thunderhead blue.

from UP AND DOWN

THE EMERALD

Hearing that on Sunday I would leave,
My mother asked if we might drive downtown.
Why certainly—off with my dressing gown!
The weather had turned fair. *We* were alive.

Only the gentle General she married
Late, for both an old way out of harm's,
Fought for breath, surrendered in her arms,
With military honors now lay buried.

That week the arcana of his medicine chest
Had been disposed of, and his clothes. Gold belt
Buckle and the letter from President Roosevelt
Went to an unknown grandchild in the West.

Downtown, his widow raised her parasol
Against the Lenten sun's not yet detectable
Malignant atomies which an electric needle
Unfreckles from her soft white skin each fall.

Hence too her chiffon scarf, pale violet,
And spangle-paste dark glasses. Each spring we number
The new dead. Above ground, who can remember
Her as she once was? Even I forget,

Fail to attend her, seem impervious . . .
Meanwhile we have made through a dense shimmy
Of parked cars burnished by the midday chamois
For Mutual Trust. Here cool gloom welcomes us,

And all, director, guard, quite palpably
Adore her. Spinster tellers one by one
Darting from cages, sniffling to meet her son,
Think of her having a son—! She holds the key

Whereby palatial bronze gates shut like jaws
On our descent into this inmost vault.
The keeper bends his baldness to consult,
Brings a tin box painted mud-brown, withdraws.

She opens it. Security. Will. Deed.
Rummages further. Rustle of tissue, a sprung
Lid. Her face gone queerly lit, fair, young,
Like faces of our dear ones who have died.

No rhinestone now, no dilute amethyst,
But of the first water, linking star to pang,
Teardrop to fire, my father's kisses hang
In lipless concentration round her wrist.

Gray are these temple-drummers who once more
Would rouse her, girl-bride jeweled in his grave.
Instead, she next picks out a ring. "He gave
Me this when you were born. Here, take it for—

For when you marry. For your bride. It's yours."
A den of greenest light, it grows, shrinks, glows,
Hermetic stanza bedded in the prose
Of the last thirty semiprecious years.

I do not tell her, it would sound theatrical,
Indeed this green room's mine, my very life.
We are each other's; there will be no wife;
The little feet that patter here are metrical.

But onto her worn knuckle slip the ring.
Wear it for me, I silently entreat,
Until—until the time comes. Our eyes meet.
The world beneath the world is brightening.

FLÈCHE D'OR

Windowglass, warmed plush, a sneeze
Deflected by the miracle
Into euphoria's
Authoritative gliding forth,
The riddle of the rails
Vitally unmoved in flight
However fast
I run racing that arrow
Lodged in my brain
Down the board platform beyond hurt or hope
Once more, once more
My life ended, having not,
Veils lifted, words from the page
Come to my senses
Eased of that last arrivederci deep
In book or view, my own
Fleet profile calmer catapulted due
North a pane floats off, desire sinks
Red upon piercing stubble—"Traveler,
Turn back!" the tracks
Outcry, din flash fade, done,
Over forever, done I say, now yet
Might somebody
Seeing it all (for once not I or I)
Judge us wisely in whose heart of
Hearts the parallels
Meet and nothing lasts and nothing ends

DAYS OF 1971

Fallen from the clouds, well-met.
This way to the limousine.
How are things? Don't tell me yet!
Have a Gauloise first, I mean.

Matches now, did I forget—
With a flourish and no word
Out came the sentry-silhouette
Black against a big, flame-feathered bird,

Emblem of your "new" regime
Held, for its repressive ways,
In pretty general disesteem

Which to share just then was hard,
Borne up so far on a strategic blaze
Struck by you, and quite off guard.

In Paris you remark each small
Caged creature, marmoset, bat, newt, for sale;
Also the sparkling gutters, and the smelly
Seine this afternoon when we embark.

And the Bateau Mouche is spoiled by a party of cripples.
Look at what's left of that young fellow strapped
Into his wheelchair. How you pity him!
The city ripples, your eyes sicken and swim.

The boy includes you in his sightseeing,
Nodding sociably as if who of us
Here below were more than half a man.

There goes the Louvre, its Egyptian wing
Dense with basalt limbs and heads to use
Only as one's imagination can.

Can-can from last night's *Orphée aux Enfers*
Since daybreak you've been whistling till I wince.
Well, you were a handsome devil once.
Take the wheel. You're still a fair chauffeur.

Our trip. I'd pictured it another way—
Asthmatic pilgrim and his "nun of speed,"
In either mind a music spun of need . . .
That last turnoff went to Illiers.

Proust's Law (are you listening?) is twofold:
(a) What least thing our self-love longs for most
Others instinctively withhold;

(b) Only when time has slain desire
Is his wish granted to a smiling ghost
Neither harmed nor warmed, now, by the fire.

Stephen in the Pyrenees—our first
Real stop. You promptly got a stomachache.
Days of groans and grimaces interspersed
With marathon slumbers. Evenings, you'd wake

And stagger forth to find us talking. Not
Still about poetry! Alas . . .
So bottles were produced, and something hot.
The jokes you told translated, more or less.

Predictably departure cured you. Stephen
Investing me with a Basque walking stick,
"How much further, James, will you be driven?"

He didn't ask. He stood there, thin, pale, kind
As candlelight. Ah, what if *I* took sick?
You raced the motor, having read my mind.

Sucked by haste into the car,
Pressing his frantic buzzer, Bee!
Suppose he stings—why such hilarity?
These things occur.

Get rid of him at once
While we can! His wrath
Is almost human, the windshield's warpath
Dins with a song and dance

In one respect unlike our own:
Readily let out into the open.
There. Good creature, also he had known
The cost of self-as-weapon;

Venom unspent, barb idle, knows
Where they lead now—thyme, lavender, musk-rose,

Toulouse, Toulon, the border. Driven?
At ease, rather among fleeting scenes.
The O L I V E T T I signs
Whiz by, and azure Lombardy is given

Back, as the Virgin of Officialdom
Severely draped twists on her throne to peek
At the forbidden crags of kingdom come
Before resuming her deft hunt and peck.

One V sticks. Venice. Its vertiginous pastry
Maze we scurry through like mice and will
Never see the likes of in our lives.

It is too pink, white, stale to taste,
Crumbling in the gleam of slimy knives.
Have your cake and eat it? Take the wheel.

Wait—now where are we? Who is everyone?
Well, that's a princess, that's the butler . . . no,
Probably by now the butler's son.
We were stopping till tomorrow with Umberto

Among trompe l'oeil, old volumes, photographs
Of faded people wearing crowns and stars.
Welcome to the Time Machine, he laughed
Leaning on us both up its cold stairs.

At table the others recalled phrases from
Homer and Sappho, and you seemed to brighten.
Your sheets would entertain the "priest" that night
(Dish of embers in a wooden frame)

And eyes glaze on the bedside book, remote
But near, pristine but mildewed, which I wrote.

Take the wheel. San Zeno will survive
Whether or not visited.
Power is knowledge in your head.
(Sorry, I must have been thinking aloud. Drive, drive.)

Time and again the novel I began
Took aim at that unwritten part
In which the hero, named Sebastian,
Came to his senses through a work of art.

O book of hours, those last
Illuminated castles built
In air, O chariot-motif

Bearing down a margin good as gilt
Past fields of ever purer leaf
Its burning rubric, to get nowhere fast . . .

The road stopped where a Greek mountain fell
Early that week. Backed-up cars glared in the dusk.
Night fell next, and still five stupid slack-
Jawed ferries hadn't got their fill of us.

Tempers shortened. One self-righteous truck
Knocked the shit out of a eucalyptus
Whose whitewashed trunk lay twitching brokenly—
Nijinsky in *Petrouchka*—on the quai.

Later, past caring, packed like sheep,
Some may have felt the breathless lounge redeemed
By a transistor singing to the doomed

At last in their own tongue. You fell asleep
Life-sentenced to the honey-cell of song,
Harsh melisma, torturous diphthong.

Strato, each year's poem
Says goodbye to you.
Again, though, we've come through
Without losing temper or face.

If care rumpled your face
The other day in Rome,
Tonight just dump my suitcase
Inside the door and make a dash for home

While I unpack what we saw made
At Murano, and you gave to me—
Two ounces of white heat
Twirled and tweezered into shape,

Ecco! another fanciful
Little horse, still blushing, set to cool.

THE VICTOR DOG

for Elizabeth Bishop

Bix to Buxtehude to Boulez,
The little white dog on the Victor label
Listens long and hard as he is able.
It's all in a day's work, whatever plays.

From judgment, it would seem, he has refrained.
He even listens earnestly to Bloch,
Then builds a church upon our acid rock.
He's man's—no—he's the Leiermann's best friend,

Or would be if hearing and listening were the same.
Does he hear? I fancy he rather smells
Those lemon-gold arpeggios in Ravel's
"Les jets d'eau du palais de ceux qui s'aiment."

He ponders the Schumann Concerto's tall willow hit
By lightning, and stays put. When he surmises
Through one of Bach's eternal boxwood mazes
The oboe pungent as a bitch in heat,

Or when the calypso decants its raw bay rum
Or the moon in *Wozzeck* reddens ripe for murder,
He doesn't sneeze or howl; just listens harder.
Adamant needles bear down on him from

Whirling of outer space, too black, too near—
But he was taught as a puppy not to flinch,
Much less to imitate his bête noire Blanche
Who barked, fat foolish creature, at King Lear.

Still others fought in the road's filth over Jezebel,
Slavered on hearths of horned and pelted barons.
His forebears lacked, to say the least, forbearance.
Can nature change in him? Nothing's impossible.

The last chord fades. The night is cold and fine.
His master's voice rasps through the grooves' bare groves.
Obediently, in silence like the grave's
He sleeps there on the still-warm gramophone

Only to dream he is at the première of a Handel
Opera long thought lost—*Il Cane Minore.*
Its allegorical subject is his story!
A little dog revolving round a spindle

Gives rise to harmonies beyond belief,
A cast of stars . . . Is there in Victor's heart
No honey for the vanquished? Art is art.
The life it asks of us is a dog's life.

Bug, flower, bird of slipware fired and fluted,
The summer day breaks everywhere at once.

Worn is the green of things that have known dawns
Before this, and the darkness before them.

Among the wreckage, bent in Christian weeds,
Illiterate—X my mark—I tremble, still

A thinking reed. Who puts his mouth to me
Draws out the scale of love and dread—

O ramify, sole antidote! Foxglove
Each year, cloud, hornet, fatal growths

Proliferating by metastasis
Rooted their total in the gliding stream.

Some formula not relevant any more
To flower children might express it yet

Like $\sqrt{\left(\frac{x}{y}\right)^n} = 1$
—Or equals zero, one forgets—

The y standing for you, dear friend, at least
Until that hour he reaches for me, then

Leaves me cold, the great god Pain,
Letting me slide back into my scarred case

Whose silvery breath-tarnished tones
No longer rivet bone and star in place

Or keep from shriveling, leather round a stone,
The sunbather's precocious apricot

Or stop the four winds racing overhead

Nought

Waste   Eased

Sought

THE KIMONO

When I returned from lovers' lane
My hair was white as snow.
Joy, incomprehension, pain
I'd seen like seasons come and go.
How I got home again
Frozen half dead, perhaps you know.

You hide a smile and quote a text:
Desires ungratified
Persist from one life to the next.
Hearths we strip ourselves beside
Long, long ago were x'd
On blueprints of "consuming pride."

Times out of mind, the bubble-gleam
To our charred level drew
April back. A sudden beam . . .
—Keep talking while I change into
The pattern of a stream
Bordered with rushes white on blue.

LOST IN TRANSLATION

for Richard Howard

*Diese Tage, die leer dir scheinen
und wertlos für das All,
haben Wurzeln zwischen den Steinen
und trinken dort überall.*

A card table in the library stands ready
To receive the puzzle which keeps never coming.
Daylight shines in or lamplight down
Upon the tense oasis of green felt.
Full of unfulfillment, life goes on,
Mirage arisen from time's trickling sands
Or fallen piecemeal into place:
German lesson, picnic, see-saw, walk
With the collie who "did everything but talk"—
Sour windfalls of the orchard back of us.
A summer without parents is the puzzle,
Or should be. But the boy, day after day,
Writes in his Line-a-Day *No puzzle*.

He's in love, at least. His French Mademoiselle,
In real life a widow since Verdun,
Is stout, plain, carrot-haired, devout.
She prays for him, as does a curé in Alsace,
Sews costumes for his marionettes,
Helps him to keep behind the scene
Whose sidelit goosegirl, speaking with his voice,
Plays Guinevere as well as Gunmoll Jean.
Or else at bedtime in his tight embrace
Tells him her own French hopes, her German fears,
Her —but what more is there to tell?
Having known grief and hardship, Mademoiselle
Knows little more. Her languages. Her place.
Noon coffee. Mail. The watch that also waited
Pinned to her heart, poor gold, throws up its hands—
No puzzle! Steaming bitterness

Her sugars draw pops back into his mouth, translated:
"Patience, chéri. Geduld, mein Schatz."
(Thus, reading Valéry the other evening
And seeming to recall a Rilke version of "Palme,"
That sunlit paradigm whereby the tree
Taps a sweet wellspring of authority,
The hour came back. Patience dans l'azur.
Geduld im . . . Himmelblau? Mademoiselle.)

Out of the blue, as promised, of a New York
Puzzle-rental shop the puzzle comes—
A superior one, containing a thousand hand-sawn,
Sandal-scented pieces. Many take
Shapes known already—the craftsman's repertoire
Nice in its limitation—from other puzzles:
Witch on broomstick, ostrich, hourglass,
Even (surely not just in retrospect)
An inchling, innocently branching palm.
These can be put aside, made stories of
While Mademoiselle spreads out the rest face-up,
Herself excited as a child; or questioned
Like incoherent faces in a crowd,
Each with its scrap of highly colored
Evidence the Law must piece together.
Sky-blue ostrich? Likely story.
Mauve of the witch's cloak white, severed fingers
Pluck? Detain her. The plot thickens
As all at once two pieces interlock.

Mademoiselle does borders— (Not so fast.
A London dusk, December last.
Chatter silenced in the library
This grown man reenters, wearing gray.
A medium. All except him have seen
Panel slid back, recess explored,
An object at once unique and common
Displayed, planted in a plain tole
Casket the subject now considers
Through shut eyes, saying in effect:
"Even as voices reach me vaguely
A dry saw-shriek drowns them out,
Some loud machinery—a lumber mill?

Far uphill in the fir forest
Trees tower, tense with shock,
Groaning and cracking as they crash groundward.
But hidden here is a freak fragment
Of a pattern complex in appearance only.
What it seems to show is superficial
Next to that long-term lamination
Of hazard and craft, the karma that has
Made it matter in the first place.
Plywood. Piece of a puzzle." Applause
Acknowledged by an opening of lids
Upon the thing itself. A sudden dread—
But to go back. All this lay years ahead.)

Mademoiselle does borders. Straight-edge pieces
Align themselves with earth or sky
In twos and threes, naive cosmogonists
Whose views clash. Nomad inlanders meanwhile
Begin to cluster where the totem
Of a certain vibrant egg-yolk yellow
Or pelt of what emerging animal
Acts on the straggler like a trumpet call
To form a more sophisticated unit.
By suppertime two ragged wooden clouds
Have formed. In one, a Sheik with beard
And flashing sword hilt (he is all but finished)
Steps forward on a tiger skin. A piece
Snaps shut, and fangs gnash out at us!
In the second cloud—they gaze from cloud to cloud
With marked if undecipherable feeling—
Most of a dark-eyed woman veiled in mauve
Is being helped down from her camel (kneeling)
By a small backward-looking slave or page-boy
(Her son, thinks Mademoiselle mistakenly)
Whose feet have not been found. But lucky finds
In the last minutes before bed
Anchor both factions to the scene's limits
And, by so doing, orient
Them eye to eye across the green abyss.
The yellow promises, oh bliss,
To be in time a sumptuous tent.

Puzzle begun I write in the day's space,
Then, while she bathes, peek at Mademoiselle's
Page to the curé: ". . . cette innocente mère,
Ce pauvre enfant, que deviendront-ils?"
Her azure script is curlicued like pieces
Of the puzzle she will be telling him about.
(Fearful incuriosity of childhood!
"Tu as l'accent allemand," said Dominique.
Indeed. Mademoiselle was only French by marriage.
Child of an English mother, a remote
Descendant of the great explorer Speke,
And Prussian father. No one knew. I heard it
Long afterwards from her nephew, a UN
Interpreter. His matter-of-fact account
Touched old strings. My poor Mademoiselle,
With 1939 about to shake
This world where "each was the enemy, each the friend"
To its foundations, kept, though signed in blood,
Her peace a shameful secret to the end.)
"Schlaf wohl, chéri." Her kiss. Her thumb
Crossing my brow against the dreams to come.

This World that shifts like sand, its unforeseen
Consolations and elate routine,
Whose Potentate had lacked a retinue?
Lo! it assembles on the shrinking Green.

Gunmetal-skinned or pale, all plumes and scars,
Of Vassalage the noblest avatars—
The very coffee-bearer in his vair
Vest is a swart Highness, next to ours.

Kef easing Boredom, and iced syrups, thirst,
In guessed-at glooms old wives who know the worst
Outsweat that virile fiction of the New:
"Insh'Allah, he will tire—" "—or kill her first!"

(Hardly a proper subject for the Home,
Work of—dear Richard, I shall let *you* comb
Archives and learned journals for his name—
A minor lion attending on Gérôme.)

While, thick as Thebes whose presently complete
Gates close behind them, Houri and Afreet
Both claim the Page. He wonders whom to serve,
And what his duties are, and where his feet,

And if we'll find, as some before us did,
That piece of Distance deep in which lies hid
Your tiny apex sugary with sun,
Eternal Triangle, Great Pyramid!

Then Sky alone is left, a hundred blue
Fragments in revolution, with no clue
To where a Niche will open. Quite a task,
Putting together Heaven, yet we do.

It's done. Here under the table all along
Were those missing feet. It's done.

The dog's tail thumping. Mademoiselle sketching
Costumes for a coming harem drama
To star the goosegirl. All too soon the swift
Dismantling. Lifted by two corners,
The puzzle hung together—and did not.
Irresistibly a populace
Unstitched of its attachments, rattled down.
Power went to pieces as the witch
Slithered easily from Virtue's gown.
The blue held out for time, but crumbled, too.
The city had long fallen, and the tent,
A separating sauce mousseline,
Been swept away. Remained the green
On which the grown-ups gambled. A green dusk.
First lightning bugs. Last glow of west
Green in the false eyes of (coincidence)
Our mangy tiger safe on his bared hearth.

Before the puzzle was boxed and readdressed
To the puzzle shop in the mid-Sixties,
Something tells me that one piece contrived
To stay in the boy's pocket. How do I know?
I know because so many later puzzles
Had missing pieces—Maggie Teyte's high notes

Gone at the war's end, end of the vogue for collies,
A house torn down; and hadn't Mademoiselle
Kept back her pitiful bit of truth as well?
I've spent the last days, furthermore,
Ransacking Athens for that translation of "Palme."
Neither the Goethehaus nor the National Library
Seems able to unearth it. Yet I can't
Just be imagining. I've seen it. Know
How much of the sun-ripe original
Felicity Rilke made himself forego
(Who loved French words—verger, mûr, parfumer)
In order to render its underlying sense.
Know already in that tongue of his
What Pains, what monolithic Truths
Shadow stanza to stanza's symmetrical
Rhyme-rutted pavement. Know that ground plan left
Sublime and barren, where the warm Romance
Stone by stone faded, cooled; the fluted nouns
Made taller, lonelier than life
By leaf-carved capitals in the afterglow.
The owlet umlaut peeps and hoots
Above the open vowel. And after rain
A deep reverberation fills with stars.

Lost, is it, buried? One more missing piece?

But nothing's lost. Or else: all is translation
And every bit of us is lost in it
(Or found—I wander through the ruin of S
Now and then, wondering at the peacefulness)
And in that loss a self-effacing tree,
Color of context, imperceptibly
Rustling with its angel, turns the waste
To shade and fiber, milk and memory.

CHIMES FOR YAHYA

1

Imperiously ringing, "Νὰ τὰ ποῦμε;
(Shall we tell it?)" two dressy little girls inquire.
They mean some chanted verse to do with Christmas
Which big homemade iron triangles
Drown out and a least coin silences
But oh hell not at seven in the morning
If you please! and SLAM the frosted glass
Spares me their tidings and themselves
Further inspection of the foreigner
Grizzled and growling in his flannel robe.
All day children will be prowling loose
Eager to tell, tell, tell what the angel said.
So, having gagged the mechanism with a towel,
Washed hands and face, put on the kettle—
But bells keep ringing in my head.
Downhill too, where priests pace in black dresses,
Chignons and hats, like Chekhov's governesses,
Their toy church on a whole block of bare earth
In central Athens (what it must be worth!)
Clangs like a locomotive—well, good lord,
Why not? Tomorrow's Christmas. All aboard.

2

Another memory of Mademoiselle.
We're in a Pullman going South for Christmas,
She in the lower berth, I in the upper
As befits whatever station we pass through.
Lanterns finger our compartment walls.
At one stop, slipping down into her dream
I lift the blind an inch. Outside, some blanketed
Black figures from a crèche, part king,
Part shepherd and part donkey, stamp and steam
Gliding from sight as rapturous bells ring.
Mummy and Daddy have gone ahead by sleigh
Packard piled with gifts I know too well.

Night after autumn night, Mademoiselle
Yielding to endearments, bringing down
From the attic, lion by tiger, acrobat by clown,
Tamer with her little whips and hoops,
The very circus of my wildest hopes,
I've seen it, memorized it all. *Choo-choo*
Goes the train towards the déjà-vu.
Christmas morning, in a Mandarin suit—
Pigtail and fan, and pipe already staled
By the imaginary stuff inhaled—
I mimed astonishment, and who was fooled?
The treasure lay outspread beneath the tree.
Pitiful, its delusive novelty:
A present far behind me, in a sense.
And this has been a problem ever since.

3

While I carry tea up to the terrace
—The day is ravishingly mild and fair—
Thirty years pass. My train of thought
Stalls near a certain tunnel's end—despair
Lit by far-off daylight . . . Isfahan.
Change of scene that might, I thought, be tried
First, instead of outright suicide.
(Looked back on now, what caused my sufferings?
Mere thwarted passion—commonest of things.)
I had been shown into a freezing room
Belonging to a man I didn't know.
"What does that matter? Simply go,"
The friend of friends had said. (These friends of friends
Were better company, that year, than real ones.)
Surrendering his letter with my shoes,
Was taking what cold comfort one can take
When one's heart is breaking, on the carpet.
The carpet? Carpet overlapping carpet,
Threadbare, opulent. Enormous carpet-
Covered cushions. On the wall a carpet
Portrait of an old forbidding man
Correct in carpet cutaway, tarboosh
And deep white pile moustache: my host's grandfather,
As I would learn, who founded the carpet works.

Rose trees in such bloom they looked unreal
(Odorless also, or had I caught cold?)
Stood in the four corners. Nearby squatted
A brazier wheezing like a bronchitic old
Bulldog, ash-white, garnet-eyed.
Smoke curled, cardings from the comb of light,
Between me and a courtyard still in shadow.
A well. A flowering tree. One tethered goat,
Her face both smug and martyred, giving suck
To a white puppy's warm, incarnate mess
Of instincts only the pure in heart confess.
Back and forth, grimly eyebrowed under shawls,
Humans passed jacketed in sheepskin.
Was that a gentle summons from within?
The person entering, as I made to rise,
Sketched a rapid unrepeatable gesture
Perfectly explicit. "I," it said,
"Am an old retainer. By these eyes
I would not have you see me otherwise—
Unless you cared to sample my poor graces,
Lampblack and henna, on a hazier basis."
Kneeling, he arranges full black trousers
To hide his striped socks full of holes,
And fusses with the kettle on the coals.

4

"Ah, you have met Hussein," the gentle voice
Just heard says at my shoulder. There
In your corduroy jumpsuit, knotting a foulard
Of camouflage greens-and-browns, you are. You are
No older or younger than I've pictured you,
No handsomer, no simpler—only kinder.
Lover, warrior, invalid and sage,
Amused, unenvious of one another,
Meet in your face. Hussein pours cups too full.
"Our friend is fidgeting. Time for his pipe.
You don't object? I used to smoke myself,
Before my father died and I became
What—the prince? the chieftain of our tribe?
We're smiling but it's serious. One belongs
To the working class of prince. The feuds alone—

Tribesmen at one's gate from miles away,
Needing a doctor or a judgment. Summers, though,
We all live *their* life, high in the foothills,
A world you wouldn't dream. Perhaps one day . . ."
Meanwhile Hussein, positioning the tar
Pearl upon his cloudy blue-green globe,
Applies a coal, is sucking peacefully
At the long polished stem. Peculiar
Sweetness—so I *can* smell—fills the air.
As for the roses, you apologize,
"Roses in Isfahan don't bloom till May.
These are imitation, from Times Square."

5

You kept me by you all that day.
I never had to think why I was there.
Figures materialized, obeyed, unraveled.
One young man brought you his smooth breast
Like an heirloom to unwrap, to probe and dress.
Hussein brought omelets, brandy, cake, fruit, lamb.
A barber shaved you. A tall blonde from Berkeley,
Gloria, doing fieldwork in the tribe,
Got asked back that evening for dinner.
After she left: "Or don't you like
The company of your compatriots?"
I liked whatever you would ask me to,
Wanted to get so many lines a week
Of you by heart. Would want tomorrow
When, to senses sharpened by the pipe
Shared with Hussein once you had gone to bed,
Jets of rigid color—the great mosque—
Rose from a pure white carpet, snowlight flowing
Through every vein and duct, would want to spend
One lifetime there as a divinity
Student niched in shallowest faience,
Pilaf steaming while the slow air
Dried his turban's green outfloating prayer.
Had there perhaps already been
Lives at your side? A paperback I read
Compares the soul to a skimmed stone
Touching the waters of the world at points

Along a curve—Atlantis, Rome, Versailles—
Where friends arrange to be reborn together.
Absurd? No more than Freud or Chemistry
To explain the joy, the jolt that had set wheels
Rolling toward some vapor-tasseled view
—And, incidentally, away from you.

6

Not a year later, ink-blue stains
Would spell the worst—a "letter" of Hussein's:

A boyhood skirmish, a (word blotted) slug
Lodged in your skull, which must . . . which finally must . . .

Prince, that the perennial gift (remember)
Unroll another time beneath your feet,

That, red with liability to bloom
And blow, the rose abstainer of your loom

Quicken a pattern ever incomplete,
Dear Prince in whom I put my trust,

Away with pipe and ember,
The real thing's dark and malleable drug;

Withdrawal rendering, as we know, more strict
Our buried craving for the habit kicked.

7

Dinner was over. Hussein spoke in your ear.
You nodded him away. We drained our beer.
Gloria went right on theorizing
About "relationships within the tribe"
I now appeared to be a member of—
Dressed by you in the black ballooning trousers,
White vest, coarse sherbet-colored shirt
And brimless derby hat your people wore.
(I wore them here once during Carnival
With burnt cork eyebrows. Nobody was fooled.)

Time for a highball? But a piercing scream
Somewhere in the household interrupted
Our flow of spirits. What on earth . . . ?
"Ah, it's too tiresome," you sighed.
"These mountain women *will* give birth
Under one's roof. They wait until their labor's
So far advanced we've no way to prepare—"
The girl from Berkeley lit up like a flare:
"In two whole years I've—oh I've told and told you—
Never seen a childbirth! Can't we just—"
You shook your head. "Ah no. The stranger
Brings bad luck, we think. Best let her be.
A doctor? No. Hussein knows an old woman.
He's gone to fetch her." "But I must, must, must!
Think of my thesis, Yahya, let me please!"
Gloria had risen to her knees.
Counterpoint of screams and argument
Making you disdainfully relent,
"All right. But quietly. Into your coats."
And into the cold courtyard black with goats.

Across, a glimmering shutter stood ajar.
Come-and-go of oil lamps, moans and shadows.
As far as we could tell on tiptoe, there
In the small room's dissolving shabbiness
Lay this veiled figure writhing on a carpet.
Gloria found the bench, I climbed beside her.
Elbows on sill, we presently were staring
While you chuckled back against the wall,
Staring like solemn oxen from a stall
Upon the mystery. "Wow," breathed Gloria,
"Smell that smell. They gave her opium."
Women were chanting. The midwife had come.
Maternal invocations and convulsions
Reaching a pitch—did I detect
In all that pain an element of play?
You also seemed convulsed, with laughter, why?—
Reaching a pitch, an infant's feeble cry
From underneath dark swathings clove the night.
These totteringly picked themselves erect.
Made for Gloria. Into her credulous
Outstretched arms laid—*not* a wriggling white

Puppy! Horrors twinkled through the brain.
Then the proud mother bared her face: Hussein.

8

Cooling tea and clouding day . . .
Over the neighborhood prevailing
Bells, triangles, tuneless treble voices
Of children one imagines. Little boys
Whose rooster tessitura, plus ça change,
Will crow above the cradle of a son.
Little girls each with her Christmas doll
Like hens a china egg is slipped beneath.
Voices so familiar by now
It might as well be silence that I sit in,
Reliving romps with my animal nature. Its ecstasy
Knocking me over, off the leash at last
Or out of the manger at least; tongue, paw and pelt,
Loyal fearless heart—the vipers it saved us from;
Unlikeness to myself I knelt embracing.
Times, too, it turned on me, or on another—
Squawks, feathers—until the rolled-up *Times*
Imposed obedience. Now by its own scale
Older than I am, stodgy, apprehensive,
For all I know, of what must soon . . .
Yet trustful, setting blurred sights on me still.
What were five or six half playful bites?
Deep no doubt, but the pain so long forgiven
It might as well be pleasure I rise in,

9

Grazing music as I do so—my bells,
Silent all this while, my camel bells
From Isfahan. Their graduated brass
Pendant hangs on the awning-frame, discolored
Shades of dully wintering
Oleander. Verdigris on fingertip
And sleeve dew-wet, to make them ring
Together, reach down for the smallest. Shake.
A tingling spine of tone, or waterfall
Crashing pure and chill, bell within bell,

Upward to the ninth and mellowest,
Their changes mingle with the parish best,
Their told tale with the children's doggerel.

YÁNNINA

for Stephen Yenser

*"There lay the peninsula stretching far into the dark gray water, with its
mosque, its cypress tufts and fortress walls; there was the city stretching
far and wide along the water's edge; there was the fatal island, the
closing scene of the history of the once all-powerful Ali."*
—EDWARD LEAR

Somnambulists along the promenade
Have set up booths, their dreams:
Carpets, jewelry, kitchenware, halvah, shoes.
From a loudspeaker passionate lament
Mingles with the penny Jungle's roars and screams.
Tonight in the magician's tent
Next door a woman will be sawed in two,
But right now she's asleep, as who is not, as who . . .

An old Turk at the water's edge has laid
His weapons and himself down, sleeps
Undisturbed since, oh, 1913.
Nothing will surprise him should he wake,
Only how tall, how green the grass has grown
There by the dusty carpet of the lake
Sun beats, then sleepwalks down a vine-festooned arcade,
Giving himself away in golden heaps.

And in the dark gray water sleeps
One who said no to Ali. Kiosks all over town
Sell that postcard, "Kyra Frossíni's Drown,"
Showing her, eyeballs white as mothballs, trussed
Beneath the bulging moon of Ali's lust.
A devil (turban and moustache and sword)
Chucks the pious matron overboard—
Wait—Heaven help us—SPLASH!

The torch smokes on the prow. Too late.
(A picture deeply felt, if in technique slapdash.)

Wherefore the Lion of Epirus, feared
By Greek and Turk alike, tore his black beard
When to barred casements rose the song
Broken from bubbles rising all night long:
"A ton of sugar pour, oh pour into the lake
To sweeten it for poor, for poor Frossíni's sake."*

Awake? Her story's aftertaste
Varies according to the listener.
Friend, it's bitter coffee you prefer?
Brandy for me, and with a fine
White sandy bottom. Not among those braced
By action taken without comment, neat,
Here's how! Grounds of our footnote infiltrate the treat,
Mud-vile to your lips, crystal-sweet to mine.

Twilight at last. Enter the populace.
One little public garden must retrace
Long after school its childish X,
Two paths that cross and cross. The hollyhock, the rose,
Zinnia and marigold hear themselves named
And blush for form's sake, unashamed
Chorus out of *Ignoramus Rex*:
"What shall the heart learn, that already knows

Its place by water, and its time by sun?"
Mother wit fills the stately whispering sails
Of girls someone will board and marry. Who?
Look at those radiant young males.
Their morning-glory nature neon blue
Wilts here on the provincial vine. Where did it lead,
The race, the radiance? To oblivion
Dissembled by a sac of sparse black seed.

Now under trees men with rush baskets sell
Crayfish tiny and scarlet as the sins

---

*"Time was kind to the reputation of this woman who had been unfaithful to her husband, vain, and grasping. She came to be regarded as a Christian martyr and even as an early heroine in the struggle for Greek independence. She has been celebrated in legend, in poetry, in popular songs and historical fiction, and surrounded with the glamour which so often attaches to women whose love affairs have been of an intense nature and have involved men of political or historical importance."

—WILLIAM PLOMER, *The Diamond of Jannina*

In any fin-de-siècle villanelle.
Tables fill up. A shadow play begins.
Painted, translucent cut-outs fill the screen.
It glows. His children by a jumping bean
Karaghiózi clobbers, baits the Turk,
Then all of them sing, dance, tell stories, go berserk.

Tomorrow we shall cross the lake to see
The cottage tumbling down, where soldiers killed
Ali. Two rugless rooms. Cushions. Vitrines
In which, to this day, silks and bracelets swim.
Above, a painting hangs. It's him,
Ali. The end is near, he's sleeping between scenes
In a dark lady's lap. Vassilikí.
The mood is calm, the brushwork skilled

By contrast with Frossíni's mass-produced
Unsophisticated piece of goods.
The candle trembles in the watching god's
Hand—almost a love-death, höchste Lust!
Her drained, compliant features haunt
The waters there was never cause to drown her in.
Your grimiest ragamuffin comes to want
Two loves, two versions of the Feminine:

One virginal and tense, brief as a bubble,
One flesh and bone—gone up no less in smoke
Where giant spits revolving try their rusty treble,
Sheep's eyes pop, and death-wish ravens croak.
Remember, the Romantic's in full feather.
Byron has visited. He likes
The luxe, and overlooks the heads on pikes;
Finds Ali "Very kind . . . indeed, a father . . ."*

Funny, that is how I think of Ali.
On the one hand, the power and the gory
Details, pigeon-blood rages and retali-

*Letter to his mother, November 12, 1809. Plomer observes: ". . . even allowing for Oriental effusiveness, it seems doubtful whether [Ali's] interest in Byron was exactly as paternal as he pretended, for a father does not give his son sweets twenty times a day and beg him to visit him at night. It is worth remarking that Ali was a judge of character and a connoisseur of beauty, whether male or female, and that the like of Byron, and Byron at twenty-one, is not often seen."

ations, gouts of fate that crust his story;
And on the other, charm, the whimsically
Meek brow, its motives all ab ulteriori,
The flower-blue gaze twining to choke proportion,
Having made one more pretty face's fortune.

A dove with Parkinson's disease
Selects *our* fortunes: TRAVEL AND GROW WISE
And A LOYAL FRIEND IS MORE THAN GOLD.
But, at the island monastery, eyes
Gouged long since to the gesso sockets will outstare
This or that old-timer on his knees
Asking the candlelight for skill to hold
The figures flush against the screen's mild glare.

Ali, my father—both are dead.
In so many words, so many rhymes,
The brave old world sleeps. Are we what it dreams
And is a rude awakening overdue?
Not in Yánnina. To bed, to bed.
The Lion sets. The lights wink out along the lake.
Weeks later, in this study gone opaque,
They are relit. See through me. See me through.

For partings hurt although we dip the pain
Into a glowing well—the pen I mean.
Living alone won't make some inmost face to shine
Maned with light, ember and anodyne,
Deep in a desktop burnished to its grain.
That the last hour be learned again
By riper selves, couldn't you doff this green
Incorruptible, the might-have-been,

And arm in arm with me dare the magician's tent?
It's hung with asterisks. A glittering death
Is hefted, swung. The victim smiles consent.
To a sharp intake of breath she comes apart
(Done by mirrors? Just one woman? Two?
A fight starts—in the provinces, one feels,
There's never that much else to do)
Then to a general exhalation heals

Like anybody's life, bubble and smoke
In afterthought, whose elements converge,
Glory of windless mornings that the barge
(Two barges, one reflected, a quicksilver joke)
Kept scissoring and mending as it steered
The old man outward and away,
Amber mouthpiece of a narghilé
Buried in his by then snow white beard.

VERSE FOR URANIA

Through the dimness, curtains drawn, eyes closed,
Where I am composing myself before tonight's excitement
(It's not quite five, yet outdoors the daylight
Will have begun to ripple and deepen like a pool),
Comes your mother's footstep, her voice softly,
Hesitantly calling. She'll have come upstairs
To borrow something for the evening, cups or chairs,
But it can't be urgent, and the footsteps fade
Before I've made my mind up, whether to answer.

Below, where you live, time will be standing cowed
Among the colors and appliances.
What passionate consumers you've become!
Second washing machine, giant second TV,
Hot saffron, pink, eyeshadow ultramarine—
Rooms like those ghostly ones behind the screen
With just the color tuned to Very Loud.
Your father's out in his new Silver Cloud
Delivering invitations. You've all been
Up since dawn—not you, of course, you're a baby,
But your mother and your sister. Between chores
Teasing each other's hair like sisters, touching
Rouged indexes to one another's cheek.
The lamb will have cooled nicely in its fat now,
Cake been iced to match the souvenir
Rosettes (two ribbons with your name and mine),
Whiskey and set-ups set up like tenpins.
According to tradition I'm affecting
Ignorance of, the post-baptismal party
Ought to be given by the godfather.
But this is your godfather speaking, calling halt.
I have already showered you with garments
Priced inversely to their tininess.
Have been shown rushes of what else my doom
Is to provide you with, world without end:
Music lessons from beyond the tomb,
Doll and dentist and dowry, that 3-D
Third television we attain so far
Exclusively in dreamland, where you are.

Would that *I* were. All too soon I'll place
Round your neck a golden chain and cross
Set with stones watery as the stars at noon;
And don't forget the fancy sheet you'll want
The moment you are lifted, born anew
Squalling and squirming out of the deep font,
While the priest lifts only his deep baritone
That makes the skull a vault of melismatic
Sparklings, and myself groan with your weight—
Renunciation of the vanities
In broken Byzantine on your behalf,
Or your father's flashbulbs popping, or your mother's eyes
Laughing to see salvation's gas inflate
Their fat peach-petal bébé-Michelin,
Not having made you, on me, a lighter burden.

Time drawing near, a clock that loses it
Tells me you must wake now, pagan still.
Slowly the Day-Glo minnow mobile twirls
Above you. Fin-glints ripple in the glass
Protecting an embroidery—your great-
Grandmother's? No one remembers. Appliquéd
On black: cross-section of a pomegranate,
Stem and all. The dull gold velvet rind
Full as a womb with flowers. Their faded silks entwine
The motto ΚΙ ΑΥΤΟ ΘΑ ΠΕΡΑΣΗ—This too will pass.

You're being named for yet another
Science whose elements cause vertigo
Even, I fancy, in the specialist.
A sleepless and unlettered urban glow
On everyone's horizon turns to gist
That rhetoric of starry beasts and gods
Whose figures, whose least phoneme made its fine
Point in the course of sweeping periods—
Each sentence thirty lives long, here below.
From out there notions reach us yet, but few
And far between as those first names we knew
Already without having to look up,
Children that we were, the Chair, the Cup,
But each night dimmer, children that we are,
Each night regressing, dumber by a star.

Still, fiction helps preserve them, those old truths
Our sleights have turned to fairy tales (or worse:
Look at—don't look at—your TV).
The storybooks you'll soon be reading me
About the skies abound with giants and dwarfs.
Think of the wealth of pre-Olympian
Amber washed up on the shores of Grimm—
The beanstalk's tenant-cyclops grown obese
On his own sons; the Bears and Berenice.
Or take those masterfully plotted high
Society conjunctions and epicycles
In a late fable like *The Wings of the Dove*.
Take, for that matter, my beanstalk couplet, above,
Where such considerations as rhyme and meter
Prevail, it might be felt, at the expense
Of meaning, but as well create, survive it;
For the first myth was Measure. Finally take
Any poor smalltown starstruck sense of "love
That makes the world go round"—see how the phrase
Stretches from Mystic to Mount Palomar
Back to those nights before the good old days,
Before the axle jumped its socket so
That genes in shock flashed on/off head to toe,
Before mill turned to maelstrom, and IBM
Wrenched from Pythagoras his diadem.

Adamant nights in which our wisest apes
Met on a cracked mud terrace not yet Ur
And with presumption more than amateur
Stared the random starlight into shapes.

Millennia their insight had to flee
Outward before the shaft it had become
Shot back through the planetarium
Cathodic with sidereality,

As ^mulKAK.SI.DI (in Sumerian)
Saw through haphazard clay to innermost
Armatures of light whereby the ghost
Walks in a twinkling he has learned to scan.

≈

Where has time flown? Since I began
You've learned to stand for seconds, balancing,
And look away at my approach, coyly.
My braincells continue to snuff out like sparks
At the average rate of 100,000 a day—
The intellect suspiciously resembling
Eddington's universe in headlong flight
From itself. A love I'd been taking nightly
Readings of sets behind the foliage now;
I wonder what will rise next from the sea—
The heart, no less suspiciously,
Remaining geocentric. Of an evening
I creak downstairs, unshaven in my robe,
Jaw with your father in his undershirt.
He's worn out by a day of spreading tar
Overtime upon America.
The TV off, you and your sister sleeping,
Your mother lifts from needlework a face
Lovelier, I find, without make-up,
Even as worry stitches her white brow:

She's written twice, and sent the photographs.
Silence from her people, weeks of it.
I've asked myself how much the godfather
They picked contributes to imbroglio.
Someone more orthodox . . . ? I'll never know.
Who ever does? From the start, his fine frank grin,
Her fine nearsighted gaze said *Take us in.*
Let them make anything they liked of me
From personal effect to destiny.
Now should he reappraise or she regret,
Fly back, why don't they? We've a daily jet.
Ah but time lost, missed payments—they're in deep.
Listen. Your sister whimpering, her sleep
Dislocated, going on three years.
Some days the silver cloud is lined with tears.
(Another day, when letters thriftily
Stamped for surface mail arrive,
Connecticut is heaven once again.)
And what if I'd done nothing, where would *you* be?
"One more baby back there in the Greece,"
Your father firmly putting his best face

On pros and cons, "when every day make seven
Bucks at the foundry? Never in my life.
Why I say to mean, this kid, she yours!"
Let's hope that my expression reassures.

Finding a moment, I've written: *Rose from bed*
Where I'd begun imagining the baptism
(In my old faith bed *was* the baptism)
To dress for it. Then all of us were racing
The highway to a dozen finishing lines
Every last one unquotable, scored through,
You bubbling milk, your sister in my lap
Touching her rhinestone treble-clef barrette
—Made-up touches. Lately I forget
The actual as it happens (Plato warns us
Writing undermines the memory—
So does photography, I should tell your father)
And have, as now, less memory than a mind
To rescue last month's Lethe-spattered module
From inner space—eternal black-on-white
Pencilings, moondusty palindrome—
For splashdown in the rainbow. Welcome home.

Let evening be at its height. Let me have stolen
Past the loud dance, its goat-eyed leader steadied
By the bull-shouldered next in line,
And found you being changed. Let your mother, proudly
Displaying under the nightie's many-eyeleted
Foam a marvelous "ripe olive" mole
Beside your navel, help me to conceive
That fixed, imaginary, starless pole
Of the ecliptic which this one we steer by
Circles, a notch each time the old bring golden
Gifts to the newborn child, whose age begins.
Nothing that cosmic in our case, my dear—
Just your parents' Iron Age yielding
To some twilight of the worldly goods.
Or myself dazed by dawnings as yet half sheer
Lyric convention, half genetic glow
("May she live for you!" guests call as they go)
Which too will pass. Meanwhile, à propos of ages,
Let this one of mine you usher in
Bending still above your crib enthralled,

Godchild, be lightly taken, life and limb,
By rosy-fingered flexings as by flame.
Who else would linger so, crooning your name,
But second childhood. When time came for him . . .

For me, that is—to go upstairs, one hitch
Was that our ups and downs meant so much more
Than the usual tralala from floor to floor.
Now I was seeing double—which was which?

No thing but stumbled toward its heavenly twin,
No thought but helped its subject to undress . . .
(Mother of that hour's muse, Forgetfulness,
Hold me strictly to the might-have-been.)

Each plate shattered below, each cry, each hue,
Any old composer could fix that
(Purcell? His "Blessed Virgin"? Strauss's "Bat"?)
Unless my taste had gone to pieces, too.

Well, light a lamp, but only long enough
To put the former on the turntable.
Head back, feet up, watch dark revolving fill
With coloratura, farthingale and ruff,

A schoolgirl's flight to Egypt, sore afraid,
Clasping the infant, thorn against her breast,
Through dotted quaver and too fleeting rest
The clavecin's dry fronds too thinly shade.

The text she sang was hackwork—Nahum Tate—
Yet ending: *Whilst of thy dear sight beguil'd,
I trust the God, but O! I fear the Child.*
Exactly my own feelings. It was late

And early. I had seen you through shut eyes.
Our bond was sacred, being secular:
In time embedded, it in us, near, far,
Flooding both levels with the same sunrise.

THE WILL

I am standing among the coal black
Walls of a living room that is
Somehow both David the Wise's and not his.
Outside, the dead of winter, wailing, bleak.

Two men and a woman, dressed in black,
Enter with a will. A will of mine?
They nod encouragement. I sign,
Give each my hand in parting. Now to pack

This canvas tote-bag. I have wrapped in jeans
With manuscript on either side for wadding
Something I'm carrying to a . . . to a wedding . . .

Then, wondering as always what it means
And what else I'm forgetting,
On my cold way. A car is waiting.

(Only last night a person more urbane
Than usual was heading for the Seine.

Here was one façade he seemed to know
From times he'd seen it all aglow

And heard its old chronologist pronounce
It not the present but the thought that counts.

He rang impulsively. No bell
Resounded from within the dark hotel.

Its front door, Roman-numeralled,
Still said, "I" in white-on-emerald.

Some humbler way into the edifice
Was chalked just legibly "I*bis.*"

Steam from a sudden manhole bore
Wetness to the dream. I woke heartsore.)

I'm at an airport, waiting. The scar itches.
Carving, last month I nearly removed my thumb.
Where was my mind? Lapses like this become
Standard practice. Not all of them leave me in stitches.

In growing puzzlement I've felt things losing
Their grip on me. What's done is done, dreamlike;
Clutches itself too late to stop the oozing
Reds, the numbing inward leak

Of pressures we have effortlessly risen
Through on occasion to a brilliant
Ice blue and white sestet

Six lines six miles above, if not rhyme, reason.
Its wingèd shadow tiny as an ant
Keeps up far down, state after sunnier state,

Or grown huge (have we landed?)
Scatters into human shadows all
Underfoot skittering through the terminal
To greet, lulled, blinded,

The mild, moist South. Che puro ciel . . .
I'm riding in a taxi. The lightskinned
Driver steering me through scenery skeined
With twitterings, flutterings, scrim of shell

Pink, shell ivory—O dogwood days—
Fleet against unutterably slow
Dynastic faces of a portico,

These float from view, lids quiver, the air dies
Upon my lips, the bag's bulk at my feet
Gone underwater-weightless, tempting fate.

My burden is an old wall-eyed stone-blond
Ibis. Over the years (I bought it with

A check my father wrote before his death)
I took to heart its funerary chic

Winged like a sandal, necked like the snakes on a wand,
Stalker that spears *and* spares . . .
Which passing into a young, happy pair's
Keeping could stand for the giver. Now, next week

I mean to remember to take
David the Fair's acrylics
And turn the wooden base to baked blue brick
With lotus frieze, blossom and pad and calyx,

Abstraction of a river, eau de Nil
Arrested by the powerful curving bill.

Gliding to a halt, the prodigal stirs.
Pays the driver. Gives himself up to home.
His mother, a year younger, kisses him.
Maids are wafting suitcases upstairs.

While sirens over seventy, with names
Like Myra, Robin, Rosalie and Midge,
Call from the sun porch, "Come play bridge!"
They love their sweetly-sung bloodthirsty games.

He is sitting at the table, dealing,
When a first tentative wrong note
Is quickly taken up ("What is it, darling?")

By the whole orchestra in unison.
The unbid heart pounds in his throat—
The bag, the bird—left in the taxi—gone!

Gone for good. In the first shock of
Knowing it he tries
To play the dummy, dreads to advertise,
"Drinks water" like a character in Chekhov.

Life dims and parches. Self-inflicted
Desolation a faint horselaugh jars.
Property lies toppled, seeing stars
Nowhere in the dry dreambed reflected.

So that tonight's pint-size amphibian
Wriggler from murky impulse to ethereal act
Must hazard the dimensions of a man

Of means. Of meanings. Codicil
And heir alike. White-lipped survivor hacked
Out of his own will.

U DID WELL JM TO DISINHERIT
YR SELF & FRIENDS OF THAT STONE BIRD
—It's June, we're at the Ouija board,
David the True and I and our familiar spirit—

SACRED TO THOTH NOW AT 310 KNOX DRIVE
MACON GA IT HAS BROUGHT DISASTER
COMME TOUJOURS PARALYZED THE DRIVERS SISTER
MAXINE SHAW BORN 1965

THESE BALEFUL PRESENCES SHAPED FOR THE DEAD
WHEN THEY CHANGE HANDS EXACT A SACRIFICE
REMEMBER ITS FIRST YEAR CHEZ VOUS YR FACE
TURNED VOTIVE GOLD JAUNDICE THE DOCTOR SD

GODS BEAK SAY I EMBEDDED IN YR SIDE
HARDLY THE BIBELOT TO GIVE A BRIDE

Ephraim, we take you with a grain of salt,
Protagonist at best of the long story
Sketches and notes for which were my missing bag's
Other significant cargo, by the way.

BY THE WAY SINCE U DID NOT CONSULT
THEIR SUBJECT YR GLUM PAGES LACKED HIS GLORY
That stings. The guide and I lock horns like stags.
What is *his* taste? Aquinas? Bossuet?

SOIS SAGE DEAR HEART & SET MY TEACHINGS DOWN
Why, Ephraim, you belong to the old school—
You think the Word by definition good.

IF U DO NOT YR WORLD WILL BE UNDONE
& HEAVEN ITSELF TURN TO ONE GRINNING SKULL
So? We must write to save the face of God?

With which the teacup pointer goes inert.
Ephraim, are you still there? Angry? Hurt?

Long pause. YR SPIRIT HAS BEEN CAUGHT REDHANDED
IT IS HIS OCCUPATIONAL FAIBLESSE
TO ENTER & POSSESS REPEAT POSSESS
L OBJET AIME   Who, me?   WELL I HAD PLANNED IT

WITHOUT SO MANY DAVIDS TO COMBAT
MY GIANT DESIGNS UPON YR ART MON CHER
SHRINK TO THIS TOPSYTURVY WILLOWWARE
IGLOO WALTZING WITH THE ALPHABET

So what is the next step?   LIVE MORE LIVE MOST
EXPECTING NO RETURN   To earth?   IT SEEMS
U WILL NOT   Hush, don't tell us— PLEASANT DREAMS
GIVE UP EVERYTHING EXCEPT THE GHOST

I'm at my desk. Paralysis.
No headway through the drafts
Before me—bleaching wastes and drifts
Of time spent writing (or not writing) this.

Then a lucky stroke unearths the weird
Basalt passage of last winter,
Tunneling black. The match struck as I enter
Illuminates . . . My word!

(At someone's bidding smooth white plaster
Had been incised with mourning slave and master

And pets with mystic attributes
In profile among goblets, fans and fruits.

Here was a manuscript. Here were
Five catgut stitches laid in lusterware.

And here in final state, where lost was found,
The ibis sat. Another underground

Chamber made ready. If this one was not
Quite the profoundest or the most ornate,

Give it time. The bric-a-brac
Slumbered in bonds that of themselves would break

One fine day, at any chance unsealing,
To shining leaf and woken shades of feeling.)

Already thickskinned little suns
Are coming back, and gusts of sharp cologne
—Lemon trees bearing and in bloom at once—

And rings exchanged for life,
And one high jet that cut to the blue's bone
Its healing hieroglyph,

While briefly over the house
A dirtbrown helicopter
Like the bad fairy Carabosse, its clatter
Drowning out the vows,

Drowning out the sweet
Voices of doves and finches
At home among the branches
In the bright, cool heat,

Hovered close, then, seeing
That it would not eclipse
The sunniness beneath it, up and went

As much had, without saying—
Leaving to lovers' lips
All further argument.

Admittedly I err by undertaking
This in its present form. The baldest prose
Reportage was called for, that would reach
The widest public in the shortest time.
Time, it had transpired, was of the essence.
Time, the very attar of the Rose,
Was running out. We, though, were ancient foes,
I and the deadline. Also my subject matter
Gave me pause—so intimate, so novel.
Best after all to do it as a novel?
Looking about me, I found characters
Human and otherwise (if the distinction
Meant anything in fiction). Saw my way
To a plot, or as much of one as still allowed
For surprise and pleasure in its working-out.
Knew my setting; and had, from the start, a theme
Whose steady light shone back, it seemed, from every
Least detail exposed to it. I came
To see it as an old, exalted one:
The incarnation and withdrawal of
A god. That last phrase is Northrop Frye's.
I had stylistic hopes moreover. Fed
Up so long and variously by
Our age's fancy narrative concoctions,
I yearned for the kind of unseasoned telling found
In legends, fairy tales, a tone licked clean
Over the centuries by mild old tongues,
Grandam to cub, serene, anonymous.
Lacking that voice, the in its fashion brilliant
Nouveau roman (even the one I wrote)
Struck me as an orphaned form, whose followers,
Suckled by Woolf not Mann, had stories told them
In childhood, if at all, by adults whom
They could not love or honor. So my narrative
Wanted to be limpid, unfragmented;
My characters, conventional stock figures
Afflicted to a minimal degree
With personality and past experience
A witch, a hermit, innocent young lovers,

The kinds of being we recall from Grimm,
Jung, Verdi, and the commedia dell' arte.
That such a project was beyond me merely
Incited further futile stabs at it.
My downfall was "word-painting." Exquisite
Peek-a-boo plumage, limbs aflush from sheer
Bombast unfurling through the troposphere
Whose earthward denizens' implosion startles
Silly quite a little crowd of mortals
—My readers, I presumed from where I sat
In the angelic secretariat.
The more I struggled to be plain, the more
Mannerism hobbled me. What for?
Since it had never truly fit, why wear
The shoe of prose? In verse the feet went bare.
Measures, furthermore, had been defined
As what emergency required. Blind
Promptings put at last the whole mistaken
Enterprise to sleep in darkest Macon
(Cf. "The Will"), and I alone was left
To tell my story. For it seemed that Time—
The grizzled washer of his hands appearing
To say so in a spectrum-bezeled space
Above hot water—Time would not;
Whether because it was running out like water
Or because January draws this bright
Line down the new page I take to write:
The Book of a Thousand and One Evenings Spent
With David Jackson at the Ouija Board
In Touch with Ephraim Our Familiar Spirit.

Backdrop: The dining room at Stonington.
Walls of ready-mixed matte "flame" (a witty
Shade, now watermelon, now sunburn).
Overhead, a turn of the century dome
Expressing white tin wreathes and fleurs-de-lys
In palpable relief to candlelight.
Wallace Stevens, with that dislocated
Perspective of the newly dead, would take it
For an alcove in the Baptist church next door
Whose moonlit tower saw eye to eye with us.
The room breathed sheer white curtains out. In blew
Elm- and chimney-blotted shimmerings, so
Slight the tongue of land, so high the point of view.
1955 this would have been,
Second summer of our tenancy.
Another year we'd buy the old eyesore
Half of whose top story we now rented;
Build, above that, a glass room off a wooden
Stardeck; put a fireplace in; make friends.
Now, strangers to the village, did we even
Have a telephone? Who needed one!
We had each other for communication
And all the rest. The stage was set for Ephraim.

Properties: A milk glass tabletop.
A blue-and-white cup from the Five & Ten.
Pencil, paper. Heavy cardboard sheet
Over which the letters A to Z
Spread in an arc, our covenant
With whom it would concern; also
The Arabic numerals, and YES and NO.
What more could a familiar spirit want?
Well, when he knew us better, he'd suggest
We prop a mirror in the facing chair.
Erect and gleaming, silver-hearted guest,
We saw each other in it. He saw us.
(Any reflecting surface worked for him.
Noons, D and I might row to a sandbar
Far enough from town for swimming naked
Then pacing the glass treadmill hardly wet
That healed itself perpetually of us—
Unobserved, unheard we thought, until

The night he praised our bodies and our wit,
Our blushes in a twinkling overcome.)
Or we could please him by swirling a drop of rum
Inside the cup that, overturned and seeming
Slightly to lurch at such times in mid-glide,
Took heart from us, dictation from our guide.

But he had not yet found us. Who was there?
The cup twitched in its sleep. "Is someone there?"
We whispered, fingers light on Willowware,
When the thing moved. Our breathing stopped. The cup,
Glazed zombie of itself, was on the prowl
Moving, but dully, incoherently,
Possessed, as we should soon enough be told,
By one or another of the myriads
Who hardly understand, through the compulsive
Reliving of their deaths, that they have died
—By fire in this case, when a warehouse burned.
HELLP O SAV ME scrawled the cup
As on the very wall flame rippled up,
Hypnotic wave on wave, a lullaby
Of awfulness. I slumped. D: One more try.
Was anybody there? As when a pike
Strikes, and the line singing writes in lakeflesh
Highstrung runes, and reel spins and mind reels
YES a new and urgent power YES
Seized the cup. It swerved, clung, hesitated,
Darted off, a devil's darning needle
Gyroscope our fingers rode bareback
(But stopping dead the instant one lost touch)
Here, there, swift handle pointing, letter upon
Letter taken down blind by my free hand—
At best so clumsily, those early sessions
Break off into guesswork, paraphrase.
Too much went whizzing past. We were too nice
To pause, divide the alphabetical
Gibberish into words and sentences.
Yet even the most fragmentary message—
Twice as entertaining, twice as wise
As either of its mediums—enthralled them.

Correct but cautious, that first night, we asked
Our visitor's name, era, habitat.
EPHRAIM came the answer. A Greek Jew
Born AD 8 at XANTHOS   Where was that?
In Greece WHEN WOLVES & RAVENS WERE IN ROME
(Next day the classical dictionary yielded
A Xanthos on the Asia Minor Coast.)
NOW WHO ARE U   We told him. ARE U XTIANS
We guessed so. WHAT A COZY CATACOMB
Christ had WROUGHT HAVOC in *his* family,
ENTICED MY FATHER FROM MY MOTHERS BED
(I too had issued from a broken home—
The first of several facts to coincide.)
Later a favorte of TIBERIUS   Died
AD 36 on CAPRI   throttled
By the imperial guard for having LOVED
THE MONSTERS NEPHEW (sic) CALIGULA
Rapidly he went on—changing the subject?
A long incriminating manuscript
Boxed in bronze lay UNDER PORPHYRY
Beneath the deepest excavations. He
Would helped us find it, but we must please make haste
Because Tiberius wanted it destroyed.
Oh? And where, we wondered of the void,
Was Tiberius these days? STAGE THREE

Why was he telling *us*? He'd overheard us
Talking to SIMPSON   Simpson? His LINK WITH EARTH
His REPRESENTATIVE   A feeble nature
All but bestial, given to violent
Short lives—one ending lately among flames
In an Army warehouse. Slated for rebirth
But not in time, said Ephraim, to prevent
The brat from wasting, just now at our cup,
Precious long distance minutes—don't hang up!

So much facetiousness—well, we were young
And these were matters of life and death—dismayed us.
Was he a devil? His reply MY POOR
INNOCENTS left the issue hanging fire.
As it flowed on, his stream-of-consciousness
Deepened. There was a buried room, a BED

WROUGHT IN SILVER   I CAN LEAD U THERE
IF   If? U GIVE ME   What? HA HA YR SOULS
(Another time he'll say that he misread
Our innocence for insolence that night,
And meant to scare us.) Our eyes met. What if . . .
The blood's least vessel hoisted jet-black sails.
Five whole minutes we were frightened stiff
—But after all, we weren't *that* innocent.
The Rover Boys at thirty, still red-blooded
Enough not to pass up an armchair revel
And pure enough at heart to beat the devil,
Entered into the spirit, so to speak,
And said they'd leave for Capri that same week.

Pause. Then, as though we'd passed a test,
Ephraim's whole manner changed. He brushed aside
Tiberius and settled to the task
Of answering, like an experienced guide,
Those questions we had lacked the wit to ask.

Here on Earth—huge tracts of information
Have gone into these capsules flavorless
And rhymed for easy swallowing—on Earth
We're each the REPRESENTATIVE of a PATRON
—Are there that many patrons? YES O YES
These secular guardian angels fume and fuss
For what must seem eternity over us.
It is forbidden them to INTERVENE
Save, as it were, in the entr'acte between
One incarnation and another. Back
To school from the disastrously long vac
Goes the soul its patron crams yet once
Again with savoir vivre. Will the dunce
Never—by rote, the hundredth time round—learn
What ropes make fast that point of no return,
A footing on the lowest of NINE STAGES
Among the curates and the minor mages?
Patrons at last ourselves, an upward notch
Our old ones move   THEYVE BORNE IT ALL FOR THIS
And take delivery from the Abyss
Of brand-new little savage souls to watch.
One difference: with every rise in station

Comes a degree of PEACE FROM REPRESENTATION
—Odd phrase, more like a motto for abstract
Art—or for Autocracy—In fact
Our heads are spinning—From the East a light—
BUT U ARE TIRED MES CHERS   SWEET DREAMS   TOMORROW NIGHT

SAMOS

And still, at sea all night, we had a sense
Of sunrise, golden oil poured upon water,
Soothing its heave, letting the sleeper sense
What inborn, amniotic homing sense
Was ferrying him—now through the dream-fire
In which (it has been felt) each human sense
Burns, now through ship's radar's cool sixth sense,
Or mere unerring starlight—to an island.
Here we were. The twins of Sea and Land,
Up and about for hours—hues, cries, scents—
Had placed at eye level a single light
Croissant: the harbor glazed with warm pink light.

Fire-wisps were weaving a string bag of light
For sea stones. Their astounding color sense!
Porphyry, alabaster, chrysolite
Translucences that go dead in daylight
Asked only the quick dip in holy water
For the saint of cell on cell to come alight—
Illuminated crystals thinking light,
Refracting it, the gray prismatic fire
Or yellow-gray of sea's dilute sapphire . . .
Wavelengths daily deeply score the leit-
Motifs of Loom and Wheel upon this land.
To those who listen, it's the Promised Land.

A little spin today? Dirt roads inland
Jounce and revolve in a nerve-jangling light,
Doing the ancient dances of the land
Where, gnarled as olive trees that shag the land
With silver, old men—their two-bladed sense
Of spendthrift poverty, the very land
Being, if not loaf, tomb—superbly land
Upright on the downbeat. We who water
The local wine, which "drinks itself" like water,

Clap for more, cry out to *be* this island
Licked all over by a white, salt fire,
Be noon's pulsing ember raked by fire,

Know nothing, now, but Earth, Air, Water, Fire!
For once out of the frying pan to land
Within their timeless, everlasting fire!
Blood's least red monocle, O magnifier
Of the great Eye that sees by its own light
More pictures in "the world's enchanted fire"
Than come and go in any shrewd crossfire
Upon the page, of syllable and sense,
We want unwilled excursions and ascents,
Crave the upward-rippling rungs of fire,
The outward-rippling rings (enough!) of water . . .
(Now some details—how else will this hold water?)

Our room's three flights above the whitewashed water-
front where Pythagoras was born. A fire
Escape of sky-blue iron leads down to water.
Yachts creak on mirror berths, and over water
Voices from Sweden or Somaliland
Tell how this or that one crossed the water
To Ephesus, came back with toilet water
And a two kilo box of Turkish delight
—Trifles. Yet they shine with such pure light
In memory, even they, that the eyes water.
As with the setting sun, or innocence,
Do things that fade especially make sense?

Samos. We keep trying to make sense
Of what we can. Not souls of the first water—
Although we've put on airs, and taken fire—
We shall be dust of quite another land
Before the seeds here planted come to light.

GRASS

The river irises
Draw themselves in.
Enough to have seen
Their day. The arras

Also of evening drawn,
We light up between
Earth and Venus
On the courthouse lawn,

Kept by this cheerful
Inch of green
And ten more years—fifteen?—
From disappearing.

THE PIER: UNDER PISCES

The shallows, brighter,
Wetter than water,
Tepidly glitter with the fingerprint-
Obliterating feel of kerosene.

Each piling like a totem
Rises from rock bottom
Straight through the ceiling
Aswirl with suns, clear ones or pale bluegreen,

And beyond! where bubbles burst,
Sphere of their worst dreams,
If dream is what they do,
These floozy fish—

Ceramic-lipped in filmy
Peekaboo blouses,
Fluorescent body
Stockings, hot stripes,

Swayed by the hypnotic ebb and flow
Of supermarket Muzak,
Bolero beat the undertow's
Pebble-filled gourds repeat;

Jailbait consumers of subliminal
Hints dropped from on high
In gobbets none
Eschews as minced kin;

Who, hooked themselves—bamboo diviner
Bent their way
Vigorously nodding
Encouragement—

Arc one by one hauled kisswise, oh
Into some blinding hell
Policed by leathery ex-
Justices each

Minding his catch, if catch is what he can,
If mind is what one means—
The torn mouth
Stifled by newsprint, working still. If . . . if . . .

The little scales
Grow stiff. Dusk plugs her dryer in,
Buffs her nails, riffles through magazines,
While far and wide and deep

Rove the great sharkskin-suited criminals
And safe in this lit shrine
A boy sits. He'll be eight.
We've drunk our milk, we've eaten our stringbeans,

But left untasted on the plate
The fish. An eye, a broiled pearl, meeting mine,
I lift his fork . . .
The bite. The tug of fate.

THE SCHOOL PLAY

"Harry of Hereford, Lancaster, and Derby,
Stands here for God, his country, and . . ." And what?
"Stands here for God, his Sovereign, and himself,"
Growled Captain Fry who had the play by heart.
I was the First Herald, "a small part"
—I was small too—"but an important one."
What was not important to the self
At nine or ten? Already I had crushes
On Mowbray, Bushy, and the Duke of York.
Handsome Donald Niemann (now himself,
According to the Bulletin, headmaster
Of his own school somewhere out West) awoke
Too many self-indulgent mouthings in
The dummy mirror before smashing it,
For me to set my scuffed school cap at him.
Another year I'd play that part myself,
Or Puck, or Goneril, or Prospero.
Later, in adolescence, it was thought
Clever to speak of having found oneself,
With a smile and rueful headshake for those who hadn't.
People still do. Only the other day
A woman my age told us that her son
"Hadn't found himself"—at thirty-one!
I heard in the mind's ear an amused hum
Of mothers and fathers from beyond the curtain,
And that flushed, far-reaching hour came back
Months of rehearsal in the gymnasium
Had led to: when the skinny nobodies
Who'd memorized the verse and learned to speak it
Emerged in beards and hose (or gowns and rouge)
Vivid with character, having put themselves
All unsuspecting into the masters' hands.

PAGE FROM THE KORAN

A small vellum environment
Overrun by black
Scorpions of Kufic script—their ranks
All trigger tail and gold vowel-sac—
At auction this mild winter morning went
For six hundred Swiss francs.

By noon, fire from the same blue heavens
Had half erased Beirut.
Allah be praised, it said on crude handbills,
For guns and Nazarenes to shoot.
"How gladly with proper words," said Wallace Stevens,
"The soldier dies." Or kills.

God's very word, then, stung the heart
To greed and rancor. Yet
Not where the last glow touches one spare man
Inked-in against his minaret
—Letters so handled they are life, and hurt,
Leaving the scribe immune?

SANTO

for Peter Hooten and Alan Moss Reverón

Francisco on his shelf,
Wreathed in dusty wax
Roses, for weeks and weeks
Hadn't been himself—

Making no day come true
By answering a prayer,
Just dully standing there . . .
What did our Grandma do?

She painted his beard black
And rinsed the roses clean,
Then hid his rags in half
A new red satin cloak,

Renaming him Martín.
Next week the baby spoke,
Juan sent a photograph
On board his submarine,

Aunt Concha went to cook
Downtown at the hotel,
The sick white dog got well
—And that was all it took!

BRONZE

In August 1972 a skin-diver off Riace, on the Calabrian coast, saw at a depth of seven or eight meters an arm upthrust from the sandy bottom. Having made sure that it was not of flesh, and remarking nearby a second, sanded-over form, he notified the local Archeological Museum. Frogmen easily raised the two figures. Even encrusted with silica and lime, they were from the start felt to be Greek originals. Their restoration, in Florence, would take nine years.

I

Birdsong. May. Tuscany. A house. Sunset
Through red or green panes falling on small print
Pored over by two figures: my companion
("David the Fair") still, after all these years,
Marvelously young, gentle in manner—yet
A certain eager bloom is lost, like wax,
To earn a new, inexorable glint;
Umberto then, our host, gnarled round his cane,
Long freckled hands refolding the timetable
Dense as himself with station and connection.
Triumphant stumps of silver light
His austere satyr's face. The morning train
To Florence will allow us, he opines,
Forty minutes with them, "all one needs.
The next train down will have you back for lunch."

Perfection—they won't be in such easy reach
Ever again. But guess who hesitates!
"Close connections," says too quiet a voice,
"Harm the soul." I stare (indeed,
So he has always thought) and check a groan.
He's been unwell—one must remember that;
Has no resistance to cold, heat, fatigue,
Or anything, apparently, but me.
Fine! Say we never see them. I'm already
Half resigned. Half fuming also. These
Two halves, a look exchanged, now choose their weapons—
Notebook and cigarette—then step outside
To settle their affair beneath the trees.

The trees! Tall domed communicating chambers,
A dark flight above ground. One duellist
Writes blind: *my piano nobile.* The other
Levels his lighter, fires into the air,
Panicking the nearest green room where
Starlings by now have joined—safety in numbers—
Forces against the Owl. A twittering dither
Fills no less the wisdom-threatened mind . . .
The starlings, though, seem rather to rewind
Our day of human speech, erasing it
At treble speed from the highstrung cassette.
If one could do as much— A last drag. Wrong
To be so—so— Saved by the dinner gong.
I run to dip my hands in water first.
How pale they turn, how innocent, immersed.

2

Umberto's meal: a tablespoon of wine
Stirred into his minestra. While we cope
With eggs and spinach, fruit and cheese, he talks.
The life inside him's like a local clay
Gritty with names, Montale, Berenson,
Edith Wharton making our eyes flash
—Mario's too, who waits in his white jacket.
Plates gleam dimly from the walls' high gloom.
Our host's gaze lidded, voice a purr,
Out comes the story long heard *of.* I wash
It down tonight a shade too greedily—
Hence this impression in blurred chalk:
The famous story of Umberto's walk.

When Italy surrendered to the Allies
In 1943, September 3rd,
The proclamation was five days deferred
Until their main force landed at Salerno.
It was imperative that liaison
Be made with them, in those five days, by (word
Meaning to me anything but certain) "certain
Anti-fascist groups." And as there were no
Lines of communication safe from the Germans,

"Withdrawn," but smelling Naples' every rat,
Umberto offered to get through alone.
The train he boarded, one warm dusk in Rome,
Left after midnight, crept an hour down
The unlit coast; sniffed peril, backed away;
Returned its passengers to Rome at dawn.

Next . . . a bus? a jeep? a peasant's cart?
The vehicle evaporates. Our friend
(To be imagined half a lifetime spryer,
Credentials drily folded to his heart,
Correct as now in city clothes—
Whatever garment, that surreal year,
Betrayed its wearer like an epithet,
Skewfoot, fleet of spirit, dressed in whose very
Visibility to glide unseen
Across a poppied or a blackened field,
A bullet- or a fullmoon-pitted square)
Kept haltingly advancing. Hillsides rang
With the cicada of one sunny parasang.

The social fabric and his place in it
Were such that he knew people everywhere—
People the war had sent like snails
Into their shells, to feed on books and air.
So the stale biscuit and tea-tainted water
Served by a scholar's maiden aunt or sister
Brought him, through a last long stretch of dark,
Face to face with—tree-tall in lamplight—
"A type of Roman hero, your Mark Clark,
Beside whom on the Prefettura balcony,
His forces having landed overnight,
I megaphoned next morning—as my one
And only 'moment' on a balcony—
The terms of peace, translated, to the crowd."

"You were the hero," David murmurs, wowed.

3

Now Florence? But a stratagem
We only later analyze—

Bared shoulder and come-hither shrug
Of hill, the spread of golden thighs—
Lures our rented Fiat bug
Away from Them.

And soon enough, to two ecstatic
Oh's, on the horizon shines
Then vanishes, then shines again,
One of those metaphysical lines
Blue-penciled through the pilgrim's brain—
The Adriatic.

Our spirit-level, salt of life!
(Unpack the picnic here?) Above
Lie field and vineyard, castle built
To nurture intellect, art, love
Together with, let's face it, guilt,
Deception, strife.

Below, in brilliant aquarelle,
Undulating dullness fans
Itself to tatters. Bubble-streamers
Betray the scuba-superman's
Downward bent or Jungian dreamer's
Diving bell.

Here at my desk, but fathoms deep,
I've known the veer and shock of schools,
The kiss of inky Mafiosi;
Perusing stanzas like tide pools,
Have seen the stranger flex a rosy
Mussel heap,

And shaken myself clear. The break
Of glib, quicksilver levity,
The plunge of leaden look or phrase
Thudding to rest where none can see . . .
I name just two of the world's ways
Picked by mistake.

Sheathed in a petrifying mitt,
A hand took mine on the sea floor.

That detour (we'll reach Florence yet)
Had to be structural before
Heroes tomorrow stripped of threat
Could rise from it.

4

—Not a moment, poor babies, too soon!
For the Mediterranean will in
Another few decades have perished,
And with it those human equivalents,
Memory, instinct, whatever
In you the first water so joyously
Answered to. These you have fed
To your desktop computers—e basta.
Yes, hard on the heels of God's death,
As reported in Nietzschean decibels,
Follows (writes Mary McCarthy
In Birds of America*) one*
Far more ominous bulletin: Nature
Is dead, or soon will be. And we
Are well out of it, who in the tempest—
Exultantly baring through coppery
Lips the carnivorous silver—
Knew best how to throw around weight
And go overboard. Thus we arrived
At the couch of the green-bearded ancient
To suffer the centuries' limpet
Accretions unwelcome as love
From a weakling, cold lessons imparted
Through waves of revulsion, yet taken
How deeply to heart! From their oozy
Sublime we have risen. Dissolving
The clay at our core, sonar probe and
Restorative poultice have brought
The high finish in which we began
Back to light. Your nostalgia completes the
Illusion with flickering tripods,
Where feasters, fastidious stucco
Pilasters, and vistas of shimmering
Water red roses rope off
Make us objects of art. We dislike it

As women in your day dislike
Being sexual objects, but were not
Consulted. To fictive environments
Blood is the fee. And this light,
This pink gel we peer out through (not gods
Like the hurler of levin in Athens,
Not tea-gowned ephebes like the driver
At Delphi, but men in their prime
With the endocrine clout so rebarbative
To the eternally boyish
Of whichever sex) is the shadow of
Light we once lived by, dealt death in,
Dividing the spoils. And it burns
But to spangle the gulf that expires
Between you—still crusted with appetite,
Armed to the teeth by your pitiful
Wish not to harm—and ourselves
Whose much-touted terribilità
Is at last this articulate shell
Of a vacuum roughly man-sized. We
Should rather be silent. Rhetorical
Postures, the hot line direct
To the Kremlin or out of Hart Crane,
Leave us cold. It's for you to defuse them.
For us, in our Dämmerung swarming
With gawkers, what trials of mettle
Remain?—short of meltdown your fantasies
Trigger, then grandly shrug off
With a sangfroid our poor old heroics
Were child's play beside. Go. Expect no
Epiphany such as the torso
In Paris provided for Rilke. Quit
Dreaming of change. It is happening
Whether you like it or not,
So get on with your lives. We have done.

5

Let's do. From the entropy of Florence, dead
Ends, wrong turns, *I told you so*'s, through rings
First torpid then vertiginous, our route

Leads outward into the bright spin of things.
Our separate routes. A month. A year.
Time for Umberto, hobbling under plane
Trees now, now cypressed-in by memory,
To take a last step, crumple, disappear.
Time for Fair David to regain
A small adobe fortress where, beset
By rodent insurrections, howl and hoot,
He turns his skylit oils to the wall rain
Exorbitantly gutters. Time for me,

Who off and on had idolized these two,
To heed a sympathetic twinge.
The doctor probes and listens. Powers failing?
A shot of hormone? The syringe he fills,
At tip one shining droplet, pure foreplay,
Sinks into muscle. And on the third day
Desire floods the old red studio.
A figure reincarnate, wings outspread,
Full quiver, eager lips, from years ago—
My Eros to the life—awaits unveiling.
Friends, here is salvation! Are you blind?
Here, *under* the dumb layers which unwind
I somehow cannot. Tanglingly opaque,
They're nothing if not me. The hidden god,
Unknelt-to, feels himself to be a fake,

The poorest jerky newsreel of dead forces
Breast-deep in waves, that strained for shore,
Bayonets flashing, helmeted young faces
Mad to provoke from the interior
Those attitudes assumed in love and war—
All fair, till peace limps forward on a cane.
The Axis fell. Its partners rose again.
Up came from vaults, for light to kiss awake,
The groggy treasures of the Glyptothek.
Out came war babies. Only the lost life
Held back, reduced to skeletal belief,
Coils of shot film, run-down DNA.
Earth saw to it as usual, clay to clay.

6

All fair? Precisely what, fair friend, umpteen
Stanzas your distance tinges haven't been.
You whom night strips to armature, whom day
Equips with tones to brush desire away,
Painting as much of sheer Experience
(Your holy mountain, that sea-born, immense
Magnet, its fatalities untold)
As one tall window facing north can hold,
Raptly, repeatedly have scaled it, if
Only to canvas. Metamorphs of cliff,
Quarry and timberline, you understand,
Haunt me, too. Come then, "because they're there,"
On with our stories. Make the telling fair.
But first, in all but liaison—this hand.

7

Off the record, but as everyone
Perfectly knew, Umberto was the son
Of his father's friend the King, whose name he bore.
A discreet match, the death of the young bride,
This phantom parentage on either side . . .
Rumor? Yet the King's bust, I recall,
Kept reigning, on its trophied pedestal,
Head and shoulders over a salon
Never in use (gilt horrors, plush, veneer),
The single, token room to have been done
Up for the Contessa. Her demise
Preserved in prelapsarian Empire
And Biedermeier the enchanting rest:
Stained glass and goat-foot chair, blue willows peeling
From gesso'd wall, tent-stripes or clouds from ceiling.

Blows that set our braver products clanging
Level categorically these hanging-
By-a-thread gardens of the West.
Umberto first intended the estate
As a "retreat for scholars." His last will
Left it intact to Mario the butler,
So long devoted and his brood so great.

The house sighed. It had entertained the subtler
Forms of discourse and behavior. Still,
There'd be the baby's tantrum, the wife's laugh,
The old man's groan. New blood. How else redeem
Spells of such cast and temper as to seem
Largely the stuff of their own cenotaph?

8

For in the odd hour made even
Odder as it dawns,
I too exist in bronze.
We were up on the deck, drinking
With summer friends, when Fred
Asked who the bust was of.
Year-round sentinel
On the domestic ramparts,
Acquiring pointlessness
As things we live with do,
It gave me a look back:
The famous, cold, unblinking
Me at six, I said—
Then drifted from his side
To stand by it. Ah yes.

Slowly the patina
Coarsened, paled—no perch
For owl or nightingale.
The local braggart gull
Flaps off and up, its shriek
Leaving a forelock white.
Where the time's flown I wonder.
A deeply-bored eye sees,
Or doesn't, the high trees
Waving in vain for sundry
Old games like Hide and Seek
Or Statues to be played,
Come evening, in their shade.

Losses of the foundry!
As chilling aftermath
Laszlo—my sculptor—made
Headlines one morning: QUEENS
MAN AXED BY SONS. Had they
Also posed for him,
Two trustful little boys . . . ?
Smoothing their brows, the maker's
Hypnotic fingertips
(I still feel my scalp crawl)
Were helpless to forestall
The molten, grown-up scenes
Ahead, when ire and yearning,
Most potent of alloys
Within us, came to grips.

Here Augie, seeing me absent,
Ambled up to rest
Tanned forearms easily
On my unruffled hair.
A tilted beer, a streak
Staining bluegreen my cheek—
Bless him, he couldn't care
Less for the Work of Art!
The stubborn child-face pressed,
Lips parted, to the heart
Under his torn T-shirt
Telling the world *Clean Air
Or Else*, was help and hurt
As much as I could bear.

CHANNEL 13

It came down to this: that merely naming the creatures
        Spelt their doom.
Three quick moves translated camelopard, dik-dik, and
        Ostrich from
Grassland to circus to Roman floor mosaic to
        TV room.

Here self-excusing voices attended (and music,
        Also canned)
The lark's aerobatics, the great white shark's blue shadow
        Making sand
Crawl fleshwise. Our ultimate "breakthrough" lenses took it
        In unmanned.

Now the vast shine of appearances shrinks to a tiny
        Sun, the screen
Goes black. Anaconda, tree toad, alpaca, clown-face
        Capuchin—
Launched at hour's end in the snug electronic ark of
        What has been.

PAUL VALÉRY: *PALME*

Veiling, barely, his dread
Beauty and its blaze,
An angel sets warm bread
And cool milk at my place.
His eyelids make the sign
Of prayer; I lower mine,
Words interleaving vision:
—Calm, calm, be ever calm!
Feel the whole weight a palm
Bears upright in profusion.

However its boughs yield
Beneath abundance, it
Is formally fulfilled
In bondage to thick fruit.
Wonder and see it grow!
One fiber, vibrant, slow,
Cleaving the hour fanwise,
Becomes a golden rule
To tell apart earth's pull
From heaven's gravities.

Svelte arbiter between
The shadow and the sun,
It takes much sibylline
Somnolent wisdom on.
Unstintingly to suffer
Hails and farewells, forever
Standing where it must stand . . .
How noble and how tender,
How worthy of surrender
To none but a god's hand!

The lightest gold-leaf murmur
Rings at a flick of air,
Invests with silken armor
The very desert. Here
This tree's undying voice
Upraised in the wind's hiss,

As fine sand sprays and stings,
To its own self is oracle
Complacent of the miracle
Whereby misfortune sings.

Held in an artless dream
Between blue sky and dune,
Secreting, dram by dram,
The honey of each noon,
What is this delectation
If not divine duration
That, without keeping time,
Can alter it, seduce
Into a steady juice
Love's volatile perfume?

At moments one despairs.
Should the adored duress
Ordain, despite your tears,
A spell of fruitlessness,
Do not call Wisdom cold
Who readies so much gold,
So much authority:
Rising in solemn pith
A green, eternal myth
Reaches maturity.

These days which, like yourself,
Seem empty and effaced
Have avid roots that delve
To work deep in the waste.
Their shaggy systems, fed
Where shade confers with shade,
Can never cease or tire,
At the world's heart are found
Still tracking that profound
Water the heights require.

Patience and still patience,
Patience beneath the blue!
Each atom of the silence
Knows what it ripens to.

The happy shock will come:
A dove alighting, some
Gentlest nudge, the breeze,
A woman's touch—before
You know it, the downpour
Has brought you to your knees!

Let populations be
Crumbled underfoot—
Palm, irresistibly—
Among celestial fruit!
Those hours were not in vain
So long as you retain
A lightness once they're lost;
Like one who, thinking, spends
His inmost dividends
To grow at any cost.

AFTER THE BALL

Clasping her magic
Changemaking taffeta
(Old rose to young spinach
And back) I'd taken

Such steps in dream logic
That the Turnstile at Greenwich
Chimed with laughter—
My subway token.

LITTLE FALLACY

Chamber of blossom, not a petal spilled,
Yesterday's Japanese cherry
—You and I charmed inside the glow—
By evening had borne fruit:

A whole day in Beirut
—According to the radio,
The first since January—
With no one killed.

ARABIAN NIGHT

Features unseen embers and tongs once worried
bright as brass, cool, trim, of a depth to light his
way at least who, trusting mirages, finds in
them the oasis,

what went wrong? You there in the mirror, did our
freshest page get sent to the Hall of Cobwebs?
Or had Rime's Emir all along been merely
after your body?

No reply. Then ("there" of course, also) insight's
dazzle snaps at gloom, like a wick when first lit.
Look! on one quick heartstring glissando, stranger
kindles to father

thirty years a shade, yet whose traits (plus others
not so staring—loyalty, cynicism,
neophyte's pure heart in erotic mufti
straight out of Baghdad)

solve the lifelong riddle: a face no longer
sought in dreams but worn as my own. Aladdin
rubs his lamp—youth? age?—and the rival two beam
forth in one likeness.

THE PARNASSIANS

Theirs was a language within ours, a loge
Hidden by bee-stitched hangings from the herd.
The mere exchanged glance between word and word
Took easily the place, the privilege
Of utterance. Here therefore all was tact.
Pairs at first blush ill-matched, like *turd* and *monstrance,*
Tracing their cousinage through consonants,
Communed, ecstatic, through the long entr'acte.

Without our common meanings, though, that world
Would have slid headlong to apocalypse.
We'd built the Opera, changed the scenery, trod
Grapes for the bubbling flutes mild fingers twirled;
As footmen, by no eyelid's twitch betrayed
Our scorn and sound investment of their tips.

GINGER BEEF

Soon to attain its famous afterglow,
The mountain drinks late sun. Below and early,
Shown to the terrace, we two pause, as always
Silenced by green fields, cottonwoods, the pond,
The two (same?) swans, their nest
Empty at this season. Close beyond's
The low clay house my friend—twelve years ago?—
Rented, only to move. And move again,
A painter's eye in quest
Of the ideal arrangement. While this scene
Didn't quite serve his purposes, no less
Radiant, forgiving and serene,
It takes him in as always, head to foot
—Where a new six-month puppy plays the fool.

They'll have found other tenants for that house—
Two rooms—in which I came to see him first:
House where, cold evenings, he and I, the dog,
Gazed, all three, into the blazing log;
Where he and I drained the last drop of red
Before he and the dog went off to bed;
From which, excited mornings, we'd all pile
Into the truck—we two in the front seat,
The dog behind us—and drive mile on mile,
Vast backdrop rippling heat . . .
When the run ended, did the cast forget
Those properties, that unstruck, sunstruck set?

Creak, offstage, of a screen door
—Our hosts? Instead, impossibly, appears
(As when "for charity" a legend acts
Despite old age, arthritis, cataracts,
The role that made her famous) who
But . . . Ouspenskaya in a dog suit? Or
Who herself! The very dog, those years
Imprinted by her master raptly crooning
"Who are you? *Who* are *you?*"
(Mix of coyote, shepherd, malamute)
Till Who at last was all she'd answer to.

Slowly now she limps the length of terrace,
Lashes gone white beneath the widow's peak,
To kiss—no prompting now or ever—
His palm, then mine: *Yes, here's*
That friend of His I grew
To tolerate, let stroke me, soul and senses
Fixed on the roadside store
He'd presently, if I kept faith, once more
Emerge from. As He did, at first. But then . . .

But then life's thrifty. Every day a bit
Gets put aside, the why and where of it
A puzzle, till the nest egg hatches—wings
Whistling through us as the pieces knit.

Isn't the right place everywhere, and found
By everyone? Some, though, turn round and round—
Ever about to settle, never quite
Able to do so—on the faithful ground.

Fear of belonging, or inflicting harm?
Friends gestured from their niches. "Pure dull charm"
Kept at arm's length—no. Make the story short.
He gave the dog to these two, for their farm.

Of course it hurt. His reasons were austere
As rainlight, as the two-or-three-per-year
Landscapes he showed us. But with what wry phrase
Of mine shall I give *him* away? For here

Our hosts come. Bright-eyed lookalikes, hair shot
With silver, smiles of puckered apricot,
Their manners—all our manners—past reproach.
I wonder how we bear it. Who does not.

For her, it's more . . . more like tonight's pièce
De résistance.—Lift from the crock, let stand;
Then chill, trim, slice, and recompose
Within its essence, clarified topaz
(Afterwards, find a moment, thank the cook)
Of a deliciousness—
                    She comes to sniff,

But is too dignified to take,
The surreptitious morsel from my hand.

Fields green still, heights their celebrated red
Well after sunset, past the panes
Flashes the puppy yapping—in Who's stead?
With passion she recalls? Yes, and disdains:
Eyes nowhere, slumping down on stone
In mute, in mortal weariness, alone.

Nambé, 1981

DEAD CENTER

Upon reflection, as I dip my pen
Tonight, forth ripple messages in code.
In Now's black waters burn the stars of Then.

Seen from the embankment, marble men
Sleep upside down, bat-wise, the sleep bestowed
Upon reflection. As I dip my pen

Thinking how others, deeper into Zen,
Blew on immediacy until it glowed,
In Now's black waters burn the stars of Then.

Or else I'm back at Grandmother's. I'm ten,
Dust hides my parents' roadster from the road
Which dips—*into* reflection, with my pen.

Breath after breath, harsh O's of oxygen—
Never deciphered, what do they forebode?
In Now's black waters burn the stars. Ah then

Leap, Memory, supreme equestrienne,
Through hoops of fire, circuits you overload!
Beyond reflection, as I dip my pen
In Now's black waters, burn the stars of Then.

LOSING THE MARBLES

for John Malcolm Brinnin

I

Morning spent looking for my calendar—
Ten whole months mislaid, name and address,
A groaning board swept clean . . .
And what were we talking about at lunch? Another
Marble gone. Those later years, Charmides,
Will see the mind eroded featureless.

Ah. We'd been imagining our "heaven"s.
Mine was to be an acrobat in Athens
Back when the Parthenon—
Its looted nymphs and warriors pristine
By early light or noon light—dwelt
Upon the city like a philosopher,
Who now—well, you have seen.

Here in the gathering dusk one could no doubt
"Rage against the dying of the light."
But really—rage? (So like the Athens press,
Breathing fire to get the marbles back.)
These dreamy blinkings-out
Strike me as grace, if I may say so,
Capital punishment,
Yes, but of utmost clemency at work,
Whereby the human stuff, ready or not,
Tumbles, one last drum-roll, into thyme,
Out of time, with just the fossil quirk
At heart to prove—hold on, don't tell me . . . What?

2

Driving its silver car into the room,
The storm mapped a new country's dry and wet—
Oblivion's ink-blue rivulet.
Mascara running, worksheet to worksheet
Clings underfoot, exchanging the wrong words.
The right ones, we can only trust will somehow
Return to the tongue's tip,
Weary particular and straying theme,
Invigorated by their dip.

Invigorated! Gasping, shivering
Under our rough towels, never did they dream—!
Whom mouth-to-mouth resuscitation by
Even your *Golden Treasury* won't save,
They feel their claim
On *us* expiring: starved to macron, breve,
Those fleshless ribs, a beggar's frame . . .
From the brainstorm to this was one far cry.

Long work of knowing and hard play of wit
Take their toll like any virus.
Old timers, cured, wade ankle-deep in sky.

Meanwhile, come evening, to sit
Feverishly restoring the papyrus.

3

body, favorite
　　　　　gleaned,　　at the
　　　　　　　　　　　vital
　　　　frenzy—

act and moonshaft, peaks
　　　　　　　　　　stiffening
　　　　Unutter[able]
　the beloved's

　　　　　　　　　　　　slowly
　　　　stained in the deep　　fixed
　　　　　　summer nights
　　　or,

　　　　　　scornful　　　　Ch[arm]ides,
　　　　　　　　decrepitude
　　　Now, however, that
　figures also

　　　　　　　　　　body everywhere
　　　　　　plunders and
　what we cannot—from the hut's lintel
　　　　flawed

　　　　　　　　　　　　　white as
　sliced turnip　　　　　the field's brow.
　　　　our old
　　wanderings

home　　　　　　　　　palace, temple,
　having　　　　of those blue foothills
　　no further　　　clear
　　　fancy[.]

4

Seven ages make a crazy quilt
Out of the famous web. Yet should milk spilt
(As when in Rhetoric one's paragraph
Was passed around and each time cut in half,
From eighty words to forty, twenty, ten,
Before imploding in a puff of Zen)
White out the sense and mutilate the phrase,
My text is Mind no less than Mallarmé's.
My illustration? The Cézanne oil sketch
Whose tracts of raw, uncharted canvas fetch
As much per square inch as the fruit our cloyed
Taste prizes for its bearing on the void.
Besides, Art furnishes a counterfeit
Heaven wherein ideas escape the fate
Their loyal adherents—brainwashed, so to speak,
By acid rain—more diatribes in Greek—
Conspicuously don't. We diehard few
Embark for London on the *QE2*.
Here mornings can be spent considering ours
Of long ago, removed and mute, like stars
(*Un*like vociferous Melina, once
A star herself, now Minister of Stunts).
Removed a further stage, viewed from this high wire
Between the elegiac and the haywire,
They even so raise questions. Does the will-
To-structural-elaboration still
Flute up, from shifting dregs of would-be rock,
Glints of a future colonnade and frieze?
Do higher brows unknit within the block,
And eyes whose Phidias and Pericles
Are eons hence make out through crystal skeins
Wind-loosened tresses and the twitch of reins?
Ah, not for long will marble school the blood
Against the warbling sirens of the flood.
All stone once dressed asks to be worn. The foam-
Pale seaside temple, like a palindrome,
Had quietly laid its plans for stealing back.
What are the Seven Wonders now? A pile
Of wave-washed pebbles. Topless women smile,
Picking the smoothest, rose-flawed white or black,

Which taste of sunlight on moon-rusted swords,
To use as men upon their checkerboards.

5

The body, favorite trope of our youthful poets . . .
With it they gleaned, as at the sibyl's tripod,
insight too prompt and vital for words.
Her sleepless frenzy—

cataract and moonshaft, peaks of sheer fire at dawn,
dung-dusted violets, the stiffening dew—
said it best. Unutterable too
was the beloved's

save through the index of refraction a fair, slowly
turned head sustained in the deep look that fixed him.
From then on veining summer nights with
flickering ichor,

he had joined an elite scornful—as were, Charmides,
your first, chiseled verses—of decrepitude
in any form. Now, however, that
their figures also

begin to slip the mind—while the body everywhere
with peasant shrewdness plunders and puts to use
what we cannot—from the hut's lintel
gleams one flawed image;

another, cast up by frost or earthquake, shines white as
sliced turnip from a furrow on the field's brow.
Humbly our old poets knew to make
wanderings into

homecomings of a sort—harbor, palace, temple, all
having been quarried out of those blue foothills
no further off, these last clear autumn
days, than infancy.

6

Who gazed into the wrack till
Inspiration glowed,
Deducing from one dactyl
The handmaiden, the ode?

Or when aphasia skewered
The world upon a word,
Who was the friend, the steward,
Who bent his head, inferred

Then filled the sorry spaces
With pattern and intent,
A syntax of lit faces
From the impediment?

        No matter, these belated
Few at least are back. And thanks
To their little adventure, never so
Brimming with jokes and schemes,
Fussed over, fêted
By all but their fellow saltimbanques—
Though, truth to tell,
Who by now doesn't flip
Hourly from someone's upper story
("That writer . . . no, on shipboard . . . wait . . . Charmides?")
And come to, clinging to the net?
And yet, and yet
Here in the afterglow
It almost seems
Death has forgotten us
—As the old lady said to Fontenelle.
              And he,
A cautionary finger to his lip:
"Shh!"

After the endless jokes, this balmy winter
Around the pool, about the missing marbles,
What was more natural than for my birthday
To get—from the friend whose kiss that morning woke me—
A pregnantly clicking pouch of targets and strikers,
Aggies and rainbows, the opaque chalk-red ones,
Clear ones with DNA-like wisps inside,
Others like polar tempests vitrified . . .
These I've embedded at random in the deck-slats
Around the pool. (The pool!—compact, blue, dancing,
Lit-from-beneath oubliette.) By night their sparkle
Repeats the garden lights, or moon- or starlight,
Tinily underfoot, as though the very
Here and now were becoming a kind of heaven
To sit in, talking, largely mindless of
The risen, cloudy brilliances above.

INVESTITURE AT CECCONI'S

for David Kalstone

Caro, that dream (after the diagnosis)
found me losing patience outside the door of
"our" Venetian tailor. I wanted evening
clothes for the new year.

Then a bulb went on. The old woman, she who
stitches dawn to dusk in his back room, opened
one suspicious inch, all the while exclaiming
over the late hour—

Fabrics? patterns? those the proprietor must
show by day, not now—till a lightning insight
cracks her face wide: *Ma! the Signore's here to
try on his new robe!*

Robe? She nods me onward. The mirror triptych
summons three bent crones she diffracted into
back from no known space. They converge by magic,
arms full of moonlight.

Up my own arms glistening sleeves are drawn. Cool
silk in grave, white folds—Oriental mourning—
sheathes me, throat to ankles. I turn to face her,
uncomprehending.

Thank your friend, she cackles, *the Professore!*
Wonderstruck I sway, like a tree of tears. You—
miles away, sick, fearful—have yet arranged this
heartstopping present.

FAREWELL PERFORMANCE

for DK

Art. It cures affliction. As lights go down and
Maestro lifts his wand, the unfailing sea change
starts within us. Limber alembics once more
make of the common

lot a pure, brief gold. At the end our bravos
call them back, sweat-soldered and leotarded,
back, again back—anything not to face the
fact that it's over.

You are gone. You'd caught like a cold their airy
lust for essence. Now, in the furnace parched to
ten or twelve light handfuls, a mortal gravel
sifted through fingers,

coarse yet grayly glimmering sublimate of
palace days, Strauss, Sidney, the lover's plaintive
Can't we just be friends? which your breakfast phone call
clothed in amusement,

this is what we paddled a neighbor's dinghy
out to scatter—Peter who grasped the buoy,
I who held the box underwater, freeing
all it contained. Past

sunny, fluent soundings that gruel of selfhood
taking manlike shape for one last jeté on
ghostly—wait, ah!—point into darkness vanished.
High up, a gull's wings

clapped. The house lights (always supposing, caro,
Earth remains your house) at their brightest set the
scene for good: true colors, the sun-warm hand to
cover my wet one . . .

Back they come. How you would have loved it. We in
turn have risen. Pity and terror done with,
programs furled, lips parted, we jostle forward
eager to hail them,

more, to join the troupe—will a friend enroll us
one fine day? Strange, though. For up close their magic
self-destructs. Pale, dripping, with downcast eyes they've
seen where it led you.

PROCESSIONAL

Think what the demotic droplet felt,
Translated by a polar wand to keen
Six-pointed Mandarin—
All singularity, its Welt-
Anschauung of a hitherto untold
Flakiness, gemlike, nevermore to melt!

But melt it would, and—look—become
Now birdglance, now the gingko leaf's fanlight,
To that same tune whereby immensely old
Slabs of dogma and opprobrium,
Exchanging ions under pressure, bred
A spar of burnt-black anchorite,

Or in three lucky strokes of word golf LEAD
Once again turns (LOAD, GOAD) to GOLD.

A DOWNWARD LOOK

Seen from above, the sky
Is deep. Clouds float down there,

Foam on a long, luxurious bath.
Their shadows over limbs submerged in "air,"

Over protuberances, faults,
A delta thicket, glide. On high, the love

That drew the bath and scattered it with salts

Still radiates new projects old as day,
And hardly registers the tug

When, far beneath, a wrinkled, baby hand
Happens upon the plug.

The ancient comic theater had it right:
A shuttered house, a street or square, a tree
Collect, life after life, the energy
To flood what happens in their shade with light.
A house in Athens does the trick for me—
Thrilling to find oneself again on stage,
In character, at this untender age.

     I

[Enters with DJ.] . . . and the kitchen. Ours,
Along with all the rest. What are those headlines
Whose upper-case demotic holds the floor—
GET THE U.S. BASES OUT OF GREECE
—That old refrain, where's their imagination?
And what's outside?
                [A sullen, peeling door
Wrenches open onto glare that weighs
So heavily on things, these August days
—And cats! The nursing mother stares appalled,
While one black kitten actually topples
Over in consternation before streaking
With three or four white siblings out of sight.]

That old shed houses them. The lilac shrub
Patient as a camel on its knees
Shades them. We used to water it—remember—
Magnanimously, with a warm, pulsing hose
From three flights up. Here in this basement flat
Lived old Miss Pesmazóglou and her cat,
Or cats. They seem to have made do without her.
Now we'll be on hand to mind them. Good of Gus
And Ab to rent the dear house back to us
While they're on tour. *You* take the upstairs. These
Half-buried rooms, so glimmeringly tiled—
The kittens also—keep me here, beguiled.

2

A dozen habits fostered by the scene
Spring back to life. Old troupers reemerge:
Tony and Nelly; from oblivion's verge
Strato himself, whose bloodshot eyes (once green)
And immense bulk confound the dramaturge.
There even comes an afternoon when, bored,
We sit down to a makeshift Ouija board.

A courtesy call merely. No big deal.
A way of letting our familiars share
In these old haunts. Instead: U MUST PREPARE
YRSELVES. It's David's and my turn to keel
Over in consternation. YES MES CHERS
A CERTAIN 8 YEAR DARLING LEAVES BOMBAY
BY PLANE FOR ATHENS ONE WEEK FROM TODAY.

I hate to say it, but the neophyte
Must take the full amazement of this news
(At least till he can purchase and peruse
A heavy volume called *The Changing Light
At Sandover*) on faith.—What? Oh. My muse,
Smiling indulgently upon the wretch,
Authorizes a quick background sketch.

Maria Mitsotáki (here in Greece
An adored, black-clad mentor) crossed the bar,
From then on dazzling our binocular
Lenses, the poem's astral Beatrice,
Its very Plato. Now—OK so far?—
This bit of doctrine vital to our text:
Souls bright as hers quit one life for the next

Conscious, to what degree I shan't here tell,
Of where they lived and whom they used to know.
Maria was reborn eight years ago
In India, as a future (male) Nobel
Prize-winning chemist. The spring overflow
Of Ganges glittering with daybreak pales
Beside our wonder. CALL BACK FOR DETAILS

3

TREMORS MES CHERS SHAKE THE SUBCON *[The teacup*
Pauses, collects itself, glides on.] TINENT
AS THE CHATTERJEE FAMILY SERVANTS BUSILY PACK.
FATHER MADLY HINDU & MADLY PUNJABI
MEMBER OF PARLIAMENT, BANKER, FIREBRAND
COMING TO ATHENS AS A MEDIATOR
IN (HO HUM) GOVT TRADE TALKS. FAMILY
STAYING AT INDIAN EMBASSY INCLUDES
PAPPA, MAMMA & YOUNG SHANTIHPRASHAD
The magic child!
                    [Concerning whom we've gleaned
Such tantalizing facts. For instance, he
Was spoken to at five by TINKLING VOICES
From test-tubes in his Junior Chemistry Kit.
At six turned WINE INTO WATER. *Lit at seven,*
While gardeners looked on goggle-eyed, HIS FIRST
SMOKELESS FIRE.]
                    That tongue-twister's a name?
CALL HIM SHANTY: THIN, INTENSE BLACK EYES,
WEARING A FLAT STRAW HAT WITH LONG BLACK RIBBON
HE WILL NOT BE PARTED FROM. THAT IS YR CUE:
HAT BLOWS OFF (WITH OUR HELP IF NEED BE)
LANDING LATE AFTERNOON SEPTEMBER 4
NEAR (IF NOT ON) YR TABLE   CAN U GUESS WHERE?

We can, of course. In Kolonáki Square,
At the Bon Goût, where we always met Maria.
TEATIME INDIAN FASHION MOTHER SLIM
IN PARIS CLOTHES, AYAH IN SARI. A LIMO
WILL WHISK THEM BACK TO PURDAH AFTER SHANTY
UTTERS THE SENTENCE HE HAS BEEN REHEARSING:
'WE WILL MEET AGAIN IN MY HOME CITY'

Well, it will be the proof we've never had
Or asked for. And if nothing happens, Ephraim?
If no hat sails our way? If D and I
Just wait like idiots? THE WIND WILL DIE

4

[*The following midday.*] David calls the cats
Our latest Holy Family. Why not?
Urania and hers have long outgrown
The Stonington arrangements. And indeed
A kind of "flight into Egypt" air pervades
The backdoor scene. Athens is full of Herods
Ready to massacre those innocents
Now suckling under leaves, now playing tag
On what to them must seem a parapet.
[*A three-foot drop divides our narrow "courtyard"*
From that of the house immediately downhill.]
Just after sunrise, watching as I set
The scraps out, which they're coming to depend on,
An old white tom, responsible and scarred—
Saint Joseph to the life—was standing guard.
He took no food; devoutly our eyes met.
The mother, too, with speaking glances said:
"Take him, my blackest and my wiliest,
Teach him the table manners of the West."
Later, the door left wide as usual,
A little bold black heart-shaped face peered in
To where I wrote, but fled my eager start.
If I could touch him—! Hasn't someone proven
That just to stroke a kitten, make it purr,
Lowers the blood pressure, both yours and its?
These kittens maddeningly don't concur:
The sight of me still throws them into fits.

[*With that, strides through the kitchen on the slender*
Chance that they're learning. Pandemonium.
The same black kitten somersaults—oh no!—
Backwards into the cement court below,
There taking refuge under an oil drum
Mounted on venerable two-by-fours
Complex and solid as the Trojan Horse.
No way to lure him out. In the other direction
A long escape route to the street leads past
The neighbors' house, promiscuously open
For renovations. Workmen come and go,
Plaster-white faces, joke and song. JM

Intends to play it cool in front of them.
Meanwhile for his—for everybody's sins
A frantic mewing back and forth begins.]

                    5

[*Two nights later.*] Talcum, loopy names
In an address book, strand of fine blond hair
Flossing a comb—God! if the Dutch au pair
Could sleep here . . . But my firework stratagems
To save the kitten fizzle in black air.
Today was Sunday. Not a soul next door.
The mother cat, cool on that canyon floor,

Suckled her black one. Ways to house and street
Were blocked, the hose hooked up. I hissed. He fled
To his old shelter. Quick! full stream ahead:
Faucet on, nozzle thumbed, a fluid sheet
Sliding beneath the oil-drum, out he sped,
Black lightning, eyes like headlights of a hit-and-run
Driver, the raison d'être of my kitten run!

With nimbleness approaching the sublime,
Seizing a bathtowel against fangs and claws
And lunging like an avatar of Shaw's
Life Force, I overtook my prey in time
To see him scuttle—not the slightest pause
Or pity for one instant laughingstock—
Into a vine-wreathed hole I'd failed to block.

The roof next door is level with our own.
It's there, as in a déjà-vu, mater-
ialized a mother dolefully—night was near—
Mewing down the drainpipe-telephone.
Feeling our eyes, "Now just see what you've done!"
Hers shone back. Such communicable pain!
From being human we grow inhumane.

We have, it seems, methodically wrecked
Her world. Analogies are rife and various
To worlds like Strato's, now disaster areas
We helped create. Hopeless to resurrect

Cradles of original neglect.
Our tidbits teach the kittens how to shit,
And day by day we put our foot in it.

6

[*Late evening, September 3.*] DJ:
Let's get some sleep. Tomorrow's the big day.

JM: All I can think about's my kitten.
It's sixty hours since we saw him last.
By now he's dying of thirst, wedged in the drainpipe . . .
I never should have opened that back door.

DJ: At least he has eight lives to go!
Remember when the Nestlé Company
Shipped its formula to Ghana, free?
The babies thrived on it. Then one fine morning,
End of shipments. No thought for all the mothers
Who weaned their babies on the formula
And had no milk left. There in a nutshell's
American policy.   JM: Say no more.
Leave every little skeleton in peace.
I never should have opened that back door.

7

[*Wednesday, 4 o'clock at the Bon Goût.*
Much harder to determine is the year.
Decades have passed since our first coffees here,
Ordered in dumbshow. Ah, if youth but knew!
The sky was then a sacramental blue,
The café's two old waiters dignified,
The tourist rare, nose buried in the Guide.]

DJ: There's a free table. It'll do . . .

[*Today's Bon Goût is more a minipark*
Cars eddy round. Yet here's a little breeze,
Respite of awnings, rustle of plane trees.
Real action won't begin till after dark.

Our glances wander—it's in fact a lark
Revisiting this former commonplace—
With guarded carelessness from face to face.]

DJ: The big thing is, they've all made money.
These young men don't have waistlines any more.
Do they still dance in pairs on the dirt floor?
JM: Would they still think our jokes were funny?

[*Sealed with red labels, wrapped in cellophane,*
Aimed at some unsuspecting hostess, boom!
Off goes the florist's grand hydrangea bomb.
Green pinks, cream blues. Beneath its weight the vain
Eternal shopboy, scion of that swain
Who piped away the War of Independence,
Whistles egregiously for his descendants.]

Waiter: Caffè, Signori? Kein Problem.

[*Living familiars infiltrate the scene.*
The lottery man. Those two crème de la crème
Canasta-playing ladies. Trailing them,
The "Diplomat"?! Don't look, there's Fritz the Queen
From Chattanooga. But in olive-green
Cords and Chanel cloud a favorite Greek
Urbanely interrupts our hide-and-seek.]

Tony: Paidiá! In public? In the Square?
Mais c'est la fin du monde! I can't, I'm late—
I've found a buyer for that desk I hate.
Tomorrow noon, then? Nelly's cut her hair.

[*Tomorrow noon we meet aboard the white*
Boat to Spetsai, where a niece's villa
Is Nelly's all this month. The island's still a
Niche for the happy few. If they invite,
Who're we to be standoffish? Our first night
A widowed Gräfin hopes that we'll drop in
For camomile or cognac after din—]

DJ: A sari, look! JM: You're right—
No, look again. The company she's chosen

Disqualifies her—sideburns, Lederhosen . . .
Our ayah would be older, more soignée.
Besides, where's little Shanty? DJ [*sighing*]:
Delayed in traffic? Well, at least they're trying.

[*We look and look. Soon it's the absent faces*
We see. Mimí. Proud Chester. His evzone
"Of hollow bronze" from Thessaly. The crone—
Gray, toothless Papagena—hung with braces
Of snipe and quail. Called up from an oasis
Watered by Lethe, which no sun can warm,
They cower from our love like a sandstorm.]

JM: It's after five. My social graces
Are crumbling. Ten more minutes, would you say?

[*As shadows lengthen we prepare to pay,*
Collect ourselves, and bend our steps uphill.
Wait, though—how beautiful the light—sit still.
Now or never, as in the old play,
Its moonbeam-dappled feats performed by day,
Titania, Oberon, wake up! Employ
Your arts, produce that little Indian boy!

Long pause.] DJ: Well, let's be. On. Our. Way.

[*Giving the magic one last opportunity,*
Clutching at straws—if it should come to that,
We'd settle for a disembodied hat,
Flutter of black somewhere in the vicinity
To pin our hopes upon, if not our sanity—
We slowly get up. Eyes front. Dignified.
Two old ex-waiters. For the wind has died.]

8

[*Spetsai.*] The Gräfin: No, no, *I* am Greek,
My husband was a Hamburger. *He* spoke
The Ursprache. Oh later, perfect Greek,
But not our first year. I'm remembering—
Nelláki tells me you adored Maria—
Didn't we all—the party where Maria

And Helmut met for the first time. Without
A single word in common they communed.
They sat down on the sofa and *communed*
All evening long. Well, forty minutes. Thirty.
Quite long enough to make a bride of twenty
Run home in tears, and lock herself in the bathroom.
I'm ashamed *for* her to this day. I am!
Helmut was knocking, frantic . . . All at once—
We lived those first years in "a wood near Athens"
As my grandfather liked to call Kifissia *then*—
No loud cafés, no traffic—all at once
Came music, music from nowhere, at one a.m.!
—Ah, don't ask me. Say the "Liebestraum"
Or something Viennese. But in this *dream*
Helmut and I met on the balcony. There
Below, like an Embarkment for Cythère,
Musicians from the party: clarinet,
Guitar, two violins. It must have been
Full moon, the garden seemed electrified,
And from the fiacre they'd come in—Maria
Waving the coachman's whip like a conductor.
We waved back, back in love. The summer night
Was young again. And then? She blew a kiss
And off they went clop-clop into the night.

Nelly [*back at the villa*]: Bah, che dream!
Moonlight and roses, pitiful old cat—
As if Maria's genre were operetta . . .

DJ: Come on, she's not so—cat? The *cat*!
I saw him—yes—this morning, our black kitten!
Meaning to tell you but it slipped my—where?
Down in the neighbors' court. No worse for wear.

9

MES CHERS WE OVERESTIMATED OURSELVES
Please don't apologize. If I may borrow
The Gräfin's genial phrase, we feel ashamed
For you already. FATHER CHATTERJEE
WD NOT ALLOW THEM OUT: SECURITY!
EMBASSY GUARDS HAD WARNED AGAINST THAT SQUARE

Innocent Kolonáki? I'll just bet.
YET (AND WE WEEP) OUR BRAVE BOY ROSE FROM HIS NAP
AS IF SLEEPWALKING & STOLE OUT UNSEEN
INTO THE STRANGE CITY. HE WAS FOUND
IN HIS PAJAMAS BY AN ANXIOUS CROWD.
'HELLO? HELLO? (IN ENGLISH, BUT SO FAINTLY)
WHERE ARE YOU?' HE WAS CALLING Ephraim, spare—
FORGIVE US. WE GREW OVERCONFIDENT.
A GRIEF FOR YOU, FAR GREATER FOR LITTLE SHANTY
SOBBING & FLAILING OUT   JM   DEAR SCRIBE
[*From whom burst certain long-pent-up reproaches*
Ending:] . . . the proof. The proof we've never had
Or, mind you, sought. Proof that you act in our theater
Not for once purely in a manner of speaking,
No: word made flesh. Flesh wailing, wide-eyed, seeking
Us! THE KITTEN LIVES! DJ'S PLAN SOUND
[*A stopgap ramp connecting the two levels.*]
I didn't mean the *kitten*— [*Here our revels*
Grind to a halt on Ephraim's shifting ground.]

Like Wise Men we'd been primed to kneel in awe
At journey's end before that child whose nature
Proved Earth at one with Heaven, and past with future.
Instead, the perfect fools we still are saw
A manger full of emptiness, dust, straw . . .
AND LIGHT! Well, yes. Light also. We weren't blind,
The sun was out. THE PLAY OF H E A V E N ' S   M I N D

10

There is a moment comedies beget
When escapade and hubbub die away,
Vows are renewed, masks dropped, La Folle Journée
Arriving star by star at a septet.
It's then the connoisseur of your bouquet
(Who sits dry-eyed through *Oedipus* or *Lear*)
Will shed, O Happiness, a furtive tear.

We've propped the rough hypotenuse of board
Between the pit to which his fall consigned
Our prodigal and the haven left behind.
Nature must do the rest. No coaxing toward

The haggard matriarch on high. A blind
Protecting us, we smile down through the slats
As our flyblown road company of *Cats*

Concludes its run. (Did T. S. Eliot
Devise the whole show from his sepulcher?)
By dusk—black, white—the kittens suck and purr.
Shanty will fly, we're told, ON MIDNIGHT'S DOT
BACK TO HIS WASTE LAND—back, if you prefer,
To our subconscious, this much being sure:
That black hole is three-quarters literature.

(Why otherwise, midway in my fifth section,
Didn't I forestall my rhyme scheme's lapse,
Its walk downtown in sleep? Although, perhaps
Thanks to a nagging sense of misdirection
Once HEAVEN'S MIND came out from under wraps,
I've caught up with it, shaken it awake,
These aren't the "risks" a poem's meant to take.)

To all, sweet dreams. The teacup-stirring eddy
Is spent. We've dropped our masks, renewed our vows
To letters, to the lives that letters house,
Houses they shutter, streets they shade. Already
Empty and dark, this street is. Dusty boughs
Sleep in a pool of vigilance so bright
An old tom skirts it. The world's his tonight.

SNOW JOBS

X had the funds, the friends, the plan.
Y's frank grin was—our common fate?
Or just a flash in just a pan?
Z, from the tender age of eight,
Had thirsted to officiate.
We hardly felt them disappear,
The crooked and the somewhat straight.
Now where's the slush of yesteryear?

Where's Teapot Dome? Where's the Iran
Contra Affair? Where's Watergate—
Liddy—Magruder—Ehrlichman?
Their shoes squeaked down the Halls of State,
Whole networks groaned beneath their weight,
Till spinster Clotho darted near
To shroud in white a running mate.
Ah, where's the slush of yesteryear?

Like blizzards on a screen the scan-
dals thickened at a fearful rate,
Followed by laughter from a can
And hot air from the candidate.
With so much open to debate,
Language that went into one ear
Came out the—hush! be delicate:
Where is the slush of yesteryear?

Omniscient Host, throughout your great
Late shows the crystal wits cohere,
The flaky banks accumulate—
But where's the slush of yesteryear?

THE INSTILLING

All day from high within the skull—
Dome of a Pantheon, trepanned—light shines
Into the body. Down that stair

Sometimes there's fog: opaque red droplets check
The beam. Sometimes tall redwood-tendoned glades
Come and go, whose dwellers came and went.
Now darting feverishly anywhere,
Manic duncecap its danseuse eludes,

Now slowed by grief, white-lipped,
Grasping the newel bone of its descent,

This light can even be invisible

Till a deep sparkle, regular as script,
As wavelets of an EKG, defines
The dreamless gulf between two shoulder blades.

MY FATHER'S IRISH SETTERS

Always throughout his life
(The parts of it I knew)
Two or three would be racing
Up stairs and down hallways,
Whining to take us walking,
Or caked with dirt, resigning
Keen ears to bouts of talk—
Until his third, last wife
Put down her little foot.
That splendid, thoroughbred
Lineage was penned
Safely out of earshot:
Fed, of course, and watered,
But never let out to run.
"Dear God," the new wife simpered,
Tossing her little head,
"Suppose they got run over—
Wouldn't *that* be the end?"

Each time I visited
(Once or twice a year)
I'd slip out, giving my word
Not to get carried away.
At the dogs' first sight of me
Far off—of anyone—
Began a joyous barking,
A russet-and-rapid-as-flame
Leaping, then whimpering lickings
Of face and hands through wire.
Like fire, like fountains leaping
With love and loyalty,
Put, were they, in safekeeping
By love, or for love's sake?
Dear heart, to love's own shame.
But loyalty transferred
Leaves famously slim pickings,
And no one's left to blame.

Divorced again, my father
(Hair white, face deeply scored)
Looked round and heaved a sigh.
The setters were nowhere.
Fleet muzzle, soulful eye
Dead lo! these forty winters?
Not so. Tonight in perfect
Lamplit stillness begin
With updraft from the worksheet,
Leaping and tongues, far-shining
Hearths of our hinterland:
Dour chieftain, maiden pining
Away for that lost music,
Her harpist's wild red hair . . .
Dear clan of Ginger and Finn,
As I go through your motions
(As they go through me, rather)
Love follows, pen in hand.

Room set at infrared,
Mind at ultraviolet,
Organisms ever stranger,
Hallucinated on the slide, fluoresce:

Chains of gold tinsel, baubles of green fire
For the arterial branches—
Here at *Microcosmics Illustrated*, why,
Christmas goes on all year!

Defenseless, the patrician cells await
Invasion by barbaric viruses,
Another sack of Rome.
A new age. Everything we dread.

Dread? It crows for joy in the manger.
Joy? The tree sparkles on which it will die.

b o d y

Look closely at the letters. Can you see,
entering (stage right), then floating full,
then heading off—so soon—
how like a little kohl-rimmed moon
o plots her course from *b* to *d*

—as *y*, unanswered, knocks at the stage door?
Looked at too long, words fail,
phase out. Ask, now that *body* shines
no longer, by what light you learn these lines
and what the *b* and *d* stood for.

PLEDGE

House on alert.
Sun setting in a blaze
Of insight kisses book and budvase
Where they hurt.

Did the page-turner yawn and slacken,
Or an omen flip by unread?
Prime cuts that once bled
Now blacken.

Her brimming eyes say
More than they see.
He is all worried probity
About to get its way.

Dance steps the world knows curiously well
Ease them asunder—
Friends "rallying round her,"
His "move to a hotel."

Which one will get
The finger-wagging metronome,
Which one make a home
For the agèd cricket

Who sang togetherness ahead
From a hearth glowing bright?
It's dark now. I write
Propped up in bed:

"You who have drained dry
Your golden goblet are about to learn—
As in my turn
Have I—

How life, unsweetened, fizzing up again
Fills the heart.
I drink to you apart
In that champagne."

FAMILY WEEK AT ORACLE RANCH

1 / THE BROCHURE

The world outstrips us. In my day,
Had such a place existed,
It would have been advertised with photographs
Of doctors—silver hair, pince-nez—

Above detailed credentials,
Not this wide-angle moonscape, lawns and pool,
Patients sharing pain like fudge from home—
As if these were the essentials,

As if a month at what it invites us to think
Is little more than a fat farm for Anorexics,
Substance Abusers, Love & Relationship Addicts
Could help *you*, light of my life, when even your shrink . . .

The message, then? That costly folderol,
Underwear made to order in Vienna,
Who needs it! Let the soul hang out
At Benetton—stone-washed, one size fits all.

2 / INSTEAD OF COMPLEXES

Simplicities. Just seven words—AFRAID,
HURT, LONELY, etc.—to say it with.
Shades of the first watercolor box
(I "felt blue," I "saw red").

Also some tips on brushwork. Not to say
"Your silence hurt me,"
Rather, "When you said nothing I felt hurt."
No blame, that way.

Dysfunctionals like us fail to distinguish
Between the two modes at first.
While the connoisseur of feeling throws up his hands:
Used to depicting personal anguish

With a full palette—hues, oils, glazes, thinner—
He stares into these withered wells and feels,
Well . . . SAD and ANGRY? Future lavender!
An infant Monet blinks beneath his skin.

3 / THE COUNSELLORS

They're in recovery, too, and tell us from what,
And that's as far as it goes.
Like the sun-priests' in *The Magic Flute*
Their ritualized responses serve the plot.

Ken, for example, blond brows knitted: "When
James told the group he worried about dying
Without his lover beside him, I felt SAD."
Thank you for sharing, Ken,

I keep from saying; it would come out snide.
Better to view them as deadpan panels
Storing up sunlight for the woebegone,
Prompting from us lines electrified

By buried switches flipped (after how long!) . . .
But speak in private meanwhile? We may not
Until a voice within the temple lifts
Bans yet unfathomed into song.

4 / GESTALT

Little Aileen is a gray plush bear
With button eyes and nose.
Perky in flowered smock and clean white collar,
She occupies the chair

Across from middleaged Big Aileen, face hid
In hands and hands on knees.
Her sobs break. In great waves it's coming back.
The uncle. What he did.

Little Aileen is her Inner Child
Who didn't . . . who didn't deserve. . . .
The horror kissed asleep, round Big Aileen
Fairytale thorns grow wild.

SADNESS and GUILT entitle us to watch
The survivor compose herself,
Smoothing the flowered stuff, which has ridden up,
Over an innocent gray crotch.

5 / EFFECTS OF EARLY "RELIGIOUS ABUSE"

The great recurrent "sinner" found
In Dostoevsky—twisted mouth,
Stormlit eyes—before whose irresistible
Unworthiness the pure in heart bow down . . .

Cockcrow. Back across the frozen Neva
To samovar and warm, untubercular bed,
Far from the dens of vodka, mucus and semen,
They dream. I woke, the fever

Dripping insight, a spring thaw.
You and the others, wrestling with your demons,
Christs of self-hatred, Livingstones of pain,
Had drawn the lightning. In a flash I saw

My future: medic at some Armageddon
Neither side wins. I burned with SHAME for the years
You'd spent among sufferings uncharted—
Not even my barren love to rest your head on.

6 / THE PANIC

Except that Oracle has maps
Of all those badlands. Just now, when you lashed out,
"There's a lot of disease in this room!"
And we felt our faith in one another lapse,

Ken had us break the circle and repair
To "a safe place in the room." Faster than fish
We scattered—Randy ducking as from a sniper,
Aileen, wedged in a corner, cradling her bear.

You and I stood flanking the blackboard,
Words as usual between us,
But backs to the same wall, for solidarity.
This magical sureness of movement no doubt scored

Points for all concerned, yet the only
Child each had become trembled for you
Thundering forth into the corridors,
Decibels measuring how HURT, how LONELY—

7 / TUNNEL VISION

New Age music. "Close your eyes now. You
Are standing," says the lecturer on Grief,
"At a tunnel's mouth. There's light at the end.
The walls, as you walk through

Are hung with images: who you loved that year,
An island holiday, a highschool friend.
Younger and younger, step by step—
And suddenly you're here,

At home. Go in. It's your whole life ago."
A pink eye-level sun flows through the hall.
"Smell the smells. It's supper time.
Go to the table." Years have begun to flow

Unhindered down my face. Why?
Because nobody's there. The grown-ups? Shadows.
The meal? A mirror. Reflect upon it. Before
Reentering the tunnel say goodbye,

8 / TIME RECAPTURED

Goodbye to childhood, that unhappy haven.
It's over, weep your fill. Let go
Of the dead dog, the lost toy. Practice grieving
At funerals—anybody's. Let go even

Of those first ninety seconds missed,
Fifty-three years ago, of a third-rate opera
Never revived since then. The GUILT you felt,
Adding it all the same to your master list!

Which is why, this last morning, when I switch
The FM on, halfway to Oracle,
And hear the announcer say
(Invisibly reweaving the dropped stitch),

"We bring you now the Overture
To Ambroise Thomas's seldom-heard *Mignon*,"
Joy (word rusty with disuse)
Flashes up, deserved and pure.

9 / LEADING THE BLIND

Is this you—smiling helplessly? Pinned to your chest,
A sign: *Confront Me if I Take Control*.
Plus you must wear (till sundown) a black eyeshade.
All day you've been the littlest, the clumsiest.

We're seated face to face. Take off your mask,
Ken says. Now look into each other deeply. Speak,
As far as you can trust, the words of healing.
Your pardon for my own blindness I ask;

You mine, for all you hid from me. Two old
Crackpot hearts once more aswim with color,
Our Higher Power has but to dip his brush—
Lo and behold!

The group approves. The ban lifts. Let me guide you,
Helpless but voluble, into a dripping music.
The rainbow brightens with each step. Go on,
Take a peek. This once, no one will chide you.

10 / THE DESERT MUSEUM

—Or, as the fat, nearsighted kid ahead
Construes his ticket, "Wow, Dessert Museum!"
I leave tomorrow, so you get a pass.
Safer, both feel, instead

Of checking into the No-Tell Motel,
To check it out—our brave new dried-out world.
Exhibits: crystals that for eons glinted
Before the wits did; fossil shells

From when this overlook lay safely drowned;
Whole spiny families repelled by sex,
Whom dying men have drunk from (Randy, frightened,
Hugging Little Randy, a red hound) . . .

At length behind a wall of glass, in shade,
The mountain lioness too indolent
To train them upon us unlids her gems
Set in the saddest face Love ever made.

11 / THE TWOFOLD MESSAGE

(a) You are a brave and special person. (b)
There are far too many people in the world
For this to still matter for very long.
But (Ken goes on) since you obviously

Made the effort to attend Family Week,
We hope that we have shown you just how much
You have in common with everybody else.
Not to be "terminally unique"

Will be the consolation you take home.
Remember, Oracle is only the first step
In your recovery. The rest is up to you
And the twelve-step program you become

Involved in. An amazing forty per cent
Of our graduates are still clean after two years.
The rest? Well . . . Given our society,
Sobriety is hard to implement.

12 / AND IF

And if it were all like the moon?
Full this evening, bewitchingly
Glowing in a dark not yet complete
Above the world, explicit rune

Of change. Change is the "feeling" that dilutes
Those seven others to uncertain washes
Of soot and silver, inks unknown in my kit.
Change sends out shoots

Of FEAR and LONELINESS; of GUILT, as well,
Towards the old, abandoned patterns;
Of joy eventually, and self-forgiveness—
Colors few of us brought to Oracle . . .

And if the old patterns recur?
Ask how the co-dependent moon, another night,
Feels when the light drains wholly from her face.
Ask what that cold comfort means to her.

OVERDUE PILGRIMAGE TO NOVA SCOTIA

Elizabeth Bishop (1911–1979)

Your village touched us by not knowing how.
Even as we outdrove its clear stormlight
A shower of self-belittling brilliants fell.
Miles later, hours away, here are rooms full
Of things you would have known: pump organ, hymnal,
Small-as-life desks, old farm tools, charter, deed,
Schoolbooks (Greek Grammar, *A Canadian Reader*),
Queen Mary in oleograph, a whole wall hung
With women's black straw hats, some rather smart
—All circa 1915, like the manners
Of the fair, soft-spoken girl who shows us through.
Although till now she hasn't heard of you
She knows these things you would have known by heart
And we, by knowing you by heart, foreknew.

The child whose mother had been put away
Might wake, climb to a window, feel the bay
Steel itself, bosom bared to the full moon,
Against the woebegone, cerebral Man;
Or by judicious squinting make noon's red
Monarch grappling foreground goldenrod
Seem to extract a further essence from
Houses it dwarfed. Grown-up, the visitor
Could find her North by the green velvet map
Appliquéd upon this wharfside shack,
Its shingles (in the time her back was turned)
Silver-stitched to visionary grain
As by a tireless, deeply troubled inmate,
Were Nature not by definition sane.

In living as in poetry, your art
Refused to tip the scale of being human
By adding unearned weight. "New, tender, quick"—
Nice watchwords; yet how often they invited
The anguish coming only now to light

In letters like photographs from Space, revealing
Your planet tremulously bright through veils
As swept, in fact, by inconceivable
Heat and turbulence—but there, I've done it,
Added the weight. What tribute could you bear
Without dismay? Well, facing where you lived
Somebody's been inspired (*can* he have read
"Filling Station"?) to put pumps, a sign:
ESSO—what else! We filled up at the shrine.

Look, those were elms! Long vanished from *our* world.
Elms, by whose goblet stems distance itself
Taken between two fingers could be twirled,
Its bouquet breathed. The trees looked cumbersome,
Sickly through mist, like old things on a shelf—
Astrolabes, pterodactyls. They must know.
The forest knows. Out from such melting backdrops
It's the rare conifer stands whole, one sharp
Uniquely tufted spoke of a dark snow crystal
Not breathed upon, as yet, by our exhaust.
Part of a scene that with its views and warblers,
And at its own grave pace, but in your footsteps
—Never more imminent the brink, more sheer—
Is making up its mind to disappear

. . . With many a dirty look. That waterfall
For instance, beating itself to grit-veined cream
"Like Roquefort through a grater"? Or the car—!
So here we sit in the car wash, snug and dry
As the pent-up fury of the storm hits: streaming,
Foaming "emotions"—impersonal, cathartic,
Closer to both art and what we are
Than the gush of nothings one outpours to people
On the correspondence side of bay and steeple
Whose dazzling whites we'll never see again,
Or failed to see in the first place. Still, as the last
Suds glide, slow protozoa, down the pane,
We're off—Excuse our dust! With warm regards,—
Gathering phrases for tomorrow's cards.

SELF-PORTRAIT IN TYVEK^(TM) WINDBREAKER

The windbreaker is white with a world map.
DuPont contributed the seeming-frail,
Unrippable stuff first used for Priority Mail.
Weightless as shores reflected in deep water,
The countries are violet, orange, yellow, green;
Names of the principal towns and rivers, black.
A zipper's hiss, and the Atlantic Ocean closes
Over my blood-red T-shirt from the Gap.

I found it in one of those vaguely imbecile
Emporia catering to the collective unconscious
Of our time and place. This one featured crystals,
Cassettes of whalesong and rain-forest whistles,
Barometers, herbal cosmetics, pillows like puffins,
Recycled notebooks, mechanized lucite coffins
For sapphire waves that crest, break, and recede,
As they presumably do in nature still.

Sweat-panted and Reeboked, I wear it to the gym.
My terry-cloth headband is green as laurel.
A yellow plastic Walkman at my hip
Sends shiny yellow tendrils to either ear.
All us street people got our types on tape,
Turn ourselves on with a sly fingertip.
Today I felt like Songs of Yesteryear
Sung by Roberto Murolo. Heard of him?

Well, back before animal species began to become
Extinct, a dictator named Mussolini banned
The street-singers of Naples. One smart kid
Learned their repertoire by heart, and hid.
Emerging after the war with his guitar,
He alone bearing the old songs of the land
Into the nuclear age sang with a charm,
A perfect naturalness that thawed the numb

Survivors and reinspired the Underground.
From love to grief to gaiety his art
Modulates effortlessly, like a young man's heart,

Tonic to dominant—the frets so few
And change so strummed into the life of things
That Nature's lamps burn brighter when he sings
Nannetta's fickleness, or chocolate,
Snow on a flower, the moon, the seasons' round.

I picked his tape in lieu of something grosser
Or loftier, say the Dead or Arvo Pärt,
On the hazy premise that what fills the mind
Shows on the face. My face, as a small part
Of nature, hopes this musical sunscreen
Will keep the wilderness within it green,
Yet looks uneasy, drawn. I detect behind
My neighbor's grin the oncoming bulldozer

And cannot stop it. Ecosaints—their karma
To be Earth's latest, maybe terminal, fruits—
Are slow to ripen. Even this dumb jacket
Probably still believes in Human Rights,
Thinks in terms of "nations," urban centers,
Cares less (can Tyvek breathe?) for oxygen
Than for the innocents evicted when
Ford bites the dust and Big Mac buys the farm.

Hah. As if greed and savagery weren't the tongues
We've spoken since the beginning. My point is, those
Prior people, fresh from scarifying
Their young and feasting in triumph on their foes,
Honored the gods of Air and Land and Sea.
We, though . . . Cut to dead forests, filthy beaches,
The can of hairspray, oil-benighted creatures,
A star-scarred x-ray of the North Wind's lungs.

Still, not to paint a picture wholly black,
Some social highlights: Dead white males in malls.
Prayer breakfasts. Pay-phone sex. "Ring up as meat."
Oprah. The GNP. The contour sheet.
The painless death of History. The stick
Figures on Capitol Hill. Their rhetoric,
Gladly—no, rapturously (on Prozac) suffered!
Gay studies. Right to Lifers. The laugh track.

And clothes. Americans, blithe as the last straw,
Shrug off accountability by dressing
Younger than their kids—jeans, ski-pants, sneakers,
A baseball cap, a happy-face T-shirt . . .
Like first-graders we "love" our mother Earth,
Know she's been sick, and mean to care for her
When we grow up. Seeing my windbreaker,
People hail me with nostalgic awe.

"Great jacket!" strangers on streetcorners impart.
The Albanian doorman pats it: "Where you buy?"
Over his ear-splitting drill a hunky guy
Yells, "Hey, you'll always know where you are, right?"
"Ever the fashionable cosmopolite,"
Beams Ray. And "Voilà mon pays"—the carrot-haired
Girl in the bakery, touching with her finger
The little orange France above my heart.

Everyman, c'est moi, the whole world's pal!
The pity is how soon such feelings sour.
As I leave the gym a smiling-as-if-I-should-know-her
Teenager—oh but I *mean*, she's wearing "our"
Windbreaker, and assumes . . . Yet I return her wave
Like an accomplice. For while all humans aren't
Countable as equals, we must behave
As if they were, or the spirit dies (Pascal).

"We"? A few hundred decades of relative
Lucidity glinted-through by minnow schools
Between us and the red genetic muck—
Everyman's underpainting. We look up, shy
Creatures, from our trembling pool of sky.
Caught wet-lipped in light's brushwork, fleet but sure,
Flash on shudder, folk of the first fuck,
Likeness breeds likeness, fights for breath—*I live*—

Where the crush thickens. And by season's end,
The swells of fashion cresting to collapse
In breaker upon breaker on the beach,
Who wants to be caught dead in this cliché
Of mere "involvement"? Time to put under wraps
Its corporate synthetic global pitch;

Not throwing out motley once reveled in,
Just learning to live down the wrinkled friend.

Face it, reproduction of any kind leaves us colder
Though airtight-warmer (greenhouse effect) each year.
Remember the figleaf's lesson. Styles betray
Some guilty knowledge. What to dress ours in—
A seer's blind gaze, an infant's tender skin?
All that's been seen through. The eloquence to come
Will be precisely what we cannot say
Until it parts the lips. But as one grows older

—I should confess before that last coat dries—
The wry recall of thunder does for rage.
Erotic torrents flash on screens instead
Of drenching us. Exclusively in dream,
These nights, does a grandsire rear his saurian head,
And childhood's inexhaustible brain-forest teem
With jewel-bright lives. No way now to restage
Their sacred pageant under our new skies'

Irradiated lucite. What then to wear
When—hush, it's no dream! It's my windbreaker
In black, with starry longitudes, Archer, Goat,
Clothing an earphoned archangel of Space,
Who hasn't read Pascal, and doesn't wave . . .
What far-out twitterings he learns by rote,
What looks they'd wake upon a human face,
Don't ask, Roberto. Sing our final air:

Love, grief etc. ★ ★ ★ ★ for good reason.
Now only ★ ★ ★ ★ ★ ★ ★ STOP signs.
Meanwhile ★ ★ ★ ★ ★ if you or I've ex-
ceeded our [?] ★ ★ ★ ~~more than time~~ was needed
To fit a text airless and ★ ★ as Tyvek
With breathing spaces and between the lines
Days brilliantly recurring, as once *we* did,
To keep the blue wave dancing in its prison.

AN UPWARD LOOK

O heart green acre   sown with salt
by the departing   occupier

lay down your gallant   spears of wheat
Salt of the earth   each stellar pinch

flung in blind   defiance backwards
now takes its toll   Up from his quieted

quarry the lover   colder and wiser
hauling himself   finds the world turning

toys triumphs   toxins into
this vast facility   the living come
dearest to die in   How did it happen

In bright alternation   minutely mirrored
within the thinking   of each and every

mortal creature   halves of a clue
approach the earthlights   Morning star

evening star   salt of the sky
First the grave   dissolving into dawn

then the crucial   recrystallizing
from inmost depths   of clear dark blue

Why is the Rising Sun aflutter from ten thousand flagpoles?
    Because the Japanese are coming today.
And why do our senators, those industrious termites,
Gaze off into space instead of forming a new subcommittee?
    Because the Japanese are coming today.
    Congress will soon be an item on their Diet.
What's gotten into the President, trading quips with reporters
As he bails out his Whitewater bubble bath? How will posterity
    judge him?
    Well, the Japanese who are coming today
    Have their own scandals. His we can forget.
Why does the waterfront swarm with clumsily bandaged apprentices,
And the garment district ring with the mirth of transvestites in
    whiteface?
    Because the Japanese are coming today,
    Bringing their sushi-bar legerdemain
    And female impersonators second to none.
But our artists and writers? Funny—somehow one had pictured
    them flocking
To greet the compatriots of Utamaro and Lady Murasaki.
    They won't be missed. The Japanese of today
    Want spicy space-pirate comics and Van Gogh.
Midnight already? Times Square is a semiologist's heaven:
Mitsubishi, Sony, Suntory, Toshiba, Kirin, Benihana . . .
But horrors! Great wings hide the moon. Are the Japanese passing
    us over,
As an in-depth update asserts, for the shores of Gimme Gucci?
    The sun has risen in Rome. By dark not a pair
    Of lizard loafers will be left unbought.
Leaving us where? With egg on our faces, or tofu. Those people
Were some sort of golden opportunity, but we blew it.

ORANGES

His mother wore, as in a fairy tale,
A fragrant crown upon her snow-white veil.
  The photograph obsessed him. Didn't she know
What grievous crops such blossomings entail?

≈

There was that sweetness just beneath the skin,
A single night of frost undid: blood kin
  To acrimony; the boy's crush rebuffed;
Sour notes drawn from a solar violin.

≈

Abroad, at the Orangerie, he came
Upon Monet's great mirrorings aflame
  With water blues, sky purples, greens and pinks . . .
The past lending no color but a name.

≈

Followed those winters when the mercury dove
Past all endurance. What could simple Love
  Hope to accomplish? Yet each night he lit
His sorry smudge-pot in the shivering grove.

≈

Segment by segment, nonetheless a mind
Made up of taste and sunlight. May the blind
  Gods who drink its juice be satisfied,
Disposing gently of the empty rind.

≈

After Jim's funeral the marmalade
Deathmask tomcat Agent Orange stayed
  Far from the house. Time passed and, mourning done,
One bright dusk up he sauntered, undismayed.

IN THE PINK

From under a duvet the pink of dunes
In first light tantalizing fragments peek,
Rosy alabaster flecked with buff:
Here a foot, there a forearm, a bent knee . . .
Their disposition so mysteriously
Right, we have no plans to trouble them
Just now. Aren't they the thermostats
That regulate the desert's warms and cools?

Armed, unamusable at the dune's crest
Our nightly Bedouin, his glance
A slit of glitter between cloak and cloud,
Stood guard, or seemed to. As the last star fades,
He mounts his camel; slowly both dissolve.
Tonight again? We have no words in common,
No way to question him, or thank—
Yet it was he who led us to the trove.

The finest, most absorbing piece thus far
Will be this lower half of a royal head
Sliced in two by a catastrophe
Lost in the mists of time. The upper half—
Eyes, forehead, serpent crown—may sooner or later
Come to light. Meanwhile notice the lips:
Work of such quality belongs
To the last great period of portraiture.

The chin rests on an incurved hand we took
At first for a second figure's—a suppliant?—
Clasping the narrow sisal "beard" required
For ritual. (Did he obtain his boon?)
This morning's theory, though, deems it the ruler's
Own knee bent, his own hand making bold
To approach its godhead, even that part
Deepest nearby in pink oblivion . . .

Wake up! It's May, it's daybreak in the City.
Already I've pulled some random selves together
Sufficiently for "us" to draft these lines

Which thus far, like the duvet, show
Stray pieces of only the Sandman's trick.
So, presto, off with that magician's cloth!
The complete sleeper stretches, blushes, yawns
A tear from either spring's lighthearted blue.

RHAPSODY ON CZECH THEMES

for Allan Gurganus

I

A mauve madness has overrun Moravia—
"Mauve" used loosely to include lavender,
Fuchsia and puce and pansy-violet,
But even the oxymoron of *strict mauve*
Is everywhere. Those posted notices,
Purple on mauve—five or six crudely-printed
Words in Czech, like losing draws in Scrabble—
What do they spell? and whom to ask? Meanwhile,
Mauve workpants, mauve shopfronts, mauve sunglasses:
Accents vividly standing out against
The obvious ochers of the Hapsburg heritage.
Or is it an early symptom of one of those
Artistic movements (mauvement in this case)
Whose hyperactive brushwork swept the Flore?
Part of the Paris Mucha's manikins
Hoped sleepy Prague would wake as—statues on bridges,
Art Nouveau . . . as if appearances
Were everything. But aren't they? and doesn't thought
—Lend me your clippers, ghastly these long nails—
Make provisions when the real thing fails?
Why else booth upon booth of marionettes?—
Our childhood intimates, known then as now
Chiefly by how they dress and do their hair.
Why else Princess and Troubadour, Hermit and Crone
(Whose joints are stiff, like mine)? Why else entangle
Ourselves for life in the Seven Deadly Strings
Or the Seven Adorable ones?—same difference.
Why else yet one more spruce façade upon
The same old miseries? The baby's vomit.
Grandfather's gunshot cough, his uniform
Faded, mildew-bemedalled. Ludmila's fits
The neighbors set their clocks by. Joys no doubt
As well. We know, we *know.* (Why bring it up?
Because, as page after notebook page blackens

With these and other musings, a small voice warns:
"James, don't leave out the humanity!")

2

A waking dream: I'm ten, I'm Dorothy
In one of the *Oz* books. Called on to set free
From their translation into bibelots
The members of a royal family.
Which of the chill cave-full will they be?
Three wrong guesses and the child that was
Becomes a nut dish of Depression glass.
(Of course the dream was telling me to set
Myself free—but from what half-humorous
Manipulative bondage I forget.)
On Dorothy's third try a purple budvase
Wakes back into a gurgling year-old princess.
So! purple was the clue, and those doomed selves
Childsplay from then on to disenchant.
As with the bloodless "Velvet Revolution,"
Its dawn till then unknown except in dream,
People now jubilantly woke—free, free!
How can you doubt the color of that velvet?

3

Far from the capital proliferates
A (what to call it?) terminal prettiness.
Houses of cards. A whole square, poker-faced,
Each frontal in broad sunset strung with gems,
Like MGM's generic frontier town.
In the antique shop, uncollectibles
Collecting dust. Gnawed cushions, carpet ends,
Postcards in savage, ego-driven script,
Dead woodcuts, loose beads, ossified crochet—
One's weakness for that terrible old stuff . . .
But look who through a pendant of chipped crystal
Exuberantly sidles in—by turns
Furnace-red, fire-emerald, glory-blue:
It's Light! snapping his fingers to a beat
Our own eyes pick up, ardently repeat.
And here's a two-foot-high medicine chest,

Oak unpainted and unhinged. Try picturing it
Painted mauve, or a purple mercy-mild,
That would at the right touch grow tall and glow,
Its baby mirror door (the mottled face
Of an old man seems to peer from) opening
In expectation—ah but you're not at home,
Just your pure concentrated know-how
Bottled in amethyst. Compounds, elixirs
Bringing us wisdom, youth, fertility . . .
In a word, change. Unstoppered as we gawk,
Those vials release through evening sun a swarm
Of whirring mothlike sprites, to do your bidding
Within the small gilt theater each of us
Reserves for rapture. Gravely they hold our gaze,
Then by imperceptible degrees
Into the afterglow of the scene played
Sink back.

4

        Woodsmoke. Night falling. Black
As one of President Havel's comedies.
Not so much as a streetlight after ten
Shining in Telč. The town's young people
Head for homework, freed from the spell of a late
Mauv—clippers again, please [*cuts the string*]—
There, no more jokes—of a late movie.
Too dark to see the kids in their true colors—
Colors, those "deeds and sufferings of light"
That flood your book's great honeycomb—But whoa!
What's this live whiteness pulsing from below?
We've all but pitched into an underground
Cube of fluorescence eerie-dense as snow
Where one lone figure in white coveralls—
Grave robber? master mechanic? have we names
For what he so candidly is and does and knows?—
Works night-shift magic. It's the school basement.
Upstairs all day the priests (in black) rehearse
A past, by termite zeal beneath our feet,
Made ever quainter and more obsolete.
What lies in store for that Old World depends
Soberingly on this dew-bright whiz and friends.

Tomorrow we'll be shown scenes from a play
They're working on ("It still needs work") performed
By eight reactors huge on the horizon,
Titans letting off steam. Some latterday
. . . Not yet Chernobyl, not yet Auschwitz. We
Trust in the dreamwork, although who's to say
What the exact works are that make us free.

5

Remember (the inner wireless crackles on)
These people have known centuries of oppression—
Magyar, Hapsburg, Nazi, Soviet
(And now the Swiss are investing—blue skies ahead)
And come through with their liveliness intact.
Would Americans be capable of that?

You're asking *me*? Oh well, America . . .
[*Deep sigh*] Who hasn't OD'd on those Carl Sandburg
WPA frescoes-in-words. Wheat sheaves,
Civic street scenes, torsos brawny-bare . . .
State art of just the sort then reaching us
From the Soviet Union. One small difference:
We had the freedom to make fun of it
And They did not. Freedom to trust all's well
Once we have made the other person smile
(As you've been doing, Reader, this whole while?).
Freedom when confronted to disarm
With openness. (Talking of other things
While stitching up my finger numb as wood,
The old blood swabbed away, *"Of course,"* said Susan,
"I'm telling you the truth, I'm from Nebraska!")
Freedom to ignore our own spellbinders
While millions behind the Iron Curtain knew
By anguished heart voices the State had schooled
In irony, shades of meaning, stratagems
Worthless now that everybody's free
To trade threadbare Camus for *Dynasty*,
Freedom to justify bad deeds by pleading
Good intentions. To shoot down those who don't
Believe what you and I do. To oust from office
The gladhander we put there in the first place.

Freedom not to wave flags on May Day
And lose our visas as a consequence
—That last detail by way of nice Jan Rippl
Who runs the pension we've settled in.
His English is piquant, he doesn't—won't?—
Speak German. His teenage children want to shame him
Into a job "worthy of his education."
Such jobs don't pay; he made more as a fireman . . .
Now, "free" to run the pension, he leads
A life that answers, sort of, to his needs.
Without TV as yet, his personal dial
Ranges from uphill Castle to The Trial
(A grim pub we avoid) downstreet. Then there's
His packed, glass-fronted bookcase below stairs
—Germaine Greer, Robert Ludlum, Wittgenstein—
To which I add a paperback of mine.
(Thank you. This dry, opinionated stretch
Has left us thirsty for the purpler patch.)

6

Eureka! Mr. Rippl, stripping beds,
"Englishes" what those crude mauve posters say:
EQUAL RIGHTS FOR SECONDARY COLORS
—A taunt "not printable" while the Red Army
Ran the show.
    (Merciful god, those "reds"
One went to school with? Their brave attitudes
Over long nights of argument and smoke
Mixed with subliminal piano blues . . .
Result? This new, seductive shade.)
       But hey,
It's our show now, as that blond kid asserts
In hoarse convulsions over his guitar.
All Prague agrees. The citywide street fair
Gathers momentum—bangles, jugglers, beer,
And yes, at every stop along our way,
Another puppet government for all
Whom ideologies of Type enthrall:
Devil and Priest, Tycoon and Commissar,
Death himself, white bones on a black robe—
Pull the right strings, and look, you've made him dance!

Our crucial selves, they're all here for the having,
All but [*ominous chords*]—all but the Golem.
Rabbi Löw's masterwork, the Golem, lurching
Unstrung, red-eyed through nightmare wails of grief,
Bent on the bonbon Child, wrapped in gold leaf.
("Will you believe," wrote Natalie reading this,
"We met the Golems at *The House of the Dead*?
She is enchanting, knows the whole world, spoke
Affectionately of you. *He's* something else,
Not—one hates to say it—a nice person.
No soul, I mean.") Just that foul Being made
Of the resurrectionist's odd limbs and organs,
Abstracted from the graves of infidels.

      7

Does the Rabbi rest in this Ghetto graveyard?
Among the markers handy to our path,
Unskewed enough for the next step,
Pause. Perform what the wisest, most
Compelling life at length comes down to:
The pious placement of a pebble
Upon the good man's golden, weather-
Gimleted stone. The whispering of a wish
Some wraith of wry complaisance underground
Will try to grant.
                Dear Heart, come, time to go.

Have we sufficiently seen? have we had our humanity?
Were our travels true, our words worthy
(As if one could say) of the unassuming
Reb Sholem of Belz, who in a minor mode
Enjoined his juniors:

*   Keep your nail-parings*
for burning and never   talmidim fail to
add when the toy fire   fondly whistles
its color-carol   two willing chips of
seasoned wood   as witnesses

CHRISTMAS TREE

To be
  Brought down at last
From the cold sighing mountain
Where I and the others
Had been fed, looked after, kept still,
Meant, I knew—of course I knew—
That it would be only a matter of weeks,
That there was nothing more to do.
Warmly they took me in, made much of me,
The point from the start was to keep my spirits up.
I could assent to that. For honestly,
It did help to be wound in jewels, to send
Their colors flashing forth from vents in the deep
Fragrant sables that cloaked me head to foot.
Over me then they wove a spell of shining—
Purple and silver chains, eavesdripping tinsel,
Amulets, milagros: software of silver,
A heart, a little girl, a Model T,
Two staring eyes. The angels, trumpets, BUD and BEA
(The children's names) in clownlike capitals,
Somewhere a music box whose tiny song
Played and replayed I ended before long
By loving. And in shadow behind me, a primitive IV
To keep the show going. Yes, yes, what lay ahead
Was clear: the stripping, the cold street, my chemicals
Plowed back into the Earth for lives to come—
No doubt a blessing, a harvest, but one that doesn't bear,
Now or ever, dwelling upon. To have grown so thin.
Needles and bone. The little boy's hands meeting
About my spine. The mother's voice: *Holding up wonderfully!*
No dread. No bitterness. The end beginning. Today's
  Dusk room aglow
  For the last time
  With candlelight.
  Faces love lit,
  Gifts underfoot.
Still to be so poised, so
Receptive. Still to recall, to praise.

KOI

Snow today, the first in seven years,
As major a blizzard as the mildness here can muster.
Big slow skydiving flakes, their floating filigrees
Aspiring to come back as a field of Queen Anne's lace.

Then it is over, and the terrain resumes its menace.
Coyotes patrol it, watchful for a small
Privileged dog to steal. Premonitions! Whole nights
Preliving the yelp of pain and disbelief

As we helplessly watch our Cosmo borne struggling off.
We keep him on a stout red leash, but still . . .
Behind these garden walls it's safe. Birds, olive trees,
A rectangular pool of koi. Twin to the urban

Gempool south of us. Last night again: a moon,
Big stars, white clouds—no, wait, clouds colorized
To the exact tint of the white patches on the koi. A white
Ever so faintly suffused by blood and gold.

And from the clouds, or far beyond them, at intervals
Our upturned faces receive a mild pinprick of dew.
Feel the world drop away it whispers. *Seven years more*
Breathes the melting snow. To which the koi can only

Reply *Carpe diem*. Next morning to their skylight comes a human
Silhouette edged by radiance, and they cluster to be fed.
Hold a fistful of pellets underwater, your hand will be kissed
By the tenderest mouths. It's too much: our "Lindbergh puppy"

Is barking—he's losing his footing—he's fallen in!

DAYS OF 1994

These days in my friend's house
Light seeks me underground. To wake
Below the level of the lawn
—Half-basement cool through the worst heat—
Is strange and sweet.
High up, three window-slots, new slants on dawn:
Through misty greens and gilts
An infant sun totters on stilts of shade
Up toward the high
Mass of interwoven boughs,
While close against the triptych panes
Rock bears witness, Dragonfly
Shivers in place
Above tall Queen Anne's lace—
More figures from *The Book of Thel* by Blake
(Lilly & Worm, Cloudlet & Clod of Clay)
And none but drinks the dewy Manna in.

I shiver next, Light walking on my grave . . .
And sleep, and wake. This time, peer out
From just beneath the mirror of the lake
A gentle mile uphill.
Florets—the mountain laurel—float
Openmouthed, devout,
Set swaying by the wake of the flatboat:

Barcarole whose chords of gloom
Draw forth the youngest, purest, faithfullest,
Cool-crystal-casketed
Hands crossed on breast,
Pre-Raphaelite face radiant—and look,
Not dead, O never dead!
To wake, to wake
Among the flaming dowels of a tomb
Below the world, the thousand things
Here risen to if not above
Before day ends:
The spectacles, the book,
Forgetful lover and forgotten love,

Cobweb hung with trophy wings,
The fading trumpet of a car,
The knowing glance from star to star,
The laughter of old friends.

Notes

Upon a Second Marriage

8   The poem is dedicated to the poet's mother, Hellen Ingram Plummer, on the occasion of her marriage to General William Plummer in 1951.

The Charioteer of Delphi

9   The title refers to a Greek bronze statue (ca. 470 BCE) of a victorious chariot driver holding the remnants of the reins of his horses is all that we have of the original sculptural group. The eyes are onyx.

Marsyas

13   In Greek mythology, Marsyas is a flute player who challenged Apollo, an expert on the lyre, to a musical duel. Apollo won the contest and the right, which he exercised, to flay Marsyas alive. He left the body dangling in a pine tree.

An Urban Convalescence

21   *The White Goddess:* A work by the British author Robert Graves (1895–1985), published in 1948, that traces the origins of poetic myth in the ancient Mediterranean and Europe to a moon goddess or muse figure dating to the Old Stone Age.

22   pousse-café: A vividly hued alcoholic drink layered (densest ingredient at the bottom) so that, viewed from the side, it has horizontal stripes of color.

Angel

32   Van Eyck: Jan van Eyck (1395–1441), the Flemish painter whose work is known for the intricacy and luminescence of its detail. Cf. the angel in *The Annunciation* in the National Gallery, Washington, D.C.

32   Satie: Erik Satie, the French composer (1866–1925), known for his idiosyncrat-
ically playful music.

The Thousand and Second Night

38   *Dahin! Dahin!:* Meaning "Back there! Back there!" A quotation from *Wilhelm
Meisters Wanderjahre* (1821, 1829) by the German poet and dramatist Johann
Wolfgang von Goethe (1749–1832). In the lyric beginning "Kennst du das
Land wo die Zitronen blühn" ("Do you know the land where the lemon
trees blossom") Mignon is remembering wistfully the idyllic setting of her
childhood.

40   Suleiman the Magnificent: (1494/5–1566) The Sultan of the Ottoman Em-
pire from 1520 to 1566, the empire's golden age, during which he commis-
sioned the building of architectural masterpieces, including Süleymaniye
Mosque in Istanbul, by the great architect Mimar Sinan (1489–1588).

40   "death-in-life and life-in-death": From the 1930 poem "Byzantium" by the
Irish poet W. B. Yeats (1865–1939).

40   "Between the motion and the act/Falls the Shadow": From "The Hollow
Men" (1925) by the American-born British poet T. S. Eliot (1888–1965).

41   l'Agneau Mystique: The Sacred Lamb, an icon for Jesus Christ and the focus
of the painting *Adoration de l'Agneau Mystique* by Jan van Eyck (cf. note to
"Angel," page 271), where the Lamb appears in a densely planted garden.

41   as even Valéry said: Cf. lines in the the last stanza of "Le Cimetière marin"
(1920) by the French poet Paul Valéry (1871–1945), "Le vent se lève! . . . Il faut
tenter de vivre!" ("The wind is rising! . . . We must try to live!").

43   A flat Methusalem of Krug: I.e., a double magnum bottle of Champagne
Krug, a famous sparkling wine, that has lost its zip.

43   Hofmannsthal: Hugo von Hofmannsthal (1874–1929), the Austrian dramatist
and librettist.

44   Germaine Nahman: A friend of Merrill's. The poet put these words in her
mouth.

44   A. H. Clarendon: A fictitious author, whom Merrill "quotes" also in "The
Book of Ephraim," section Q.

45   Scheherazade: The narrator's cat, named for the storyteller in *A Thousand and
One Nights,* or *The Arabian Nights.* The storyteller herself appears with the Sultan
in this poem's fifth section. There is a poem, "Maisie" (not included here), for
Merrill's actual cat, in *Nights and Days.*

46   Spender's phrase: From the poem by the English poet Stephen Spender
(1909–1995) known by its first line, "I think continually of those who were truly
great."

52 Merrill's parents were Charles E. Merrill (1885–1956), co-founder of the Merrill Lynch brokerage firm, and Hellen Ingram (1898–2000) (cf. note to "Upon a Second Marriage," page 271).

53 Al Smith: The Democratic politician (1873–1944), who advocated reform in labor laws and other areas and was the first American Roman Catholic nominee for president (defeated by Herbert Hoover in 1928).

53 José María Sert: The Spanish painter (1876–1945), whose large mural *American Progress* (1934) occupies a wall in the main lobby of what is now Rockefeller Center, replacing, at Nelson Rockefeller's behest, one by Diego Rivera that showed leftist sympathies.

53 Clemenceau: Georges Clemenceau (1841–1929), the prime minister of France (1917–1920), radical Republican turned right-wing nationalist, who favored more severe treatment of Germany at the end of World War I and thus clashed with Woodrow Wilson and Lloyd George.

53 *war mongerer:* I.e., warmonger. The furious woman has made a mistake.

54 a stone guest: In the 1787 opera *Don Giovanni* by the Austrian composer Wolfgang Amadeus Mozart (1756–1791), the Stone Guest is the cemetery statue of the Commendatore, whom Don Giovanni has killed. The Commendatore has his revenge when the statue delivers Don Giovanni to Hell.

54 Poor Tom: In Shakespeare's *King Lear,* 2.3., Poor Tom is Edgar—the loyal son of Kent, the Duke of Gloucester—banished from the kingdom and disguised as a madman on the heath.

From the Cupola

58 Psyche: Merrill bases his poem on the novel *Metamorphoses* (better known as *The Golden Ass*) by the Roman Lucius Apuleius (second century CE). Merrill's use of the Greek names for the characters suggests that he read Erich Neumann's 1956 *Amor and Psyche*, a translation of and commentary on Apuleius. Psyche is a royal princess who had failed to find a mortal husband because she, unlike her two spiteful sisters, was intimidatingly beautiful. She was abandoned by her parents to the elements, only to be rescued by Eros, who whisked her off to his palace, where he visited her only at night and made her promise never to look at his face. In spite of her happiness with Eros, nostalgia eventually overcame her, and she made a visit to her home, where her sisters, envious of her new life, persuaded her to view her lover, who they implied hid himself because he was a monster. One night after she had returned to Eros's palace, Psyche lit an oil lamp to see her sleeping husband, who turned out to be a stunning youth. A drop of hot oil fell on Eros's shoulder, and he woke to leave her for breaking her vow. Psyche was turned out into the world and, without his protection, was imprisoned by a jealous Aphrodite in her

palace, where she was tormented and made to perform nearly impossible tasks. Eros, who had missed her sorely, finally rescued her. The two received Zeus's permission to marry and Aphrodite's forgiveness. The name Psyche means "soul" in Greek.

64   L'Africana: Or *L'Africaine*, the 1865 opera by the German composer Giacomo Meyerbeer (1791–1864).

70   la vie en rose: "Life in the pink" or "a beautiful life," a phrase that is also the title of a romantic song written and popularized by French chanteuse Edith Piaf (1915–1963).

Days of 1964

72   Kyria Kleo: The poem is set at the house at 44 Athinaion Efivon Street in Athens that Merrill and Jackson shared beginning in the 1960s. "Kyria" is a Greek honorific comparable to "madam," and "Kleo" is a first name or nickname.

72   Palmyra matron: Palmyra was an important caravan city in ancient Syria. Excavations of burial sites have yielded limestone slabs with busts representing the souls of the interred.

Lorelei

74   In German legend, Lorelei was a young woman who drowned herself in the Rhine River because of an unfaithful lover, was turned into a siren, and sang from a rock and lured sailors to their death.

The Friend of the Fourth Decade

75   Fannie Farmer: Fannie Merritt Farmer (1857–1915) wrote *The Boston Cooking-School Cook Book* in 1896. It became so popular that American housewives referred to later editions as merely "Fannie Farmer's cookbook."

Words for Maria

80   Maria: Maria Demertzí Mitsotáki (1907–1974), an Athenian friend of Merrill's who is featured also in *The Changing Light at Sandover*.

80   the Bon Goût: Merrill's name for a café (actually called Lykóvrisi) he frequented on Kolonáki Square in Athens. It comes up also in "Nine Lives," page 224.

To My Greek

82   kaló-kakó: The words "good-bad" in Greek.

Matinées

88   Alberich: The villain in the epic operatic cycle *Der Ring des Nibelungen (The Ring of the Nibelungs)*, composed between 1848 and 1874 by the German composer

Richard Wagner (1813–1883). Alberich's theft of gold from the Rhine River at the opening of the cycle precipitates the tragic action that follows.

88   Comique: The Opéra-Comique is a theater in Paris, now a national monument.

89   Jan Kiepura: the Polish-born tenor and actor (1902–1966), here recalled singing the role of the Duke of Mantua in the 1851 opera *Rigoletto* by Italian composer Giuseppe Verdi (1813–1901).

89   Lehmann's Marschallin: The German soprano Lotte Lehmann (1888–1976) starred in many roles of the German operatic repertory, but most critics consider her performances as the Marschallin in *Der Rosenkavalier*, by the German composer Richard Strauss (1864–1949), her greatest role.

90   *Lulu:* An opera by the Austrian composer Alban Berg (1885–1935), left unfinished at his death, and first performed in that version in 1937. After the death of Berg's widow, the opera was completed by Friedrich Cerha and first performed in its entirety in 1979. Its lurid plot turns on a heroine who seduces both men and women, then murders those whom she has not already driven to their deaths. In the end, working as a prostitute in London, she is herself murdered by Jack the Ripper.

The Summer People

91   The epigraph quotes the French poet Stéphane Mallarmé (1842–1898): ". . . and winter would remain the intellectually creative season." The quotation is from a response, published in *Echo de Paris*, that Mallarmé wrote to a man who wanted to know how spring affects a writer's creative faculty.

92   "Go grasshopper! Go ant!": The allusion is to Aesop's fable. The diligent ant works through the summer to lay in supplies for the winter, while the happy-go-lucky grasshopper wastes the summer in play and suffers the consequences.

93   Mendelssohn's augmentations: Felix Mendelssohn-Bartholdy (1809–1847), the German composer.

95   Cointreau: Orange-flavored liqueur.

97   "I have seen / The fuchsia, and it works": In 1921, after his return from a visit to post-revolutionary Russia, the American journalist Lincoln Steffens (1866–1936) made the following optimistic pronouncement: "I have seen the future and it works." By the time of his death, he had become disillusioned with communism.

97   Frans Hals: The Dutch painter (ca. 1580–1666) whose revelers often have rubicund cheeks.

102   The Jungfrau: The name of the highest peak in the Bernese Alps in Switzerland; the word means "virgin" in German.

102   "venerable beads": The Venerable Bede (ca. 672–735) was an Anglo-Saxon ecclesiastical historian and theologian of the Roman Catholic Church.

105   *Emma:* By the English novelist Jane Austen (1775–1817).

108 "Where do the years go": The question alludes to the *ubi sunt* (Latin, meaning "where are") tradition exemplified in the fifteenth-century "Ballade des dames du temps jadis" ("Where are the ladies of yesteryear?"), a lament for the transience of life by the French poet François Villon (1431–after 1463).

109 "One by one, like swallows": The quotation is from the poem "Pilgrims" by the English poet Mary Botham Howitt (1799–1888).

After the Fire

112 yiayia: Greek word for "grandmother."

113 "Ah Monsieur Tzim . . .": Panayióti is saying in this stanza in his Greek-accented French:

> "Ah, Mr. Jim, hello and welcome back!
> Excuse my casual dress. All night
> I decorated the church for the festival
> and made love, the priest and I,
> in an alcove behind the Holy Icon.
> Well then, I have a present for you,
> a pretty foulard which doesn't suit me.
> You take it, it's not stolen—
> I'm no longer a thief, just fickle!"

Days of 1935

115 the Lindbergh baby: The twenty-month-old son of the celebrated aviator Charles Lindbergh (1902–1974) was abducted from his bedroom at the family's home in Hopewell, New Jersey, on March 1, 1932, two days before Merrill's sixth birthday. The case quickly became what H. L. Mencken called "the biggest story since the Resurrection." A ransom of $50,000 was paid, but a child's body thought by some to be the Lindberghs' son was found in May. Bruno Hauptmann, a German immigrant, was charged with the kidnapping and murder and was executed by electric chair in 1936. The case remains controversial.

118 Claire Coe in *Tehuantepec:* A fictional starlet. Probably coincidentally, a short documentary, entitled *Tehuantepec* after the town in the state of Oaxaca, and directed by the Mexican painter Roberto Montenegro (1887–1968), was released in 1935. Perhaps more to the point, the place name recurs in "Sea Surface Full of Clouds" by the American poet Wallace Stevens (1879–1975).

119 *Belshazzar's Feast:* The 1931 oratorio by English composer William Walton (1902–1983).

120 Spider lightly running forth: Cf. "The Spider and the Fly" by English poet Mary Botham Howitt (1799–1888).

124 Sazerac: Venerable cocktail usually made of bourbon or cognac, bitters, Pernod, and sugar.

125   This is the address of the brick townhouse in New York City where Merrill's parents lived at the time of his birth. On March 6, 1970, members of the radical group the Weathermen were making bombs in the basement when one device exploded, killing three people. Two members of the group, Cathy Wilkerson and Kathy Boudin, escaped from the house. It was Wilkerson who, stumbling naked from the ruins, kept asking "Where is Adam?" The two women escaped and were fugitives for decades.

125   Aquarians in the basement: The American musical *Hair* (1967)—book by James Rado and Gerome Ragni and music by Galt McDermot—focuses on a group of counterculture youths, "Hippies of the Age of Aquarius," who oppose the Vietnam war and sexual repression.

126   *Les Sylphides:* The 1893 ballet by the Polish-born composer Frédéric Chopin (1810–1849) and the Russian-born choreographer Michel Fokine (1880–1942). The plotless ballet involves sylphs dancing in moonlight with a young man.

132   The title is French for "golden arrow." *Flèche d'Or* was an expensive and elegant train linking Paris and London during the 1930s.

133   Gauloise: The name of a French brand of cigarette.

133   Bateau Mouche: A sightseeing boat on the River Seine in Paris.

134   *Orphée aux Enfers: Orpheus in the Underworld,* the 1858 operetta by the French composer Jacques Offenbach (1819–1880).

134   Stephen in the Pyrenees: Stephen Yenser (b. 1941), the American poet and critic and Merrill's friend, whom JM visited during this trip in Jurançon, France, near Pau.

135   The O L I V E T T I signs: Signs beside the road that, letter by letter, advertise the Olivetti typewriter.

135   Umberto: Umberto Morra (1897–1981), an Italian friend of Merrill's, whom he visited in Cortona. See note to "Bronze" (page 283).

136   San Zeno: San Zeno Maggiore, an elegant twelfth-century Romanesque church in Verona, Italy.

136   Nijinsky in *Petrouchka:* Vaslav Nijinsky (1890–1950), the Russian ballet dancer and choreographer who danced the principal role of the puppet in the premiere of *Petrouchka* by the Russian composer Igor Stravinsky (1882–1971).

137   Strato: Strátos Mouflouzélis (b. 1942), Merrill's Greek friend who was the driver on this road trip from Paris to Athens. (See chronology, page 292.)

137   Murano: An island north of Venice, famous for its glassmaking factories.

138   Bix: Leon Bismark ("Bix") Beiderbecke (1903–1931), the American jazz cornet player and pianist.

138   Buxtehude: Dietrich Buxtehude (ca. 1637–1707), the Danish-born composer and organist.

138   Boulez: Pierre Boulez (b. 1925), the French composer and conductor.

138   the Victor label: The label of the early recordings produced by The Victor Talking Machine Company featured a small terrier named Nipper listening to a Victrola.

138   Bloch: Ernest Bloch (1880–1959), the Swiss-born American composer.

138   the Leiermann: "Der Leiermann" ("The Organ-Grinder"), a poem by the German Wilhelm Müller (1794–1827) set to music by the Austrian composer Franz Schubert (1797–1828) as the final song in his cycle *Die Winterreise*.

138   Ravel's "Les jets d'eau du palais de ceux qui s'aiment": "The palace fountains of those who are in love." Maurice Ravel (1875–1937), the French composer, wrote "Jeux d'eau," a piano solo, inspired by "Jeux d'eau à la Villa d'Este" by the Hungarian pianist and composer Franz Liszt (1811–1886). The line Merrill quotes is of obscure origin. It could well be his own *jeu de mots*.

138   the Schumann Concerto: The 1845 Piano Concerto in A Minor by the German composer Robert Schumann (1810–1856).

138   *Wozzeck:* The 1925 opera by the Austrian composer Alban Berg (1885–1935).

138   his bête noire Blanche: Cf. Shakespeare, *King Lear*, 3.6.

138   Jezebel: A Biblical queen (1 Kings), whose name has become the shorthand term for a corrupt woman.

139   No honey for the vanquished: Merrill's phrase, the counterpart to "To the victor go the spoils," alludes to the now proverbial dictum, "Vae victis" ("Woe to the vanquished") by the Roman historian Livy (59 BCE–17 CE). "Vae victis behavior" is also known as "Victor's justice."

Syrinx

140   In Greek mythology Syrinx was a nymph with whom the god Pan fell in love. To frustrate his pursuit, the gods changed her into a reed on the riverbank. Hearing the wind in the reeds, Pan cut some down and invented the pan-pipes, which he called the syrinx in memory of her.

140   A thinking reed: Translation of "un roseau pensant," the definition of humanity in the *Pensées* (#348) of the French philosopher Blaise Pascal (1623–1662).

140   the great god Pain: In his *Lives*, the Greek historian Plutarch (ca. 46–120) tells the story of a crew of sailors during the reign (14–37) of Roman emperor Tiberius (42 BCE–37 CE) who, when near the Echinades islands in the Ionian Sea, heard a voice call out three times, "When you reach Palodes, proclaim that the great god Pan is dead." The story has often been interpreted to

announce the passage of the classical age and the beginning of the Christian era.

Lost in Translation

143   Epigraph: These lines are a translation of part of the seventh stanza of Paul Valéry's poem "Palme": "Ces jours qui te semblent vides / Et perdus pour l'univers / Ont des racines avides / Qui travaillent les déserts," as translated by the German poet Rainer Maria Rilke (1875–1926). For Merrill's own translation, see "Paul Valéry: *Palme*," page 201.

143   Verdun: This town in northeastern France, in Lorraine, was the site of one of World War I's bloodiest battles and its longest (February through December, 1916).

143   curé: A parish priest in France.

143   Alsace: A region in eastern France annexed with Lorraine by Germany in 1871. A bone of contention between France and Germany, it was recovered by France after World War I, then occupied by Germany in World War II and returned to France after that war.

144   Patience dans l'azur: "Patience beneath the blue," a phrase from Valéry's "Palme" followed by a faulty recollection of Rilke's translation of it into German (Rilke's version is "Gedulden unter dem Blau").

146   "cette innocente mère,/Ce pauvre enfant, qui deviendront-ils?": "This innocent mother, / This poor child, what will become of them?"

146   "Tu as l'accent allemande": "You have a German accent."

146   Speke: John Hanning Speke (1827–1864), the English officer who explored Africa and was the first Westerner to reach (with Sir Richard Burton [1821–1890]) Lake Tanganyika and (by himself) Lake Victoria.

146   "Schlaf wohl, chéri": "Sleep well, dear one." Mademoiselle is again mixing German and French.

146   Kef: Literally "pleasure" in Arabic; hence, hashish smoked to induce that state.

146   Insh'Allah: "God willing," an Islamic formula in Arabic.

146   Richard: Richard Howard (b. 1929), the American poet, critic, translator, friend of Merrill's, and the dedicatee of this poem.

146   Gérôme: Jean-Léon Gérôme (1824–1904), the French academic painter and printmaker who often rendered Middle Eastern scenes.

147   Thebes: The ancient capital of Egypt, on the Nile in Upper Egypt.

147   Houri and Afreet: A female attendant spirit in the Moslem paradise and an evil demon in Arabian mythology respectively.

147   sauce mousseline: Hollandaise sauce with whipped cream folded in.

147   Maggie Teyte: The English soprano (1888–1976).

148   verger, mûr, parfumer: "Orchard, ripe, to perfume."

157 Ioannina, or Jannina, a lake city, now the capital of Epirus in northwestern Greece, described in the epigraph by English painter and nonsense poet Edward Lear (1812–1888). Under Turkish control for centuries, its most famous period was when it was ruled by Ali Pasha (1741–1822), the "Lion of Epirus," whose flamboyant life, including his meeting with Byron, is vividly recounted in the biography Merrill quotes, *The Diamond of Jannina* (first published in 1936 under the title *Ali the Lion*) by the South African writer William Plomer (1903–1973).

157 Frossíni: A wife of Ali Pasha.

159 Karaghiózi: The main Greek character in the eponymous Turkish shadow theater, a venerable genre with complex materials that is now almost extinct. The stage is separated from the audience by a fine white sheet of cotton or other material stretched taut and illuminated by oil lamps. The puppeteer holds the puppets, on horizontal rods, between the lights and the screen. The puppets (each about a foot high), silhouettes made of animal skin stained with translucent dyes, show up in brilliant color on the screen. Their operation is an intricate and delicate matter. The comic dramas, which mix slapstick with sophisticated literary devices, involve stock characters and formulaic structures, the details of which are improvised in presentation.

159 Vassilikí: A wife of Ali Pasha.

159 höchste Lust: "Highest bliss [desire]," from Isolde's last aria in the 1865 opera *Tristan und Isolde* by the German composer Richard Wagner (1813–1883).

Verse for Urania

162 In 1969, Christos Alevras, a friend of the poet's in Athens, moved with his wife Vaso and their daughter Georgia into the apartment below Merrill's on Water Street in Stonington. Their second daughter, Urania, was born in 1973. Urania, which means "heavenly" in Greek, was the Muse of astronomy; it is also one of Aphrodite's bynames.

163 bébé-Michelin: A miniature version of the Michelin Man, the familiar inflated figure advertising the French automobile tire company.

164 *The Wings of the Dove:* The 1902 novel by the American-born writer Henry James (1843–1916).

164 Mystic: A town in Connecticut near Merrill's Stonington.

164 Before mill turned to maelstrom: See Giorgio de Santillana and Hertha von Dechend, *Hamlet's Mill: An Essay Investigating the Origins of Human Knowledge and Its Transmission through Myth* (1969) for this and other arcane astrophysical and astrological concepts and terms in this poem.

164 Pythagoras: The Greek philosopher (ca. 570–490 BCE), born on Samos, revered in Plato's day and often afterwards as a mathematician, scientist, and

cosmogonist and sometimes associated with the idea of "the harmony of the spheres," an early version of the unified field theory.

164 Ur: A Mesopotamian city near the original mouth of the Tigris and Euphrates rivers and close to what is now Nasiriya, Iraq, the site of one of the oldest civilizations.

164 ^{mul}KAK.SI.DI (in Sumerian): *Hamlet's Mill* (see note on page 280 for "Before mill turned to maelstrom") tells us that this is the term for the star we know as Sirius and that it has been thought of as instrumental in the cosmic "whirlpool" treated in that study. Sumerian was the earliest language written in Mesopotamia.

165 Eddington's universe: The English astronomer Arthur Stanley Eddington (1882–1944) was a founding figure in modern astrophysics. His 1933 book *The Expanding Universe* explores the concept of the recession from one another of remote galaxies.

167 Purcell? His "Blessed Virgin"? Strauss's "Bat"?: The English composer Henry Purcell (1659–1695) wrote the music for the sacred song "The Blessed Virgin's Expostulation," and the Austrian Johann Strauss II (1825–1899) composed the 1874 opera *Die Fledermaus. Fledermaus* is the German word for "bat."

167 Nahum Tate: The Irish-born man of letters (1652–1715) who wrote the text for Henry Purcell's "The Blessed Virgin's Expostulation" (see note above).

The Will

168 David the Wise: Merrill's friend the American literary scholar David Kalstone (1933–1986). See note to "Farewell Performance," page 284.

168 I*bis:* I.e., as in a French address, where the *bis* indicates a small habitation that takes its address from an adjacent residence.

169 Che puro ciel: "What a clear sky," an aria from the 1762 opera *Orfeo ed Euridice* by the German composer Christoph Willibald Gluck (1714–1787).

170 David the Fair: Merrill's friend the American painter David McIntosh (b. 1938), also mentioned in "Bronze" (see page 190).

171 David the True: Merrill's longtime companion, the American writer and painter David Jackson (1922–2001). See note to "The Book of Ephraim," page 282.

171 Ephraim: The otherworldy spirit and central figure in "The Book of Ephraim," with whom Merrill and David Jackson communicated for years by way of the Ouija board. Cf. section A from "The Book of Ephraim" (page 175).

171 Aquinas: St. Thomas Aquinas (ca. 1225–1274), the Roman Catholic theologian and philosopher.

171 Bossuet: Jacques-Bénigne Bossuet (1627–1704), the French bishop, scholar, prolific writer, and illustrious orator.

173 Carabosse: The evil fairy in the tale of Sleeping Beauty, she casts upon the princess a spell that is mitigated by the Lilac Fairy.

175   Northrop Frye: The Canadian literary theorist (1912–1991), whose 1957 *Anatomy of Criticism* is cited. See the chapter "Theory of Mythos: An Introduction."

175   Woolf not Mann: The English writer Virginia Woolf (1882–1941) and the German novelist Thomas Mann (1875–1955).

176   Grimm, / Jung, Verdi, and the commedia dell' arte: Jacob and Wilhelm, the Brothers Grimm, the German folklorists who published their first collection of fairy tales in 1812. Carl Jung (1875–1961), the Swiss psychiatrist noted for his writings on the idea that the psyche can be best understood through art, mythology, and astrology. Giuseppe Verdi (1813–1901), the Italian composer of often melodramatic operas. Commedia dell' arte, an improvisational theater style popular in eighteenth-century Italy and elsewhere, based on a repertory of stock situations and characters.

176   "The Will": Merrill's poem (see page 168 and notes on page 281).

176   David Jackson: "David the True" in "The Will" (see page 168). An American writer and painter, Jackson (1922–2001) shared homes with Merrill in Stonington, New York City, Athens, and Key West. Their communication with spirits by way of the Ouija board (they made their own on many occasions and used the handle of a teacup as a pointer) continued for decades. The first of Merrill's poems to mention the Ouija board, which also plays a part in his novel *The Seraglio* (1957), is "Voices from the Other World" (page 16). Communications through the Ouija board also figure in "The Will" as well as being the basis for *The Changing Light at Sandover*.

176   Ephraim: See note to "The Will," page 281.

177   Wallace Stevens: The American poet (1879–1975), who appears throughout *The Changing Light at Sandover*.

178   Willowware: Popular and inexpensive household china, imitating the blue-on-white patterns of Chinese export porcelain.

180   The Rover Boys: A popular series of books for children published between 1899 and 1926 that turn on the adventures of three brothers, Tom, Sam, and Dick Rover.

182   Samos: A Greek island in the eastern Aegean Sea, near Turkey.

183   "the world's enchanted fire": The quotation is from the 1951 opera *The Rake's Progress* (1, 2), with music by Igor Stravinsky and a libretto by W. H. Auden and Chester Kallman (see note to "Nine Lives," page 285).

183   Pythagoras: See note to "Verse for Urania" (page 280).

183   Ephesus: An ancient Greek city in Ionian Asia Minor, now a major tourist attraction in Turkey near the Aegean and the village of Selçuk.

The School Play

187   The school cast is performing Shakespeare's *Richard II*. The "school play" was an annual event at St. Bernard's School in New York City that Merrill attended as a boy.

Page from the Koran

188   "How gladly with proper words . . . the soldier dies": From the last tercet of the sequence "Notes toward a Supreme Fiction" by the American poet Wallace Stevens (1879–1975).

Bronze

190   David the Fair: See note to "The Will" (page 281).

190   Umberto: Count Umberto Morra di Lavriano (1897–1981) was named for Umberto II, the last king of Italy, who reigned for only thirty-three days, May 9–June 12, 1946. Morra was rumored to be the sovereign's illegitimate son. Merrill met him in Rome in 1951 and visited him at his villa in Cortona on several later occasions. Morra was an anti-Fascist activist during the 1930s and 1940s. After World War II, he served as director of the Italian Cultural Institute in London. He published a book entitled *Colloqui con Berenson* in 1963. Cf. note on Berenson below.

191   Montale: Eugenio Montale (1896–1981), the Italian poet.

191   Berenson: Bernard Berenson (1865–1959), the American art critic of impressive reputation whose home near Florence, I Tatti, was a retreat for artists and scholars. Thanks to his bequest, I Tatti became the Harvard University Center for Italian Renaissance Studies.

191   Edith Wharton: The American novelist (1862–1937) who spent much of her life in Europe.

192   Mark Clark: Mark W. Clark (1896–1984), the illustrious American career army officer who was Commander of the Fifth Army Group in Italy in much of World War II. He led the liberation of Naples (1943) and of Rome (1944) and finally accepted the surrender of the German forces in Italy and Austria in May 1945.

195   *Dämmerung:* "Twilight" in German.

195   *the torso / In Paris provided for Rilke:* The sonnet "Archaïscher Torso Apollos" by the German poet Rainer Maria Rilke (1875–1926) was inspired by a fragmentary marble statue in the Salle Archaïque of the museum of the Palais du Louvre.

196   Glyptothek: The austere neoclassical museum in Munich commissioned by King Ludwig I of Bavaria (1786–1868) to house ancient and modern sculptures.

197   Empire: The grand, elaborate, neoclassical furniture style, often combining

ancient Egyptian and classical Greek and Roman motifs, that Napoleon encouraged during his First Empire (1804–1815).

197 Biedermeier: The style that flourished from 1815 to 1848 (after Empire), which was simpler, less massive, more practical.

199 Laszlo: The original cast of the bronze head of the poet is now at the Stonington Historical Society in Stonington, Connecticut. Merrill kept a copy on his sundeck in Stonington. Nothing is known about the sculptor.

Paul Valéry: Palme

201 The original poem by Valéry is an important element in Merrill's "Lost in Translation." See page 143.

Ginger Beef

208 Ouspenskaya: Maria Ouspenskaya (1876–1949), the diminutive Russian-born character actor with distinctive physical features, student of Stanislavsky's and teacher of his method, known especially for roles in "Wolf Man" films of the 1940s.

210 *Nambé:* Nambé Pueblo, New Mexico, is north of Santa Fe, at the foot of the Sangre de Cristo Mountains.

Losing the Marbles

212 Charmides: A character in Plato's dialogue of this name, which concerns the nature of temperance or self-restraint.

212 "Rage against the dying of the light": A line from the 1951 villanelle "Do Not Go Gentle into That Good Night" by Welsh poet Dylan Thomas (1914–1953).

213 *Golden Treasury:* A widely read anthology of English poetry first compiled by Francis Turner Palgrave in 1861.

215 Melina: Melina Mercouri (1920–1994), the Greek film actor who became a member of the Hellenic Parliament and served as Minister for Culture from 1981 to 1989, and again from 1993 to 1994.

215 Phidias and Pericles: Phidias (ca. 480–430 BCE), the most eminent Greek sculptor of the Golden Age, designed (among many other works) the Parthenon and the monumental statue of Zeus at Olympia, both of which were probably commissioned by Pericles (ca. 495–429 BCE), the exemplary Greek statesman, friend of writers, and patron of culture.

217 Fontenelle: Bernard le Bovier de Fontenelle (1657–1757), the French man of letters.

Farewell Performance

220 palace days, Strauss, Sydney: Merrill's friend the American scholar David Kalstone (1933–1986), whose book *Five Temperaments* includes a chapter on

Merrill and to whom this elegy is dedicated, for many summers rented rooms in the Palazzo Barbaro in Venice. The palazzo was owned in the 1880s by Daniel and Ariana Curtis, whose guests included the expatriate Americans painter John Singer Sargent (1856–1925) and novelist Henry James (1843–1916), who used it as a model for the character Milly Theale's residence in his 1902 novel *The Wings of the Dove*. Among Kalstone's favorite artists were the German composer Richard Strauss (1864–1949) and the English courtier poet Sir Philip Sidney (1554–1586), on whose work Kalstone also wrote a book.

220   Peter: Merrill's friend Peter Hooten (b. 1950), an American actor.

Nine Lives

224   A house in Athens: The house on Athinaion Efivon Street where Merrill and David Jackson ("DJ" in this poem; "David the True" in "The Will," see page 168) lived for a number of years. The house also figures in "Days of 1964" (see page 72) and the "heavy volume called" *The Changing Light at Sandover*. Merrill gave the house to the American School of Classical Studies at Athens and at the time of this poem had rented it back from its traveling occupants.

225   Tony and Nelly: Merrill's old Athenian friends Tony Parigory (1925–1992), the subject of the elegy "Tony: Ending the Life" in *A Scattering of Salts*, and Nellie Liambey (b. 1910), the poet's companion in "Santorini: Stopping the Leak" in *Late Settings*. The latter is "Nelláki" in section eight of this poem.

225   Maria Mitsotáki: See "Words for Maria" (page 80) and the note on page 274.

226   In Kolonáki Square / At the Bon Goût: See note to "Words for Maria" (page 274).

226   Ephraim: See note to "The Will" (page 281).

228   Shaw's / Life Force: The Irish-born British playwright George Bernard Shaw (1856–1950) came to believe that the essence of our existence is a life force that evolves in the direction of God.

228   Strato: See note to "Days of 1971" (page 277).

230   Paidiá!: Literally "children" in Greek, the term is used to address one's friends.

230   *Spetsai:* Spetses, a small island close to Athens that is a resort especially for wealthy Athenians.

231   *Mimí. Proud Chester:* Dimítra Atsídes Vassilikós (1934–1978), a Greek friend of Merrill's and wife of novelist Vassíli Vassilikós (b. 1934). Chester Kallman (1921–1975), American poet and librettist and W. H. Auden's longtime partner.

231   *Papagena:* A character in Mozart's 1791 opera *The Magic Flute.*

231   *Titania, Oberon:* Characters in Shakespeare's *A Midsummer Night's Dream.*

232   Kifissia: Now an upscale suburb of Athens.

232   "Liebestraum": Piano piece by the Hungarian composer Franz Liszt (1811–1886); the title means "dream of love."

232   Embarkment for Cythère: The title of a painting of an ostensibly joyful scene by French painter Jean-Antoine Watteau (1684–1721).

Snow Jobs

235   Teapot Dome: A 1922 scandal involving bribes from oil magnates that tainted the administration of President Warren G. Harding (1865–1923).

235   the Iran / Contra Affair: A 1987 scandal involving illegal arms sales to Iran and help to Nicaraguan rebels known as the Contras. It tainted the administration of President Ronald Reagan (1911–2004).

235   Watergate: A 1972 burglary of the Democratic National Committee offices in the Watergate Office Buildings and the subsequent revelation of other illegal activities eventually led to the resignation of President Richard M. Nixon (1913–1994) two years later. G. Gordon Liddy (b. 1930), a political operative, masterminded the burglary. Jeb Magruder (b. 1934), an aide to Nixon, was convicted of conspiracy for his role in the burglary and cover-up. John Ehrlichman (1925–2000), Nixon's domestic affairs adviser, was also convicted in the scandal.

235   Clotho: One of the three Fates of Greek mythology, the spinner of the thread of life.

Overdue Pilgrimage to Nova Scotia

249   "New, tender, quick": The last words of "Love Unknown" by the English poet George Herbert (1593–1633), a favorite of the American poet Elizabeth Bishop (1911–1979).

Self-Portrait in Tyvek(™) Windbreaker

251   Roberto Murolo: The Neapolitan singer and scholar (1912–2003) whose encyclopedic collection of Neapolitan songs ranges from 1200 to 1962.

252   Nannetta: A character in *Falstaff* (1893), the last opera by Italian composer Giuseppe Verdi (1813–1901).

252   the Dead: The Grateful Dead, a group of rock musicians who started out in San Francisco in 1965 and became known for their eclectic mix of influences.

252   Arvo Pärt: The Estonian composer (b. 1935) of experimental music, recently the kind he calls "tintinnabulation."

253   Ray: Ray Izbiki (1921–2007), who became Merrill's friend, rented an apartment in the poet's building on Water Street in Stonington and, in Merrill's will, was granted life tenancy.

253   Pascal: Blaise Pascal (1623–1663), the French philosopher and mathematician. See Pascal's complex argument in "Trois Discours sur la condition des grands."

256   This poem was inspired by "Waiting for the Barbarians" by the Alexandrian (Greek) poet C. P. Cavafy (1863–1933).

256   Utamaro and Lady Murasaki: Utamaro Kitagawa (ca. 1750–1806), the Japanese painter known for his lovely portraits of female prostitutes. Murasaki Shikibu (ca. 973–1025), the author of *The Tale of Genji*, sometimes regarded as the first "modern" novel, based on Japanese court life.

Oranges

257   Orangerie: The Musée de l'Orangerie in the Tuileries Gardens in Paris, which contains an oval gallery created to house eight of the panels known as the *Water Lilies* or *Nymphéas* by the French impressionist painter Claude Monet (1840–1926).

Rhapsody on Czech Themes

260   the Flore: The Café de Flore, on the Left Bank, was a famous meeting place for intellectuals in Paris after World War II.

260   Mucha: Alfons Mucha (1860–1939), the Czech artist most famous for his posters in the Art Nouveau style.

261   "Velvet Revolution": The name given to the series of nonviolent demonstrations in Czechoslovakia during November and December of 1989 that led to the downfall of the ruling Communist regime.

262   President Havel: Václav Havel (b. 1936), the Czech dramatist and writer who served as the last president of Czechoslovakia (1989–1992) and the first president of the Czech Republic (1993–2003).

262   Telč: Town in the Czech Republic, registered in the UNESCO World Cultural Heritage list, that looks today much as it did in the fourteenth century.

263   Carl Sandburg: American poet and folklorist (1878–1967).

263   Camus for *Dynasty:* The French philosopher and novelist Albert Camus (1913–1960). *Dynasty* was a popular U.S. television series broadcast between 1981 and 1989, concerned with the Carringtons, a rich oil family from Colorado.

264   Germaine Greer, Robert Ludlum, Wittgenstein: Greer (b. 1939) is an Australian scholar, leftist, and feminist whose best-known work is *The Female Eunuch* (1970); Ludlum (1927–2001) was an American writer of thriller novels, including the Bourne series; and Ludwig Wittgenstein (1892–1951) was an Austrian analytic philosopher who wrote *Tractatus Logico-Philosophicus* (1922), which helped to shape logical positivism, and *Philosophical Investigations* (1953), which influenced language philosophy.

265   Rabbi Löw: Judah Löw ben Bezalel (1525–1609), the Czech scholar and mystic

known as the "Maharal of Prague," said to have devised the legend of the golem, a living creature made of inanimate matter.

265   *The House of the Dead: From the House of the Dead* is the 1930 opera by Czech composer Leoš Janáček (1854–1928).

265   Reb Sholem of Belz: Belz is a town in western Ukraine, birthplace and namesake of a Hasidic dynasty founded by Reb Sholem or Reb Shalom (the latter is the classical Hebrew and the former the Chassidic version of the name) in the early nineteenth century. A version of the passage Merrill quotes can be found in Stephen Jolly's 1961 translation of the 1937 *Nine Gates to the Chassidic Mysteries* by the Czech mystical writer Jiri Langer (1894–1943), in the chapter "The First Gate."

265   *talmidim:* The Hebrew term for disciples of a rabbi and students of the scriptures.

Koi

267   "Koi" is the Japanese word for ornamental carp.

267   Cosmo: The Jack Russell terrier owned by Merrill and his friend Peter Hooten (see note to "Farewell Performance," page 285).

Short Chronology

1926   Born in New York City, on March 3. His father, Charles Edward Mer-
rill (1885–1956), was a co-founder of the Merrill Lynch brokerage firm.
In 1925 Charles Merrill married his second wife, Hellen Ingram
(1898–2000), a society reporter from Jacksonville, Florida. JM's half sib-
lings, Charles and Doris, were the children of Charles Merrill's first mar-
riage. The family lived in Manhattan and in a grand house designed by
Stanford White in Southampton on Long Island.

1936–38   Attended St. Bernard's School in Manhattan.

1939–42   His parents concluded a bitter divorce in 1939. After the divorce, Merrill
lived with his mother and maternal grandmother at the latter's Manhat-
tan apartment, 164 East Seventy-second Street. Attended Lawrenceville
School in New Jersey and started writing poetry. In 1942, as a sixteenth-
birthday gift, his father published his poems in a limited edition called
Jim's Book. His close friend and literary collaborator at Lawrenceville was
Frederick Buechner, later a prominent novelist.

1943–44   Graduated from Lawrenceville in 1943 and enrolled at Amherst College,
his father's alma mater. While at Amherst, he met Robert Frost and
undertook intensive literary studies.

1944–45   Inducted into the U.S. Army, he served eight months, largely in training
camps, and described himself as "scared, lacerated with hatred." Re-
enrolled at Amherst in September and fell in love with his teacher, Kimon
Friar, who introduced him to W. H. Auden, the experimental filmmaker
and anthropologist Maya Deren, and the writer Anaïs Nin. His parents'
discovery of the affair led to unhappy and sometimes melodramatic mis-
understandings. Played the lead role in a college production of Jean
Coctcau's *Orphée*.

1946   Friar arranged for the publication in Athens of Merrill's short volume of poems *The Black Swan,* in an edition of one hundred copies, with a drawing by the Greek artist Nikos Ghika on its cover. JM's verse play, *The Birthday,* performed at Amherst. First publications in *Poetry* magazine. Met Dutch poet Hans Lodeizen, who was studying at Amherst.

1947   Completed honors thesis on Marcel Proust (" *'À la recherche du temps perdu':* Impressionism in Literature") and graduated summa cum laude from Amherst in May.

1948–49   Taught at Bard College. First read Elizabeth Bishop. Won *Poetry*'s Levinson Prize. Became friend of Irma Brandeis, professor of Italian at Bard, who was associated with the Italian poet Eugenio Montale and later wrote a book on Dante. Traveled to Paris.

1950–53   Fell in love with Claude Fredericks. Read with Richard Wilbur at Amherst and was dissatisfied with both his own voice and his poems. Visited Friar in Athens and went to Rhodes and Poros. Traveled with Fredericks to France, Switzerland (where Hans Lodeizen was suffering from leukemia and where he died in 1950), Austria, Mallorca, and Italy. Mother remarried, to William Plummer, a retired Army general. First full-fledged book, *First Poems,* published in an edition of 990 copies by Knopf in 1951. In Rome, began psychoanalysis with Dr. Thomas Detre. Wrote *The Bait,* produced in New York at the Comedy Club in 1953, and began work on his novel *The Seraglio,* a roman à clef. Returned to New York. At Christmas Buechner gave him his first Ouija board. Met David Jackson, who was to be his lifelong companion.

1954   Attended Wallace Stevens's birthday party, hosted by the Knopfs in connection with the publication of Stevens's *Collected Poems.* Merrill sat at the table for the guest of honor, and Stevens later wrote to his friend Witter Bynner, "There were a lot of people there whom you would have enjoyed quite as much as I did, including young James Merrill, who is about the age which you and I were when we were in New York." With Jackson, rented the top floor of a commercial building at 107 Water Street in Stonington, Connecticut.

1955   His play *The Immortal Husband* produced at the Theater de Lys in New York. His chapbook of poems, *Short Stories,* published by Fredericks's Banyan Press. Experimented with the Ouija board with Jackson—and first contacted Ephraim on August 23. Began reading Yeats's *A Vision.* Taught at Amherst. Purchased the building on Water Street and began renovations.

1956–57   *The Immortal Husband* published by New Directions in *Playbook: Five Plays for a New Theatre.* Began a round-the-world trip with Jackson: Japan (where he befriended Donald Richie, the film critic and travel writer), Thailand, Ceylon, India, Turkey, West Germany, Italy, and France (where he visited Alice B. Toklas). Father died in 1956, while JM was in Japan. *The Seraglio* published by Knopf. Created the Ingram Merrill Foundation for the purpose of funding grants to writers, artists, and organizations.

1958   Spent summer of 1958 in Santa Fe. Traveled in Denmark, Spain, Italy, and Austria. First stay in Greece with Jackson.

1959–60   *The Country of a Thousand Years of Peace* published by Knopf. *The Bait* published by Grove in *Artists' Theatre*, edited by Herbert Machiz. Spent October in Munich, and December in Alexandria, where he met puppeteer Bernard de Zogheb. At about this time, after his grandmother's death and his mother's move to Atlanta, he inherited the apartment on East Seventy-second Street, and used it as a pied-à-terre. Close friends in New York included the poets John Hollander, Richard Howard, and Howard Moss.

1961–62   Traveled in Greece, West Germany, and Sicily. Knopf turned down his next collection, *Water Street*. Harry Ford, his longtime editor, left Knopf to co-found Atheneum, which published *Water Street* in 1962. Began work on an "experimental" novel, based on his experience in Greece and his relationship with Friar, to be entitled *The (Diblos) Notebook*.

1963–64   Traveled to Istanbul, Rhodes, San Francisco, and Rome. In Greece began friendships with Tony Parigory and Maria Mitsotáki. Studied modern Greek, in which he was to become fluent. In May 1964, purchased a house in Athens, at 44 Athinaion Efivon, near Kolonáki Square, with its views of Mt. Lycabettos to the north and Mt. Hymettos to the south. His friends there over the years would include the poet Alan Ansen; Chester Kallman, the poet and librettist and Auden's partner; and the Greek novelist Vassílis Vassilikós and his wife Mimí. Met Strátos (called Strato) Mouflouzélis, with whom he had a passionate affair for some years.

1965   *The (Diblos) Notebook*, published by Atheneum, nominated for National Book Award. Began friendship with critic David Kalstone.

1966   Traveled to Greece (as he did habitually for many years), Iran (with Richie), and Rome. *Nights and Days* published by Atheneum.

1967   Won the National Book Award for *Nights and Days*. In their citation, judges W. H. Auden, James Dickey, and Howard Nemerov wrote, "The 1967 National Book Award in poetry is awarded to *Nights and Days*, by James Merrill, for his scrupulous and uncompromising cultivation of the poetic art, evidenced in his refusal to settle for any easy and profitable stance; for his insistence on taking the kind of tough, poetic chances which make the difference between esthetic success or failure." Taught at the University of Wisconsin in Madison, where his students included Stephen Yenser and writer Judith Moffett. Visited Chicago to see his friend Daryl Hine, poet and editor of *Poetry*, and to read at the magazine's Poetry Day.

1968   Awarded honorary LittD degree by Amherst. Met painter David McIntosh, a love who inspired much of JM's poetry for the next several years, and traveled with him in Wyoming. Visited Auden and Kallman in Kirchstetten, Austria.

1969   Visited McIntosh in Santa Fe. Stepfather William Plummer died. *The Fire Screen* published by Atheneum.

1970–71   In Peru with his brother Charles. Visited Elizabeth Bishop in Brazil, who in turn visited him in Stonington later in 1970. Elected to the National Institute of Arts and Letters. In spring of 1971 flew to Paris and drove with Mouflouzélis through France and Italy to Greece. Went to Yánnina with Yenser, who had spent the summer in Greece. Accepted position as Fanny Hurst Visiting Professor at Washington University, St. Louis, for November 1971.

1972   Visited Yenser in Los Angeles and McIntosh in Santa Fe. Introduced to Transcendental Meditation. *Braving the Elements* published by Atheneum. In her *New York Times Book Review* notice, Helen Vendler wrote, "The time eventually comes, in a good poet's career, when readers actively wait for his books: to know that someone out there is writing down your century, your generation, your language, your life. . . . He has become one of our indispensable poets." Began friendship with J. D. McClatchy.

1973   Awarded Bollingen Prize, a choice criticized on the editorial page of *The New York Times* for its elitism. Traveled to Venice and Greece. Attended Yenser's wedding in Los Angeles. Using the Ouija board, through the spirit Ephraim contacted Auden, who had died in September.

1974   His Athens friend María Mitsotáki died. "The Book of Ephraim" begun. *The Yellow Pages* published by Temple Bar Bookshop, Cambridge, Massachusetts.

1975   Finished "The Book of Ephraim." David Jackson's parents died in Athens, where they had moved to be near Jackson and Merrill. Taught at Yale.

1976   *Divine Comedies*, published by Atheneum, was awarded the Pulitzer Prize.

1977–79   In California, Florida, Greece. *Mirabell: Books of Number*, published by Atheneum, won Merrill a second National Book Award and was hailed by the judges as "nothing less than monumental in scale and execution." With Jackson bought a house in Key West, at 702 Elizabeth Street. JM began spending winters there, and his annual New Year's Eve party included the writers John Malcolm Brinnin, John Ciardi, John Hersey, Harry Mathews, Alison Lurie, and Richard Wilbur.

1980   *Scripts for the Pageant* published by Atheneum.

1982   *The Changing Light at Sandover* and *From the First Nine: Poems 1946–1976* published by Atheneum. *Sandover*, which gathered into a single volume the trilogy of Ouija board poems and added a coda, won the National Book Critics Circle Award. Interviewed by McClatchy for *The Paris Review*'s Art of Poetry series. Awarded honorary LittD by Yale.

1983   Visited Friar in Greece and Kalstone in Venice. Began judging the Yale Series of Younger Poets competition. Met actor Peter Hooten, with whom he began a relationship that lasted until JM's death. Traveled to Holland with Hooten. Took canoe trip on the Connecticut River in New Hampshire with Peter Tourville.

1985   In Key West. Visited Green Cove Springs, his father's birthplace, with Hooten. Spent time with Kalstone in Venice and with Jackson in Greece. Visited Paris with Hooten. *Late Settings* published by Atheneum.

1986   Traveled to Japan with Hooten, where he visited Richie. Kalstone died of AIDS. While undergoing tests at the Mayo Clinic, Merrill learned that he was HIV-positive, a fact he revealed only to a few friends. *Recitative: Prose*, a collection of essays and interviews, edited and introduced by McClatchy, published in San Francisco by North Point Press. The one-act verse play *The Image Maker*, based on Santeria, produced at UCLA in May (and the following year at Seton Hall College in New Jersey).

1987   Harry Ford returned to Knopf, Merrill's first publisher. JM's next collection, *The Inner Room*, published by Knopf.

1988   *Voices from Sandover*, a staged reading for three actors adapted from *The Changing Light at Sandover*, performed in Cambridge, Massachusetts, at Royce Hall at UCLA, and at the Guggenheim Museum in New York, with Merrill and Hooten as two of the actors. Went to Atlanta to celebrate his mother's ninetieth birthday.

1989   Key West friend James Boatwright died of AIDS. Traveled with Hooten to Elizabeth Bishop's childhood home in Nova Scotia. Inducted into the American Academy of Arts and Letters.

1990   A new version of *Voices from Sandover*, this time with eight actors (including Merrill as himself), videotaped in August at the Agassiz Theater at Harvard University. Honored with the first Bobbitt National Prize for Poetry, awarded by the Library of Congress.

1991   With Hooten in Los Angeles, Key West, New York, and Arizona.

1992   Took literary tour of London, Rotterdam, Copenhagen, Glasgow. Hosted Jackson's seventieth birthday party in Stonington. Visited mother in Atlanta. *Selected Poems 1946–1985* published by Knopf. Release of the film *Lorenzo's Oil*, directed by George Miller, in which Merrill has a small but pivotal role as a physician in a symposium.

1993   Visited Parigory in Greece. Parigory died of AIDS. *A Different Person: A Memoir* published by Knopf.

1995   Wintering in Tucson, JM died of a heart attack on February 6. AIDS and the treatments he had sought for it had undermined his health during his last year. Throughout this time he had continued to work—on the day before his death he had drafted a new poem in his hospital room. On February 13, after a burial service in Stonington, his ashes were interred in the Stonington Cemetery. A memorial tribute was held at the New York Public Library on May 13. *A Scattering of Salts*, which Merrill saw through press, was published posthumously by Knopf.

Suggestions for Further Reading

Bauer, Mark. *The Composite Voice: The Role of W. B. Yeats in James Merrill's Poetry.* New York and London: Routledge, 2003.

Bloom, Harold, ed. *James Merrill.* New York: Chelsea House, 1985.

Farrell, Frank B. *Why Does Literature Matter?* Ithaca, NY, and London: Cornell University Press, 2004.

Forbes, Deborah. *Sincerity's Shadow: Self-Consciousness in British Romantic and Mid-Twentieth-Century American Poetry.* Cambridge and London: Harvard University Press, 2004.

Gallou, Claire Louise. *A Virgin's Lovers: James Merrill, Stéphane Mallarmé, and the Symbolist Quest.* Ann Arbor: UMI Dissertation Services, 2006.

Gwiazda, Piotr. *James Merrill and W. H. Auden: Homosexuality and Poetic Influence.* New York: Palgrave Macmillan, 2007.

Halpern, Nick. *Everyday and Prophetic: The Poetry of Lowell, Ammons, Merrill, and Rich.* Madison: Unversity of Wisconsin Press, 2003.

Kalstone, David. *Five Temperaments.* New York: Oxford University Press, 1977.

Kenniston, Ann. *Overheard Voices: Address and Subjectivity in Postmodern American Poetry.* New York and London: Routledge, 2006.

Labrie, Ross. *James Merrill.* New York: Twayne, 1982.

Lehman, David, and Charles Berger, eds. *James Merrill: Essays in Criticism.* Ithaca, NY, and London: Cornell University Press, 1983.

Lurie, Alison. *Familiar Spirits: A Memoir of James Merrill and David Jackson.* New York: Viking, 2001.

Materer, Timothy. *James Merrill's Apocalypse.* Ithaca, NY, and London: Cornell University Press, 2000.

McHale, Brian. *The Obligation toward the Difficult Whole: Postmodern Long Poems.* Tuscaloosa: University of Alabama Press, 2004.

Moffett, Judith. *James Merrill: An Introduction to the Poetry*. New York: Columbia University Press, 1984.

Nickowitz, Peter. *Rhetoric and Sexuality: The Poetry of Hart Crane, Elizabeth Bishop, and James Merrill*. New York: Palgrave Macmillan, 2006.

Perkins, David. *A History of Modern Poetry*, vol. II. Cambridge and London: Harvard University Press, 1987.

Polito, Robert. *A Reader's Guide to James Merrill's "The Changing Light at Sandover."* Ann Arbor: University of Michigan Press, 1984.

Rotella, Guy. *Castings: Monuments and Monumentality in Poems by Elizabeth Bishop, Robert Lowell, James Merrill, Derek Walcott and Seamus Heaney*. Nashville: Vanderbilt University Press, 2004.

Rotella, Guy, ed. *Critical Essays on James Merrill*. New York: G. K. Hall, 1996.

Sastri, Reena. *James Merrill: Knowing Innocence*. New York and London: Routledge, 2007.

Selinger, Eric Murphy. *What Is It Then Between Us?: Traditions of Love in American Poetry*. Ithaca, NY: Cornell University Press, 1998.

Vendler, Helen. *The Music of What Happens: Poems, Critics, Writers*. Cambridge and London: Harvard University Press, 1988.

———. *Part of Nature, Part of Us: Modern American Poets*. Cambridge and London: Harvard University Press, 1980.

———. *Soul Says: On Recent Poetry*. Cambridge and London: Harvard University Press, 1995.

Yenser, Stephen. *The Consuming Myth: The Work of James Merrill*. Cambridge and London: Harvard University Press, 1987.

Yu, Christopher. *Nothing to Admire: The Politics of Poetic Satire from Dryden to Merrill*. New York: Oxford University Press, 2003.

Index of Titles

A NOTE ABOUT THE EDITORS

J. D. McClatchy and Stephen Yenser are James Merrill's literary executors. J. D. McClatchy is the author of six volumes of poems and three collections of essays. He teaches at Yale and is the editor of *The Yale Review*. Stephen Yenser has written two volumes of poems and three books of criticism (one about Merrill). He is Distinguished Professor of English and the director of creative writing at UCLA.

A NOTE ON THE TYPE

This book was set in a type called Baskerville. The face itself is a facsimile reproduction of types cast from the molds made for John Baskerville (1706–1775) from his designs. Baskerville's original face was one of the forerunners of the type style known to printers as "modern face"—a "modern" of the period A.D. 1800.

Composed by Creative Graphics,
Allentown, Pennsylvania

Printed and bound by R. R. Donnelley,
Harrisonburg, Virginia